THE AUTHOR

Graham Campbell McInnes was born in London in 1912. His mother was the indomitable Angela Mackail, later famous as the novelist Angela Thirkell, his father the singer James Campbell McInnes. His brother Colin MacInnes (his preferred spelling) also became a well-known novelist and social commentator.

After her divorce from McInnes, Graham's mother married an Australian, George Thirkell, who formally adopted the boys. The Thirkells sailed from England in 1919, living first in Hobart before a loan from Angela's cousin Stanley Baldwin enabled them to buy a house in Melbourne. Graham was educated at Scotch College and won a scholarship to Melbourne University, where he met his future wife Joan Burke, and in 1933 gained a first-class degree in history. He then set off for Canada to find his father, whom he had not seen for fifteen years. From 1938-41 McInnes was the art critic for the Toronto paper *Saturday Night*, and an extra-mural lecturer for Toronto University; from 1942-8 he worked for the Canadian National Film Board. At the age of thirty-six, he switched to a diplomatic career, spending four years in Ottawa before postings to New Delhi and then Wellington. Later he attended the Imperial Defence College and served in the Canadian High Commission in London from 1959-62, finally as Minister. After a period as Canada's first High Commissioner in Jamaica he became the permanent Canadian delegate to UNESCO in Paris and was made Ambassador in 1969.

Graham McInnes wrote articles, art books and novels such as *Lost Island* (1954) and *Shushila* (1957), but his lasting fame rests on his classic series of memoirs: *The Road to Gundagai* (1965), *Humping My Bluey* (1966), *Finding A Father* (1967), all to be published by The Hogarth Press, and culminating in *Goodbye Melbourne Town* (1968). He died in Paris in 1970.

THE AUTHOR, MELBOURNE 1930

HUMPING MY BLUEY

Graham McInnes

New Introduction by
Barry Humphries

THE HOGARTH PRESS
LONDON

FOR JOAN

Published in 1986 by
The Hogarth Press
Chatto & Windus Ltd
40 William IV Street, London WC2N 4DF

First published in Great Britain by Hamish Hamilton Ltd 1966
Copyright © The Estate of Graham McInnes 1966
Introduction copyright © Barry Humphries 1986

British Library Cataloguing in Publication Data

McInnes, Graham
Humping my bluey.
1. McInnes, Graham   2. Diplomats –
Canada – Biography
I. Title
327.2'092'4   JX1730.A59

ISBN 0 7012 0594 6

Printed in Great Britain by
Cox & Wyman Ltd
Reading, Berkshire

INTRODUCTION

Although I knew Colin MacInnes pretty well in Soho in the sixties, I never met his brother Graham, the author of this remarkable volume and its companions. I wish I had; yet, in a sense, his four-part autobiography published twenty years ago forms such a vivid self-portrait that it gives the reader the illusion of intimate acquaintance.

In spite of his Pre-Raphaelite antecedents (his great-grandfather was the painter Edward Burne-Jones), Graham McInnes was a Melbourne Man, who wrote about my home town and Australia's 'grey and cryptic land' more evocatively and with more wit and affection than anyone else. The truth is that Melbourne and its comfortable, leafy, and exhilaratingly depressing suburbs has not often fired the literary imagination. Many of the talented people born there have 'humped their bluey' elsewhere, and devoted their energies to forgetting their native city rather than to its commemoration.

In the 1950s, when I was still a student, I tried my hand at writing satirical monologues about my birthplace. It seemed to me that all those bungalows – Californian style, Spanish mission, Queen Anne, neo-Georgian, jazz *moderne*, and that great Australian contribution to domestic architecture, the triple-fronted cream brick veneer – all set in their own tiny parks amongst birches, liquid ambers, pinoaks and pittosporums, deserved some sort of literary doing-over.

Our writers were then too busy exploring the Outback – 'the real Australia' – and our dramatists too anxious to provide T. S. Eliot, Terence Rattigan or Tennessee Williams with an antipodean rival, to look around them at the places where most Australians really lived.

A couple of my suburban sketches appeared on a small 'microgroove' (quaint period word) and when I first read the

McInnes autobiography in the mid-sixties I was flattered to find that my privately circulated 'Wild Life in Suburbia' records had earned a generous footnote. But when I first began to home in on my home town they had begun to pull it down. Not, happily, the suburbs which never seemed to change even as they proliferated, but the City itself, the commercial heart, an impressive and homogeneous Victorian monument which suffered the worst depredations of provincial 'progress'. Graham McInnes describes all the old familiar places, the streets, the shops, stations, pubs, theatres and schools, but as they were *before the War*. Enchanted by distance, intact, before the rot set in.

There it is, ante-bellum Melbourne. All the things the town planners and suburban developers of the Swinging Sixties have succeeded in either disfiguring or razing to the ground.

Autobiography is not a form which one would at first suppose comes naturally to the Australian temperament, either from a native circumspection or the covert suspicion that life in Australia may be too boring to merit a literary record. And yet we have produced a number of fine writers like Frederic Manning, Hal Porter, Randolph Stowe, George Johnson and Clive James, who have all given us brilliant memoirs, sometimes cast in the form of fiction, sometimes a faithful chronicle. Most recently, the publication of A. B. Facey's autobiography, *A Fortunate Life*, aroused huge public interest in the reminiscences of persons with no pretensions to literary ability and no thought of publication. As a result, publishers are now tending to accept MSS, many handwritten and difficult to decipher, which would undoubtedly have been returned with thanks in former years.

Humping My Bluey and its companion volumes stands amongst the few great Australian self-portraits. It is not merely valuable for its precisely recollected urban detail, for its evocation of Melbourne and Sydney and Adelaide in the decade just before I was born, but for its moving and memorable portraits of the author's mother Angela Thirkell, his stepfather and, in a subsequent volume, father. The precise observation, the humour, and the author's apparently flawless powers of recollection have produced an absorbing and joyous narrative, as fresh and direct as Sassoon or Isherwood, and, thank God, free of those arch autobiographical mannerisms which have long given sensitivity a bad name. In short, you feel you are reading a classic.

Graham McInnes died in 1970, but his youth, humour and intelligence robustly and triumphantly survive on the pages of this book.

Barry Humphries, Sydney 1986

CONTENTS

ILLUSTRATIONS

MAPS
(Drawn by Archie Harradine)

Back to Croajingalong
For that's the place where I belong;
Where a sun-kissed maid
Neath a gum tree's shade
Waits for me to go along to Croa-jinga-long;
No longer will I roam
From my old Australian home;
I'll hump my bluey
And I'll shout a coo-ee
Back to Croa-jinga-linga-linga-long.
                                    —PAT DUNLOP

FOREWORD

To 'hump your bluey'—the phrase is taken from Pat Dunlop's song *Back to Croajingalong*—means to shoulder your swag and, by implication, hit the trail. This particular trail is still 'the road to Gundagai', but we are a bit further along now. For whereas in *The Road* it was a boy, in this instalment it is a youth, and even a very young man. Though life at that epoch is full of a sudden sense of glory—'just a bowl of cherries', as we used to say—it is also a period when one does have to start to hump one's bluey if one is ever to amount to anything.

As with *Gundagai*, this story of the Australia I knew thirty to forty years ago is liberally sprinkled with the names of real people: friends, acquaintances and public figures. To them may I express the hope that any resemblance between them and the characters in these pages is acceptable.

I am again indebted to my friend Mr. J. Barton Hack of Melbourne for his tireless assistance in tracking down certain more precise details of a vanished glory. I am also indebted for the same service to his daughter Iola and to Mr. Max Paton of Sydney. But if the research is theirs, any errors still remain mine.

I have to make the following acknowledgements: to Allans Music (Aust.) Pty. Ltd., Melbourne, owners of the copyright of *Back to Croajingalong* by Pat Dunlop; to Mr. Kenneth Slessor and Angus and Robertson Ltd. for permission to quote the passage from *South Country* which appears in his *Poems*; to Cole Publications of Melbourne for permission to quote from *Cole's Funny Picture Book*.

G. McI.

Chapter One

PROLOGUE: THE SINISTER COP

'Hey! You boys! Pull over there.'

'Christ, it's a cop!'

From the doorway of a bank building opposite our floodlit town hall stepped a short dark man in plain clothes.

'That's not Murphy!' said Tiger. 'That's a new bloke. Plain-clothes.'

'Then we're for it,' I said, because we were riding without lights.

I looked at my own dead bicycle lamp with its freight of mushy carbide and felt a creeping chill. The cop's approach was leisurely. He clumped slowly up to us and stood in the circle of light cast by the street lamp. He wore a brown serge suit beneath a tight blue overcoat; a black velours hat was jammed onto his head. His face was pale in the yellow light and his dark eye surveyed us keenly.

'Well, well, well,' he said nodding his head. 'Riding without lights.'

We remained silent.

'Or maybe my sight isn't what it used to be,' said the cop. 'Maybe this lad here—' he removed a hand from his overcoat pocket and pointed a long finger at me '—maybe he really *has* a light and just can't be bothered using it. Likes to make work for the police. Eh?'

'No sergeant. The light won't work.'

'Don't suck up to me, my lad, I'm no sergeant.'

Tiger said, 'Well, sir, I mean officer, it didn't seem right to have to walk.'

'And why not?' asked the cop. 'Why can't a healthy lad walk his bike on a fine evening? Eh? I'll tell you,' he thrust his face forward. 'It's because you boys are all the same. Bone lazy! You've been warned time and time again about riding without lights. But you keep right on with it. You think the police are just a bunch of fools, eh?'

There was a pause, then with ostentatious boredom the cop took out a notebook.

'Let's have your name.'

'Tiger Webb.'

'No fancy nicknames here.'

'Gordon Russell Webb.'

'And where do you live, Gordon Russell?'

'Six Haverbrack Avenue.'

'And *your* name?'

I told him.

'And where do you live?'

'Four Grace Street.'

'Parents' names?'

'George L. Thirkell—he's my stepfather, and Angela Thirkell, that's my mother.'

'H'm. Grace Street. Quite close eh?'

'Yes sir.'

The policeman snapped his book shut. 'So you're the lad that's causing the trouble. What's the matter with your light?'

'The carbide's wet.'

The cop nodded reflectively. 'You should use an oil lamp: more reliable.'

'Yes.'

'It's not just traffic we have to consider. It's you. All sorts of things can happen to a boy at night.'

He spat on the sidewalk and erased the spittle with his boot.

'Now, both of you, listen to me,' he said sharply. 'This is your last chance. You'll walk your pushbikes home. Understand? *Walk.* And on Friday at four you'll present yourselves at the station with lights in good order for inspection, see?'

We bobbed our assent.

'All right then, off you go! Vamoose!'

We walked our machines down hill in silence for a few minutes.

'We didn't get run in. We can be thankful for that.'

'Is he still looking?'

'Nope, he's gone. Probably hiding in a door-way to cop the next poor bastard that rides by without a light.'

Tiger straddled his machine with his feet on the ground and wiggled his handle-bars.

'I think I'll hop along.'

'That's okay. See you tomorrow.'

Down Harvey Street the brilliant arcs of the main road gave way to lamps slung far apart on overhead wires, and swaying in a new-born breeze so that gigantic shadows swung in a dizzy rush. The pools of darkness ebbed and flowed like surf on a beach. 'The Germans will get you!' The oft-repeated rubric leaped to mind and I quickened my pace, tingling with anticipation. Soon I was

14

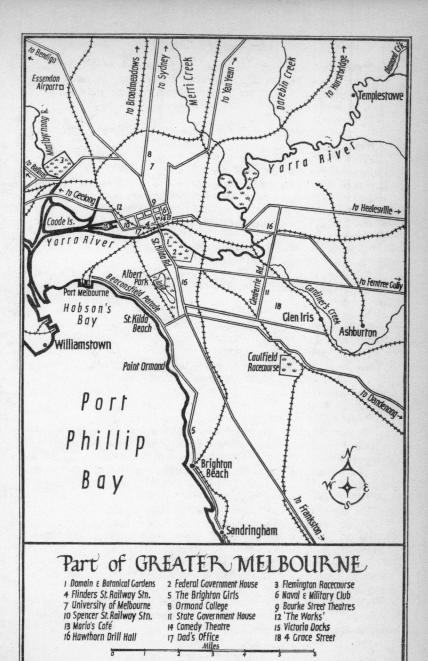

Part of GREATER MELBOURNE

1 Domain & Botanical Gardens   2 Federal Government House   3 Flemington Racecourse
4 Flinders St. Railway Stn.   5 The Brighton Girls   6 Naval & Military Club
7 University of Melbourne   8 Ormond College   9 Bourke Street Theatres
10 Spencer St. Railway Stn.   11 State Government House   12 'The Works'
13 Mario's Café   14 Comedy Theatre   15 Victoria Docks
16 Hawthorn Drill Hall   17 Dad's Office   18 4 Grace Street

Miles

avoiding cracks in the sidewalk. If I reached home without treading on a crack, the Germans, stealthily advancing in their steel helmets, and held at bay by the ebbing and flowing pools of light, would bite the mud !

'Hey, you !'

I stopped, uncertain whether the voice was in my own imagination.

'Yes, you !'

There was no mistaking it this time. From the shadow of a pittosporum hedge at the corner of my own street, Grace Street, the john hop came slowly forward. The borderland between nightmare and reality really wavered until I saw, behind the cop's advancing figure, the light in my own home. Now came panic of another kind: fear of the law. What had I done? How had the cop got there so fast? The cop stopped a few feet off.

'I told you to walk home.'

I found my voice. 'I did, sir.'

The man looked at his wrist watch under the lamp. His hat seemed to be further down over his face now, and his coat collar was turned up.

'You were pretty quick.'

'Walked fast.'

'Frightened, eh?'

'No, sir, it was pretty cool.'

His hands still in his pockets, the man beckoned with his head.

'I think you and me'd better have a talk. Where do you live?'

'On this street.'

'Which way?'

'That way.'

'Then we'll just go around the block *this* way.'

We walked without speaking; that is until I got a momentary glimpse at the man's face. Then I wanted to break and run, for I'd caught a flash of something, as through a half open door into blackness.

'I think I'd better go home.'

The cop's reply was injured yet cajoling.

'Now, now: we can't have you talking like that.'

He tried to take my arm as we turned another corner, and began to speak almost in the accents of a friend.

'You've got the police all wrong, you boys. You think the johns are your enemies, don't you?'

I didn't answer.

'Oh yes you do,' the cop went on. 'But we hate to see boys in trouble. Hate to see them punished for things they ought to know better than to do.'

He stopped, gripping my elbow. I was paralysed with fear. We stood beneath a lamp which cast a pool of yellow light on the road, and onto the strip of trampled buffalo grass between it and the cracked sidewalk. The leaves of a nearby plane tree gave a dry rustle.

'Let's have a look at you,' said the cop. There was no heat in his voice, only a feline smoothness. I wrenched my elbow from his grasp and put the bicycle between us. The cop stood quite still and laughed softly, he beckoned with a coy stubby finger.

'Don't try anything funny. Remember, I'm the law.'

For an irresolute split second I looked him in the eye and saw something small and faraway leap out as if on the stalk of a snail. The next instant I was running like the wind. I heard a metallic crash and an oath as the policeman fell across the bicycle. In a moment, it seemed, I was fumbling at my gate, was through it, and pounding with my fists on the front door. A light went on and my stepfather was standing there in pyjamas while my fists beat at the empty air.

'Hey, what the devil! Easy, boy, easy . . . what's wrong?'

*　　*　　*

The familiar jangle of suburban traffic stilled and I stood in shadowy silence smelling stale wood and rancid linoleum, hearing the distant clack of a typewriter, and aware of the faint tang of old cigars and, somewhere far off, the murmur of indistinguishable conversation. Slowly my eyes adjusted to the dim light and I saw a blank wall with a dark band of stained distemper from many generations of despondent shoulders; a notice—NO SMOKING NO SPITTING NO LOITERING; over against the wall a worn leather chair, and in it my stepfather.

'You're late.'

He heaved himself up out of the chair and stared down at me. Musty memories of his own boyhood must have stirred sluggishly and he certainly seemed to feel a vague pity for my scared discomfort, and perhaps even the instinct of a father of sorts, to do battle for the family. But I think he was embarrassed at finding himself here to explain a story that seemed both ludicrous and improbable.

He patted my shoulder and said, 'I've talked over the 'phone to the Super. He can't see us himself this morning: but he's asked one of the specials to see us.'

I nodded absent-mindedly.

'Now this is a serious business. So before we go in I want to make sure we're on the right track.'

I stared at him in blank incomprehension.

'What do you mean, Dad?'

He hastened to reply. 'Now, now, don't get excited,' though it was he who was getting excited. 'All I mean is, you're quite certain about last night? I mean, we'll have to—um—substantiate what we say. Maybe we'll have to make a written statement; so—you're sure, now?'

'Of course, Dad.'

'That's fine. Just wanted to make certain.'

A thin-lipped woman in steel-rimmed spectacles came down the corridor.

'The sergeant will see you now.'

'Thanks miss.'

We walked down the hall with its grimy walls and scuffed linoleum. Dad's doubt had left me with only my own vivid memory for support, and I felt a bit deserted.

The room was high, dark and gloomy. It was lined with green filing cabinets and hung with spotted sepia photographs of bygone police football teams, all alike. It smelled of duplicating ink and stale tobacco and the must of leather-bound statutes. At the far end, with his back to the window, sat the constable. He rose to meet us and in the gloom I knew at once the unforgettable silhouette, and heard as from a great distance the well remembered voice.

'Mr. Thirkell, I believe? Sit down, sir; and this is your boy?'

'Yes, this is my boy Graham.'

'Pleased to meet you, sonny.'

The cop was examining me with blank but friendly unrecognition, and holding out his hand. I shrank back. The cop smiled, let his hand fall and offered Dad a cigarette.

'Your boy seems worried. There's nothing to be concerned about. The police are here to help, you know.'

'Yes, yes, of course,' said Dad testily.

He wanted to get back to work and dispense with long-winded formalities. 'Still, you can hardly blame him for being scared.'

The cop nodded perfunctorily and shuffled the papers on his desk. 'I have your story here, Mr. Thirkell, as reported to me by the Super and—ah—frankly it's an unusual statement. I must tell you,' he went on in his low voice, 'the Chief finds it a little hard to credit. You see, anything like that would mean instant dismissal from the force, and it seems hard to believe that any officer would be so downright foolish.' He turned his head and looked me in the eye. 'Tell me, sonny,' he said slowly through the smoke, 'just what did the man look like?'

I was silent. To say 'He looked like you' seemed hopeless. I tried to appraise the chances of being heard out in the adult world and knew the scales were weighted against me. Hopelessness gave way to resignation. In an instant I'd cut my cables from the treacherous adult shore and drifted out onto the certain currents of boyhood's ocean. Here I could at least foresee the consequences of my acts, in terms of tangible rewards and punishments.

'Come on, Graham; what did the man look like?'

'I don't remember, Dad.'

'Don't remember?' He sounded surprised, a bit annoyed.

'You're quite sure about that, sonny?' said the policeman softly, easing his bulk in the old swivel chair.

'It was . . . very dark.'

The policeman raised his eyebrows. Dad ground his cigarette butt into the floor and stood up.

'I think maybe we'd better go. I know the boy isn't a fibber. Something funny did happen last night.'

'Of course,' said the policeman, 'we're not denying that. We'll keep an extra watch out for any of these fancy characters.'

'The boy was upset and he may have been confused; but there's no doubt he was stopped by a policeman at the town hall, because we checked up with his pal.'

The cop rose to his feet, placed his palms flat on the desk and leaned slightly towards us.

'Of course. I stopped him. I stopped both of them. Those boys were riding without lights, and our instructions . . .'

'I'm not questioning that, but . . .'

'I quite appreciate that you're not. But your boy should be more careful. I told them to walk home, for their own and the public's safety. He had no light and, mind you, I'm not denying the boy's story; it's quite possible he was spoken to. We have the details as to time and place and believe me, we'll keep a sharp look out, as we always do.' He paused and dragged his forefinger slowly down the side of his nose. 'But the point I'm trying to make is: these lads invite trouble if they won't obey the law. If he'd had a light, this wouldn't have happened.' He smiled pleasantly.

Dad picked up his hat and said heavily, 'Well, yes, but . . . thanks for your trouble. I'll see that he gets his light in shape.'

'That's fine. Good day, Mr. Thirkell. Good day, son.'

He held out his hand and this time I took it; it was moist but not retentive. It was given and withdrawn as if absent-mindedly and, as we turned to go, the policeman slumped back in his swivel chair and began reading papers.

We walked off in silence, down the dingy corridor and out through the worn doors. We paused irresolute at the top of the flagged steps, blinking in the sunlight.

'You're not angry with me, Dad?'

'No, old chap. I'm not angry. But, tell you what; let's go down to the bike shop and get an oil lamp. After all, best to do what the police tell you, eh?'

'Oh sure, Dad.' I heard in my voice the toneless quality of obedience.

It was the last day of my boyhood.

Chapter Two

THE BRIGHTON GIRLS

Bᴜᴛ at sixteen one suddenly believes oneself a man. The days start perceptibly to accelerate as one moves inexorably forward in the scale of biological time to the point where, at fifty, years will last six months and recede into the past like telegraph poles along a railway track. At fifteen I had grown five inches to the accompaniment of the usual boils and warts, wens and bilious attacks, furred tongues and blinding headaches. At sixteen, as a gangly six footer, they miraculously disappeared. Suddenly I was in a new world of heightened awareness, living in a state of perpetual excitement. It was not solely the unexpected discovery that a cupid's bow mouth or a kiss-curl beneath a bashed-in school felt hat could send you capering jauntily on your way with ludicrous lightness; that you sang out loud in the street; that you lengthened your stride and took deep breaths. It was the towering realization that you could take decisions and could exercise a will; that you had a personality which people knew and to which they responded; that the world stretched out before you gleaming and glittering; that you were immortal.

The earliest intimations of immortality came prosaically enough in the Melbourne suburb of Brighton. The first thing the nostalgic English settlers did when they disembarked from the emigrant vessel was to defend themselves against the harsh indifference of the sun-burnt continent with the sure shield of English names. The bolder spirits might welcome Woolloomoolloo or Caddabarrawirracanna, but the majority preferred to be reminded of Home; and thus there were Brightons all over Australia: in Queensland, in Tasmania, in Victoria and in South Australia. But none as exciting as ours. First of all, Brighton had 'the beach' which meant that even a modest weather-board bungalow with a tin roof was within a five minute scamper of yellow sands. But unlike our own Malvern with its cramped red brick villas and its endless terracotta roofs baking in the sun, Brighton was a suburb of generous space. Enormous rambling nineteenth-century gingerbread castles lay somnolent behind cedar hedges in the shade of flowering gums, or else, excitingly modern, presented daring cantilevered concrete aprons and pioneer picture windows to the windswept ti-tree scrub and sand dunes, across which the sticky salt breeze blew in from 'The Bay'. And instead of the dull old green and yellow tramcars of the M. & M.T.B., Brighton was served by great clattering maroon giants, a subsidiary of the majestic Victorian Railways. Indeed the insignia V.R. was long thought by us to mean Victoria Regina even as G.R. on the station post box was ignorantly translated as Government Railways.

From behind tall hedges came the plangent thwack of ball on tennis racquet, and on summer nights the beaches were strewn with picnic parties and couples, while the strains of *Valencia* and *Don't Bring Lulu* floated tinnily but romantically from the horns of H.M.V. portables with their pile of 78 r.p.m. discs half buried in the sand.

Because it was so far from our car-less 4 Grace Street, and because inaccessible, therefore improbable and enjoyable, we regarded Brighton for some time as entirely beyond our reach. I did, it is true, make tentative excursions before the Great Awakening. An old A.I.F. friend of Dad's, Brigadier-General Lamb, put us up for a week at his home in Brighton Beach. There were two hulking daughters in their teens who overwhelmed us by their sheer size; for if you are ten the sight of a giantess's black muscular cotton-clad thigh emerging from beneath the pleated navy blue serge skirt of a school uniform can be unnerving in the extreme. However they introduced us to Susan Coolidge, and reading *What Katy Did* in the long hot summer days at Conic Section brought alive the problems of a large family. Katy's Mother had seven or was it eight children? ('Mother, why don't *you* have more children?' 'Because three rowdy boys are quite enough.')

But the terrifyingly delightful Lamb girls were left behind at the entrance to the Brighton Beach Baths. There, in chilling pre-breakfast dips as the sea slashed through the shark-proof piles and the waves arched their silky necks among the shiny festoons of black mussels, the bluff Brigadier taught me to swim. Later his decades of military training caused him to write 'C. R. Lamb, B.G.' in my autograph book when I'd hoped he would write grandly 'General Lamb'.

The second Brighton excursion was to the mansion of a famous legal family, who inhabited a large square stone house draped in Virginia creeper and set behind a sixteen-foot hedge well back from the busy hum of men and maroon tramcars. How we loved those stately sleepy wide-verandahed Victorian mansions compared with the pinched red brick terracotta bungalows in our part of Malvern. Only occasionally did we see behind the cedar hedges and the flowering gum-trees to the sweeping springy lawns of buffalo grass above which sprinklers twisted lazy shimmering arms in the heat, amid the distant hum and clatter of a horse-drawn mower. But Mother's sprightly conversation made her persona grata, and though we usually only went once (did they tire of her sharp tongue or of our boyish rowdiness?), glimpses of these great mansions whetted our appetite for wider worlds.

Stonnington, the house of the Governor of Victoria, Lord Stradbroke, hardly counted (even if his two sons had briefly attended our school) because it was official and hence sui generis. But next door to it, sunk in a mysterious bed of tall rhododendrons, melancholy blue-gums and droopy elms, was an enormous Tuscan palazzo briefly glimpsed from the speeding tramcar and filling us with awe and longing. Occasionally a sleek but rachitic Rolls could be seen leaving the palazzo : its body was encased in yellow basketwork; the upholstery inside was of green leather; and snuggled in its depths, smothered in furred rugs with scalloped edges of navy blue felt, was a little girl of ten or so. Where was she bound? Certainly not to St. Margaret's school, whose leggy young ladies leaped deftly from the tramcar at the next stop. Possibly to some esoteric private school or arcane convent? We never learned, any more than we ever knew to whom the great palazzo belonged; though clearly the poor little girl was in the clutches of some diabolical Central European Count (what was *he* doing in Australia?) who was holding her to ransom. She was probably tuberculous too; not long for this world. The basketwork Rolls receded down Glenferrie Road and its small high oval-shaped rear window yielded no hope, no clue.

Bicycles made possible tours further afield. There was a visit to a judge who had a large spreading bluestone house with a sixteen foot verandah covered by a concave curving galvanized iron roof. The great house lay somnolent in the midst of an acre of ground in East St. Kilda surrounded by a cedar hedge about five hundred feet tall. It was also about fifty feet thick and impenetrable both to the eye and the schoolboy arm which emerged from its crackling depths scored with tiny grazes and covered with a thick layer of dust. The house was in an area where the streets were named after the battles of the Crimean War; the dust probably belonged to at least as far back in time. The immense garden pulsated in the summer heat, and rang with the rasping chant of locusts whose shed skeletons, whiteish and paper-thin, we used to pry from the back of trees as we climbed in bare feet to get at the loquats and lichees which hung in clusters above. Sometimes we were allowed to play there when the judge was out. If our thirst became unbearable and the house was closed we would bicycle over to Dandenong Road down the middle of which ran a wide strip of ornamental turf. Embedded in the grass were the nozzles of water sprays, and even if the water was shut off you could, by dint of lying on your face and sucking until it was purple, conjure from the hidden pipe a draught of metallic-tasting water, warm to start with then cooler as you sucked, and wonderfully refreshing.

Over towards the river lay the Domain with the white turret of the Federal Government House at its centre. Beyond were the Botanical Gardens, unnumbered acres of sloping greens, dark tunnels through exotic trees, and little gazebos and temples overlooking the Yarra which flowed down below, and in the far distance the Jolimont Railroad Yards. They were always just about to roof over the Jolimont Yards but somehow it never happened, other ways having been found to cope with the city's traffic problems.

The Domain was sacred ground to us, forbidden policed territory where in Government House dwelt the representative of King George V. Melbourne was then the provisional seat of Government of the Commonwealth of Australia, until such time as the new Houses of Parliament could be built at Canberra. The compromise had been made, as part of the invincible Melbourne-Sydney rivalry, when Australia federated in 1901. It was agreed that the new federal capital should be located 'not less than two hundred miles' from Sydney, and also that, until it was built and ready for its new tenants, the federal capital should be Melbourne. Thus for twenty-six years, until the Duke and Duchess of York opened Canberra in 1927, Melbourne was the seat of two parliaments of both a Governor and a Governor-General. This conferred on us an adventitious pomp and circumstance and also generated a painful snobbery.

Melbourne, in any case, was in those days particularly avid of any act or gesture which conferred on the doer the cachet of Englishness. The large mansions of Toorak fizzed and bubbled with society doings which were duly reprinted as society gush by the local news-hens. This gossip reached us in the social page of the Sydney *Bulletin* and the glossy centre spread of the Melbourne *Table Talk* with which we thoughtfully stoked the chip-heater that warmed Dad's bath water. But the gush was even better, because at once more brittle and more silken in style, in the copies of the *Tatler* and the *Bystander*. These magazines, imported from England and anything from two to four months late, were the preferred reading (if dog-ears mean preference) in every doctor's and dentist's waiting room.

An Englishman told me many years later that he thought Melbourne the most snobbish city he had ever visited. He cited as an example the fact that he was required to pack tails in his economy class air baggage en route to an international conference because his Australian hosts had said that they would almost certainly be needed. They were, but at a reception graced only by a mayor, not even a Lord Mayor; and he regarded this straining after conspicuous gloss as very suburban. Very Streatham Ballroom and Victor Sylvester was the phrase he actually used. Perhaps this suggests his own snobbery in reverse, but he concluded with the memorable dictum: 'Melbourne people's notion of London is that it's as starchy as Toorak actually is.' This social gossip, though we found it fascinating, had for us a strong air of unreality. It never occurred to us that we could be involved in any of these high class shenanigans, so that when we actually did visit Government House I didn't connect the visit with society at all.

Mother had an acquaintance of some sort with the Governor-General, Lord Forster, as a result of which we were all invited to tea at Government House by his daughter Mrs. Pitt Rivers, (inevitably, in the schoolroom, Mrs. Spit Rivers and the author of *Great Expectorations*) to play with her children. A large open green Daimler, with crown instead of licence plate, called for us and caused an immense sensation in Grace Street. But the memorable aspect of the afternoon was climbing with the Pitt Rivers boys to the top of Government House tower. From here we surveyed, in a breathtakingly unfamiliar panorama, the Botanical Gardens, the Domain and the river, the smoky city beyond it and, in the distance, girdling the horizon, the blue ranges of the Australian Alps. It was late winter and there was even a dramatic trace of snow high up on the shoulder of Donna Buang. We returned home in a state of euphoria and received from Mother a piece of homely advice.

'I wouldn't boast about this at school, if I were you.'

'Why not, Mother? I mean—I wasn't going to anyway.'

'Because nobody would believe you,' she said succinctly.

She was both right and wrong. We were quite unable to refrain from boasting about having gone to the top of Government House tower, but the response was mixed. Some of the boys yahed and made faces of disbelief; but others, among whom the story of the green Daimler had already spread like a grass fire, were overcome with admiration, and eventually it was they who carried the day. We thus learned that association with the great, however adventitious, confers lustre. Maybe this is not confined to Melbourne, but it seemed that Melburnians were prone to confer the lustre on slight or specious grounds, as in the case of Dad and the Duchess.

When he was on leave during the War, my stepfather, 'Thirk' then, had been briefly a guest along with other Australian officers at Glamis Castle, the home of Lady Elizabeth Bowes-Lyon, daughter of the Earl of Strathmore. Dad kept photographs of this happy period in his study at our home, and impressed on us what a wonderful person she was. So indeed she appeared in her fringe and bun, her sweet expression and her long-sleeved blouse and ankle-length pleated skirt of the day. The photograph became a fixture on the wall and we thought no more about it. But the years rolled by and in 1927 the former Lady Elizabeth Bowes-Lyon, now Duchess of York, arrived in Melbourne with her husband en route to the opening ceremonies at Canberra. In the midst of her multifarious activities which included, in addition to the chores at Canberra, shouldering the loyal lampoons of university students, she found time to remember the A.I.F. Captain and to grant him the honour of a dance with her at the Government House ball. Dad was of course deeply touched but he was a simple man and the cataract of social outpouring which this incident unleashed in the women's columns he found highly disconcerting. Once again, though, we couldn't help noticing that our 'izzat' at school rose by many notches and we became, momentarily, figures of mark.

Sometimes the bicycle took us further afield, especially in the spring time to gather wattle at Ashburton. Here amid the mouldering ruins of the old Outer Circle line was a curious wild heath, utterly remote from the red brick rash creeping eastward from the city towards the Dandenong Ranges. The open parkland was covered with rough grass and scrub; and in among the ti-trees were stagnant billabongs of Gardiner's Creek, lined with trees whose knees and feet were splotched with bright orange fungus, and covered in their more foetid reaches by a scum of watercress. I became an enthusiastic collector of fungi and took home great swatches of dripping cress, which nobody would ever eat because it stank so strongly of mud.

Nearer at hand was the Caulfield Racecourse where, by dodging past the gatekeeper, one could slalom endlessly on a bicycle in and out of the bookmaker's poles set in asphalt behind the main grandstand. On off days the racecourse was silent and deserted; and in place of Honest Joe Cohen or Ben Green, with his greasy fedora, bookie's bag and hoarse entreaties, was an empty surrealist world of endless freewheeling permutations. The height of skill was to thread your way through a line of steel posts 'no hands', demanding a degree of expertise attained only by a shock-headed albino friend with pale blue eyes, who earned our left-over sandwiches for his efforts.

I never saw such a place as Melbourne for sandwiches, and for morning and afternoon teas. About eleven o'clock the women shoppers or suburban housewives and their children, or even salesmen and business acquaintances, would start to thicken in the entrance

lobbies of such emporia as *The Wattle*, *The Georgian*, or *The Chocolate Bowl*. Here they would consume not just tea, but immense
quantities of sandwiches, asparagus squares, cold sausage rolls, rock
cakes, scones, chocolate eclairs, cream puffs, and great mounds of
iced fruit cake. It was sheer gormandising; but it was also a ritual
of the most demanding kind. A university student or even a favoured
nephew who received an invitation to 'Meet me at the *Wattle* for
morning tea' knew that he would have to turn up sharp on the
hour, be prepared to stay at least an hour, and also to make a show
of consuming these immense mountains of saccharine carbohydrates.
Morning tea also had a social cachet and (if those drinking it were
sufficiently important) would be reported in the gossip columns.
The whole performance was a monument to 'ghastly good taste' and,
while it was wonderful for a boy on holiday to be able to stuff
himself thus, the ritual produced a painful obesity in the suburban
housewife as she puffed stertorously back to Moonee Ponds or Glen
Iris to prepare the hot mid-day 'dinner'.

Being a snob myself I of course naturally preferred St. Kilda and
Brighton to places like Moonee Ponds. Down St. Kilda way for
example was the Michaelis home on Acland Street with delicate
white-painted lace ironwork falling in a filigree between slim cast
iron pillars that supported two storeys of verandah and balcony.
Michaelis-Hallenstein were tanners by trade, but aesthetes by avoca-
tion, and their house filled me with an exquisite longing to shed my
suburban lineaments and strut about in an imaginary Graustarkian
atmosphere of high tasselled boots, hussars with six-inch collars
bowing stiffly from the waist, and ladies with ringlets, décolleté
ball gowns and flirtatious fans. I was entirely oblivious of the fact
that just up the hill from the Michaelis house the St. Kilda skyline
was pierced by a tall sewer ventilator known to us all as 'the stink
pipe'. Acland Street was not of this world; perhaps I just ignored
the pipe.

So that what with the prospect of Brighton mansions and Brighton
maidens my curiosity for this far off unattainable pleasure dome by
the dreamy sea (last tram 11.40 p.m.) grew apace. It was satisfied
in an unexpected manner, through The Play. Voice firmly broken
and with the 1920's equivalent of my G.C.E. 'O' behind me, it was
possible to emerge from the pupa of girls' parts into the chrysalis
of young manhood (eyes romantically shadowed by the 'foots',
sticky-out ears mercifully flattened by the 'pros') and to wow the
girls—or at least to wow oneself—by one's acting ability.

The stellar vehicle, as they say, was *A Safety Match* by Ian Hay
and I was well content to leave the lead to Charlie Jacobs who, as
the producer said, could play everything from the Emperor of China

to the confused noise outside and who, unlike me, was commendably interested in acting rather than in simply making an impression. I was quite satisfied with the subordinate but by no means lean part of his secretary, Jim Carthew, an officer and a gentleman, the kind of fellow who wins V.C.s and gets done in wholesale, who carries out the Juggernaut's orders with unfailing devotion and precision, who sings stirring evangelical hymns with a group of entombed miners and eventually, against all probability, emerges with a bloodied head from a shroud of coal dust and fallen timbers on the arm of the flibbertigibbet Bright Young Thing, Vane, whom he has long worshipped from afar but who hitherto has revealed her tinselly worthlessness by spurning him and who is redeemed (in the eyes of the playwright at any rate) by her discovery that Jim is a hero.

'Lean on me, Jim, dear boy. I want you to *lean* on me,' she chirrups (in the person of Jock Frew, fifth form science), as she leads me staggering through the fumes to open air and to thunderous applause. A natural, you'd say, for a tall self-opinionated but basically insecure lad of sixteen, now shaving every other day. And so, miraculously, did it appear to the Brighton maidens. Through the agency of their friends in The Play and mine, Barton Hack and Kevyn Hume-Cook, I was now about to enter their magic world.

Barton Hack was a dry cool fellow with a firm jaw, tight curly blond hair, and a grim sense of moral rectitude through which ran a wild streak of mordant and rebellious humour. He played the part of an elderly clergyman in our school play, and we thought it perfect type-casting. Then, one dress-rehearsal, during a pause to re-set the lighting, there emerged from above the parsonical adam's apple and the dog collar the startling announcement, delivered dead-pan, that he had just perfected a rotary mechanical self-renewing bum-wiper which could be automatically raised and lowered to the required position. Purchase of this piece of equipment included its free installation in your toilet bowl. He was in the market for share capital; was anyone interested? He gazed around the vicarage breakfast table with a benign ferocity. We were too taken aback even to laugh, and just then the lights came on, the producer yelled 'On cue', and the dress-rehearsal continued. 'Are you serious?' someone whispered. 'Oh yes,' said Barton judiciously. 'I'm taking out a patent.'

We all knew of course that Barton's father was the head of a firm of patent attorneys in Collins Street. His name was Clement A. Hack and he was, to boys, a most daunting man. I never saw him in his private lair in Collins Street, but he could transform the drawing-room in his Brighton house into a den quite as terrifying as any 'headmaster's office. When Barton first took me to his home one evening after school I was impressed by its soaring two-storeyed solidity and delighted by his mother, a small neatly built woman with a bun, a quizzical expression and long rustly clothes which somehow assuaged and made bearable the, to me, terrifying bark of Clement A. Hack.

This formidable man, with a head of close-cropped greyish-blond hair, was usually sighted by the invading horde of post tea-time boys in possession of the drawing-room. One entered the vast dimly lit room behind Mrs. Hack whose finger was to her lips, and descried the Great Man at a vast, brilliantly lit distance, like an altar in the dim recesses of a European cathedral. He was ensconced at the far corner of the great square room seated in an armchair with a biblical reader propped in front of him, its white pages and his blond-grey hair bathed in the refulgent splendour of a green shaded precursor of the anglepoise, the sole source of light in the darkened room: an explosion of terrifying intensity in the arc-lit corner of an underwater cave. The power of his intense concentration radiated in waves across the room. Beneath the bluff forehead and the grizzled hair a fierce intelligence blazed in concentrated fury on the task before him.

Mrs. Hack whispers, 'Say good evening to him, Graham; he won't notice you otherwise.'

It is like disturbing a judge summing up, a bishop in communion with his God, or a scientist on the verge of discovering $E=MC^2$. The patent cases he reads with such voracious intensity may relate to the mundane affairs of Coca Cola or Shell Oil or Broken Hill Proprietary; but for all we know he may be about to thunder out the Mosaic law, to utter a piercing Socratic cry, or to roar out some crushing Johnsonian apophthegm.

'Good evening, sir.'

There is a breathless pause. Eventually the head rises like that of a dinosaur in pain, and looks vaguely outward, blinded by the light and still steeped in the juices of judicial enquiry.

'Who's that?' It is a bark, but being faintly querulous is therefore vaguely reassuring. Evidently we're all not going to be put in irons tonight; not just yet, anyway.

'Me sir, Graham.'

'Ah Graham.' Pause. 'Enjoying yourself?'

'Oh yes sir.'

'Barton looking after you?'

'Oh yes sir.'

'Good. Get along then.'

Mrs. Hack holds the door open and, with a rustle of skirts, ushers us through. The relief is enormous. Banished from the drawing-room in which it would be, and later did, become possible to have eight tables of bridge or a dance for twenty couples, we return to the dining-room. Barton's sister Lindsay, a severe girl with gold braids, and her friend who has brown hair and a slightly supercilious expression, are setting up a ping-pong net on the dining table. Lindsay is in a difficult mood. We don't seem to see eye to eye on whether you should bat from beneath the table or whether it's all right to do a spin serve on the sandpapered side of the bat from *above* the table. While we are arguing in a pointless, well-I'm-sure-I-don't-care-it-couldn't-mean-less-to-me manner Barton and the friend have disappeared. Lindsay and I are stuck with each other.

'Why do you do your hair in pigtails, Lindsay?'

'Don't call them pigtails. It's rude.'

'What do you want me to call them?'

'I don't particularly want you to call them anything; but if you must mention them, they're plaits.'

'O.K., plaits then. Why do you do your hair in plaits?'

'Because I like them. What business is it of yours?'

'It makes you look like a little girl.'

'Well that's suitable for a little boy isn't it?'

'Don't get sore at me.'

'Then don't make personal remarks. There's the door-bell.'

'That's just an excuse not to talk to me.'

'No, it really is the bell. Excuse *me*.'

She flounced—she really did—out of the room, pigtails and all, and in a surge of greetings and hallos in burst Kevyn Hume-Cook and a quiet girl whom I didn't know. Lindsay's face brightened perceptibly.

'It's Kevyn.' He gave an elaborate ballet-esque bow.

At once the atmosphere oozed a sort of roguish duplicity and everyone looked as though they expected Kevyn to pick a white rabbit out of the air. He just stood there all liquid arms and legs, bouncing delicately on the balls of his feet with his curly well-brilliantined hair falling in a juicy lock over his forehead. His nose was long and slightly tip-tilted. He had beautifully even white teeth behind a pair of curvy lips. He was all nods and becks and wreathed smiles and no matter what attitude he struck (and he never adopted but always struck an attitude) he seemed to glide and pour himself over the furniture like a couple of yards of water in a polythene bag.

From his liquid coils and curves exuded a naked and unabashed charm which floored us all : school friends, girls, schoolmasters, old ladies. He was a mental spiv and disarming roguish Pan who weaved his way through school life without, so far as we could see, doing a stroke of work or playing any organized games. Yet he was sought after by schoolmasters to whom he did amusing imitations of their colleagues' voices, and by the big tough football and rowing bruisers whose love-life he helped to straighten out by sage and disinterested counsel, given with an air of enormous worldly wisdom. He was an elderly exquisite of seventeen and when he gangled and gesticulated with his liquid delicacy and his feathery fluttery hands it was quite impossible to resist him. Girls sat with lips slightly parted; fellows with an amused twinkle in their eye; the expression they wore was that of a mistress who waits for her favourite dog to perform a well-known and complicated trick.

Kevyn oozed out of an armchair and put his hand in mine; somehow it didn't seem cissy when he did it.

'Who's afraid of the Big Bad Wolf?' he asked.

'Not me, Gallagher,' I replied.

'Attaboy, Captain Cook,' he said and patted my knee. He looked genially at us: 'How's about a game of winks?'

We tried to look wise and said nothing. The strange girl looked in my direction and gave a timid smile. It dawned on me that everybody seemed to know her but me. I was just going to ask Kevyn to introduce us when the lights went out in preparation for 'winks'. There was a certain amount of scuffling in the dark and a suppressed giggle or two. I felt my way carefully over to where the strange girl had been sitting. Though I wasn't very bold where girls were concerned, the darkness made me enterprising and I lunged onto the sofa and made a grab. The lights blazed on. Lindsay regarded me with a freezing disdain which I'm sure was mirrored by my own disconcertment. She rose swiftly without looking at me. 'I'm going to get some ginger ale,' she said as she swept out to the kitchen. Kevyn came in with the strange girl.

'So it was you?' said Barton.

'Who doused the glim? That's right. I'm the oldest inhabitant around here and I know where all the switches are.'

He gangled into a chair; the strange girl paused awkwardly beside it. I knew from long experience that Mr. Hack would shortly emerge from his lair in a highly ropable state, so I suggested we vamoose.

'No need,' said Barton. 'The old man's deep in a case. Nothing we do would disturb him.'

Kevyn laid his finger to his long tip-tilted nose.

'There's where you drop the molasses jug,' he said. 'I pulled the wrong switch and my hunch is he was in the gloom for several minutes. Let's get over to my place, eh? Those in favour? Contrary? Carried!'

Lindsay came in with bottles of ginger ale and glasses on a tray, her pigtails swinging.

'Dad's mad,' she said. 'We have to break it up.'

The strange girl looked alarmed. Kevyn spread broad spatulate fingers in an arc of shrugging.

'Over to my place, eh? By the way Graham this is Cec. Oh sorry, I should have done it the other way round. Cec, Graham. We'll all go in the family barouche. I've managed to borrow it for the night.'

Lindsay chucked her eyes up to heaven.

'What about my ginger ale?'

'Don't be a nark,' said her brother.

Kevyn put his finger to his lips.

A muffled bellow came from the rear of the house.

'His Master's Voice,' said Kevyn. 'This way.'

We piled into a Crossley convertible; Kevyn at the wheel—illegal and exciting—with two girls beside him, he insisted on that. Barton and I shared Cec in the back seat. Kevyn considerately put a rug over all three of us. We zoomed off into the night with the sticky salt breeze in our hair, and the salt rust clinging to the lamp standards as they rushed by. The great clumsy maroon tramcars complete with cowcatcher thundered past. I saw that with a little adroit dallying I could contrive to miss the last tram back to 4 Grace Street and be compelled to spend the night at either the Hacks' or the Hume-Cooks'.

The Hume-Cooks' house was called Girrahween, an 'Abo' name which somehow fitted in perfectly with Kevyn's liquid movements and long eyelashes. If Clement A. Hack seemed brusque and withdrawn, James Hume-Cook was lean, willowy and distinguished with a long sad nose, a carefully tended cavalry moustache and, most daring of all, white piping to the vee of his waistcoat. In point of fact he was the Hon. James Hume-Cook, the title having been conferred for life on all who had been members of the first Federal Parliament of the Commonwealth of Australia which opened in 1901. Kevyn's father had been a Member of the House of Representatives and was therefore the Hon.

He was at the time Secretary-Manager of the Australian Industries Protection League and we used to read his publicity on billboards in vacant lots and above the windows in trains and tramcars:

Wherever you trade
Buy Australian-made.

A memorable jingle, but somehow not entirely worthy of the flowing flowery James Hume-Cook—as lean and elegant as Clement A. Hack was rough and craggy—with his white piping, his gold Prince

32

Albert chain, his grey homburg hat and his buttoned boots, clearly marking him as a fastidious eccentric in Melbourne of the late 1920s. He acquired great stature in my eyes by being able to pronounce correctly—though of course, surprisingly—such exotic American place names as Yosemite and Schenectady. Mrs. Hume-Cook was pretty and loving, specially of Kevyn who was the 'baby'. His sister Madge was often at home when we called, and would tactfully withdraw to her own room leaving the 'lounge' to the youngsters to hold hands while gazing into the electric fire to the strains of *Rhapsody in Blue*.

Kevyn felt he had to account for his sister's presence, presumably in case one of us was crass enough to ask why she wasn't out with a boyfriend.

'She's the serious type,' he'd say. 'Thinks she's on the shelf because she's twenty-two and single, but I say to her "Sweetie, save yourself for your Knight Errant. He'll come along don't you worry".'

We were prepared to take Madge on trust so long as she didn't barge in when we were 'scrondling' (a cross between a scramble and a fondle) as it was known to the young bucks of the day.

Kevyn's elder brother Keith was too manly and glamorous for our timid teenage diversions. Whenever I spent a weekend, or even an evening, at Girrahween he was always on the point of going out; either to fetch his girl of the moment in a rakish beat-up sports car, or else rushing to drive away a girl who was already waiting in the car at the kerbside, the cynosure of admiring or curious eyes from behind the paling fences and the lace curtains of treeless Manor Street. One evening when Kevyn and I were larking with a couple of girl-friends in the back garden gloaming of Girrahween, Keith came bursting out in a fresh dress shirt, but minus the tie which was streaming from his left hand.

'Graham,' he yelled, 'make yourself useful for once—will you? I've cut myself shaving and I can't tie this bloody tie in the mirror.'

'Why don't you wear a made-up tie,' asked Kevyn innocently.

His brother favoured him with a blistering look. 'Here Graham, try and fix it for me will you.'

I was willing enough but he stood before me with his neck thrust out and his arms akimbo like a rampaging bull at the arena gate. He breathed heavily through his nostrils and was obviously panting to be off.

'Hurry, I'm late, there's a good bloke,' he said. He made me nervous and I fumbled cursorily with the tie while his impatience mounted. Finally he could bear it no longer and jerked his own hands up to feel a rudimentary knot.

33

'That's okay, that's okay,' he bellowed in a frenzy. 'I can manage from here on.'

I saw to my alarm that blood from his cut neck had got onto his tie where, since the tie was black, it was mercifully invisible. But I gazed in horrid fascination lest it should somehow slide off and spot his spotless collar.

'What the hell are you staring at?'

I couldn't say it. I just nodded, gagging in my throat with my mouth open. Then he did it. As the neat bow was tweaked into place, his finger slipped and a red blob appeared on the shirt collar. He felt the stickiness that I saw, but to my amazement didn't upbraid me. He was in too much of a hurry and all he said was,

'Hell, got a blood spot on my collar? Thought so. Madge'll get it off with warm water. Hey, Madge!'

With a bound he was off up the garden and into the house throwing a 'Thanks, kiddo' at me over his shoulder.

But tonight when the ancient Crossley slid to the kerb outside Girrahween no one was in. The house was silent and we six were alone. I was discomfited to find, when Kevyn pulled the rug off the three of us in the back seat, that the girl's right hand was in mine and her left in Barton's. She didn't seem to mind a bit—or even notice. I considered myself very ill used. However we pulled up the carpet in the 'lounge', and after dancing for a while to the strains of *You're the Cream in my Coffee* and *Deep Night* it dawned on me with a delicious sense of relief that the last tram had already left.

'Hey Bart, I'll have to stay the night.'

'Want to telephone your people?'

'Why bother, it's Saturday.'

Kevyn executed a pirouette in the middle of the improvised ball-room floor and said,

'On with the dance, let joy be unrefined.'

*　　*　　*

Brighton now opened out unbelievably into the Timmins home. Here mildly cynical but inexhaustible affection reigned supreme under the tempestuous and kindly eye of Mrs. Timmins who provided a well chaperoned paradise for very young men, no less than three daughters, and a son who was still in the stage between teddy bears and railways when I came on the scene.

Mrs. Timmins was the daughter of Theodore Fink, chairman of *The Herald* (read by 186,734 people daily) and her marriage to

Walter Timmins joined her Jewish drive, shrewdness and *gemüt-lichkeit* to his charm, good looks and mechanical inventiveness. Between them they produced three really smashing girls. Theodore Fink was to us only a vague grandfather in the background, but we knew that his discovery of Keith Murdoch (later Sir Keith or 'Lord Southcliffe' as he was irreverently known) had been a spectacularly successful venture into mass journalism. You couldn't live in Melbourne and not know it. In those days *The Herald* was the sole evening paper in a city of one million people. Even today, close to forty years later, when the population of Melbourne is now two million, *The Herald* is still the only evening paper. This astonishing feat was due to a combination of Fink's financial shrewdness and Murdoch's organizing drive, and the empire expanded to include the morning *Sun News-Pictorial* (known to my kid brother as the 'piotrical') based on a similar success by the London *Daily Mirror*; *Table Talk* (the local *Tatler* and *Bystander* combined), the Adelaide *Advertiser* and an enormous job printing business.

Walter Timmins was an engineer of placid disposition and wonderful good looks who seemed a bit outdistanced by his wife and took refuge in the amiable superiority that is conferred by offering young men pints of beer in silver tankards with glass bottoms and asking them their opinion on world affairs. Always sure fire. Rival courtiers for his daughters' favours would pontificate warily, as in a mediaeval joust, under the benign eye of Walter Timmins while Margery was readying the girls upstairs.

It was only rarely that we were allowed to bring friends back home to 4 Grace Street. Mother took the view that, broadly speaking, we three boys existed in the house on sufferance. She had left a life of elegance and wit in W.8 for what she was pleased to call The Underworld. This in itself was sufficient tribulation without having rowdy boys bring their friends home to leave mud on the carpets and dirty finger marks on the door jambs.

What was home anyway? I was ashamed of it: ashamed of the Morris wallpaper and the outside lavatory and chip-heater and the tiny garden and the pools of oil left by Dad's bike and the general air of scrape and save. The atmosphere lacked generosity and for a long time after I met Barton and Kevyn I put off inviting them to the house until my excuses ran out. Then one evening when I complained of feeling sick they simply accompanied me bodily back to 4 Grace Street. It turned out to be the 'flu and when they neither derided this weakness nor sneered at our humble red brick bungalow the snobbishness inherent in all children was stilled, and thereafter they often visited me. But girls; well, in the first place, I wouldn't want to bring them to the house where the new-found gallantry of my conduct and brilliance of my wit would be exposed to the jaundiced comments of parents and family. And secondly, what girl would ever want to visit 4 Grace Street? Let them admire me for myself not for my home (it was the parents' home anyway, not mine). Finally Mother herself was sufficient discouragement for any girl to face.

If I were unfortunate enough not to reach the mail box first, Mother would hand me across the breakfast table, with a sibylline smirk, billets-doux from young ladies of the Melbourne Church of England Girls' Grammar School or the Presbyterian Ladies' College. If the envelope was pink or purple, as they often were, (I used to *beg* my girl-friends not to nail their colours so assertively to the mast), or scented (which did happen once or twice) Mother would say

'Well well, another prospective daughter-in-law' in a loud clear voice. And one evening when I rashly brought a girl home for a breather between a tea party and a dance Mother accosted her with such a coruscation of fireworks that the poor thing never came near me again.

'Good evening, Mavis. Mavis is Scottish—though why the Scotch should prefer to be so pedantic about naming themselves I cannot imagine—for blackbird. Did you know that, Mavis?'

'Well I . . .'

'I expect you sing like a blackbird, don't you? "I have heard the Mavis singing her love-song to the morn." You know that charming ballad of Burns' I expect?'

'I . . .'

'But I mustn't talk about singing love songs, must I? Come along, you little goose, *don't* be so sensitive. I'll show you where the lavatory is. Outside I'm afraid. Unfortunately in this uncivilized country we live in a sort of Irish cabin, but no doubt you'll find your way . . .'

And the only time we ever did have a dance at 4 Grace Street it was Mother's idea, reluctantly accepted by me; and all the initiative, the food and the *placement* were hers. The girls and boys danced glumly to music on the H.M.V. portable, grimly handcranked by Mother between numbers. They sat stiffly on rush-bottomed wooden chairs in the Lady Help's bedroom (she had been banished to a movie for the evening), eating bought ice cream and odious 'squashed fly' biscuits and drinking barley water. Conversation froze before Mother's literary sallies.

'Are you enjoying yourself, Eric?'

'The time's just flying, Mrs. Thirkell!'

'Time flies; you cannot; they go too fast.'

'Er . . .'

'*Aspice faciem*. Come come, where's your Latin?'

'Um—I think maybe it's time . . .'

'Not in the least. Have some more barley water. A house full
a hole full, you cannot gather a bowl full.'

Later when the 'men', contrary to all instructions, were 'watering
the daisies' on the darkened back lawn I heard a pal say

'Is his Mum dotty?'

'No, but she's very highly educated.'

The party sank without trace about eleven p.m., Mother watching
with benevolent ferocity from the glaringly lit front porch ('I *won't*
have any spooning in my house') as I gloomily saw my guests off,
and my particular girl for the evening wedged like a frightened
pullet between two other companions in the back seat of someone
else's car. No wonder we preferred Brighton.

By contrast, the Timmins home seemed to be, on week-ends at
least, an almost perpetual round of gaiety and excitement, aided of
course by a tennis court, an enormous new playroom upstairs at
the back of the house, and a wide verandah with access to cooling
drinks of an innocent nature, for we were all so full of bounce that
we could burn for a whole afternoon and evening on a simple mixture of Kia Ora lemon squash and raspberry vinegar. Mrs. Timmins
moved with large kindly poppy eyes and a ponderous but somehow
nimble walk, not exactly in the background but not exactly in the
foreground either: rather a sort of invisible but perpetual warp-and-
woof, strengthening the fabric of any party. Lovers' tiffs, Galahads'
quarrels, the mooning of young men about unattainable girls or
unattainable aspects of the universe always found in her a kindly
but astringent listener.

'Do you believe in love at first sight, Mrs. Timmins?'

'It's not impossible, Graham, but at first sight by whom?'

'By the man of course. At least . . .'

'What about the woman?'

'Well I suppose that's important too, in a way.'

'You bet your sweet life it is!'

'But I was thinking more of romantic love, you know. Like some
fellow suddenly seeing a girl for the first time and, you know, getting
smitten on her?'

'You mean he thinks he is?'

'That's right.'

'But he doesn't worry too much what the girl thinks?'

'Oh I see what you mean. Well naturally I suppose it's important
to him that the girl should, well, reciprocate. At least he hopes she
will.'

'Yearns for it I should think,' said Mrs. Timmins drily.

'Oh yes, but the most important thing is his own sudden sense of glory and hopelessness.'

'Why hopelessness?'

'Well I mean to say, if the girl doesn't respond. I mean she *knows*, doesn't she? A girl knows when a man is smitten on her even if he says nothing?'

'A girl can almost always tell when a man's interested in her, yes. But she's apt to distrust this "love at first sight" as you call it.'

'But why? Isn't that very . . . cautious of her?'

'Girls have to be more cautious than men; they have more at stake.'

This certainly sank in.

'Mrs. Timmins.'

'Yes?'

'Did you . . . I mean do you think a man falling in love at first sight makes a girl fall in love with him?'

'At first sight?'

'Well, at any sight.'

'It may. If it's powerful and tempestuous enough, it's bound to have a very profound effect on a girl. But not all to the good. It can be very upsetting to her.'

'But why should it be so upsetting to be loved?'

'Because a young man's love—particularly this love at first sight— is really a very selfish emotion.'

'Selfish !'

'That's what I said. The young man is usually thinking about himself, *his* feelings, *his* unhappiness. And he really doesn't think much about the girl at all—except as the mere object of his affections. I mean he doesn't consider what *she* feels.'

'Perhaps he's so overwhelmed by his own feeling that he can't?'

'That's just my point. Real love is a matter of giving as well as taking, or reducing the fortress of your own personality by letting someone breach it—if you want a military metaphor.'

'Oh but, doesn't that mean surrender?'

'Of course it does !'

'I thought only women surrendered.'

'Don't you believe it ! There's a mutual exchange of hostages and that enlarges the fortress of your personality.'

'Did Mr. Timmins surrender to you?'

'No personalities now ! You'll have to learn to keep conversations on love confined to—abstract principles.'

'Then you can't help me? I mean with my problem?'

'Your problem, as you call it, will stop being a problem when you start considering the other person. Now get me a drink like a good boy.'

'Is Mummy putting you through the hoops? You poor man!'

It was dark-eyed Prudence, the youngest, most intense and least manageable of the three Timmins sisters; barely in her teens, yet the asker of diabolical and fiendish questions. She hopped about on one leg, barley-sugared herself round a verandah pillar and observed,

'I'm absolutely *embedded* in *Rewards and Fairies*. You must of course know all about that because you're related to Kipling aren't you, Graham?'

'Remotely, yes.'

'Oh but my dear, to think of being related at all! I think it's positively *unmanning*! How do you pronounce the title? Do you say *Rewards and Fairies* as if you were being offered a reward, say five pounds? Or do you pronounce it *Rewards* to rhyme with *Stewards*?'

'I never heard . . .'

'I have a theory, mind you, that a reward, as in steward, is just another sort of fairy, a gnome or elf or troll; and that that's what Kipling *really* meant when he linked the name with fairies.' She untwisted herself with lightning rapidity and lunged forward, her eyes popping at me with intense and fearful concentration. 'I mean, Graham, you must know, being a relative or a connection. Call it what you will; it's a touch of consanguinity, and that puts you *en rapport*, doesn't it? So you say Rewards or Rewards? Now come, do tell me.'

'I just say *Rewards*.'

'Oh do you? Oh I think that's most unenterprising and disappointing of you. I don't know how Cec can possibly be interested in such a dull young man.'

'Now, wait a minute . . .'

'Prue you just shut up!' Cec appeared from the tennis court and looked menacing.

'So that you two can be alone eh?'

'Prue, I'm warning you.'

'Oh she's so brutal, Graham. She'll twist my arm like anything when you've gone. Great big bully you are, Cec. Ow! That hurts. Let me go! Let go or I'll tell Graham all about you and—Ow!'

Cec flushed and she shot out between clenched teeth,

'Honestly Prue, I'll murder you if you don't shut up.'

'Oh very well.' Cec relaxed and Prue shook herself free with a frenzied feline grace and stalked huffily away. 'Though I'm bound to observe,' she shot over her shoulder at her sister, 'that you don't look absolutely at your best when you're upset.'

'Who's upset?' said a crisp contralto. It was Ruth the middle sister, an exquisitely and coolly beautiful girl with the most perfect oval Raphael face and a great mass of honey gold hair.

'No one!' snapped Cec.

Ruth raised an enquiring eyebrow and glided gracefully past us into the pantry. Cec said

'Well at least we can go upstairs.'

But upstairs we found young Rod, the sole and prideful male heir, playing with his train on the floor and beside him his father whom I could see from the rapt expression on his face was enjoying it even more than Rod, perhaps because he was an engineer. Cec gave a deep sigh. Mr. Timmins looked up with his endearing smile.

'Hullo, did you want to use this room?'

'Rod,' Cec snapped, 'you know this part of the house is supposed to be ours after six o'clock. Can't you take your blessed train somewhere else?'

'I like it here,' said Rod phlegmatically.

Mr. Timmins moved gracefully to his feet and extended his hand to me with a wink.

'Sorry about this,' he said. Cec sighed again. He had a jolly smiling face with a thin nose and neatly sculptured lips and a permanent twinkle in his eye. A bit like Cec, I used to think.

'Give me a hand to dismantle this apparatus,' he said 'and then we'll see about a beer. Come on young man.' He picked up Rod under one arm and a fistful of Hornby rails in his free hand and off we all went downstairs leaving Cec alone in the upstairs room.

It often went like that at the Timmins' because they were so kind and agreeable that one's affections became diffused among the entire family. And there were compensations too in the interplay of the generations. It was rather flattering, as you danced the *Yale Walk* or the *Varsity Drag* with Cec or Ruth or Beryl or Lindsay to have Mrs. Timmins walk level with you for a couple of tours round the living room while she sought your opinion of *Elmer Gantry*.

'Well frankly Mrs. Timmins I don't think it's as good as *Babbitt*.'

'Isn't that funny, neither do I. What's the reason do you think?'

'It seems to me too forced' (treading on my partner's toes).

'Yes I suppose that's it. The snapshots came just a little too quickly; and the camera shutter clicks too fast.'

'Oh Mum, *do* let us dance.'

'Sorry dear. But it's better than *Main Street* don't you think?'

'I found *Main Street* a bit beyond me, actually Mrs. Timmins. There were parts of it I couldn't understand' (Bump!)

'Oh *Mum*!!'

'We must talk about it sometime, Graham. I find your views so refreshing.'

Fun too, to leave the girls for a bit to their mysterious prettifying and discuss early makes of cars with Mr. Timmins: the Palm, the Crossley, the Stutz Bearcat; how he'd courted Mrs. Timmins (funny somehow to think of her as Margery Fink) in a Stanley Steamer owned jointly by himself and his brother when they were establishing the engineering works in South Melbourne; how he once went to Flemington Racecourse for the Melbourne Cup in an old Canadian McLaughlin (God knows how *that* crossed the Pacific in those far off days); and how he bought shares in a company that manufactured the ill-starred Australian Six.

'But all I've got now is a Rolls-Canardly.'

'I've heard of a Rolls, sir, but never . . .'

'Haven't you? It's a very well known make. Rolls down the hills and can 'ardly get up 'em. How about another beer?'

Most weekend parties ended up, if you waited long enough, in a moonlight excursion to the beach with three boys and three girls crammed into someone's Baby Austin or Hillman. We essayed hurried kisses with imminent danger of a horribly anti-climactic clashing of teeth as the elated driver bumped too fast over an intersection. Then on the beach itself the moonlight washed like surf against the dim outline of the houses and hedges at our rear, and before us lay a long bright shimmering pathway across the oily waters of The Bay. And after the chaff and the pleasantries came the pairing off for which we'd all been pretending not to wait for the whole weekend, and then even gritty grains of sand between them couldn't mar the excitement of soft lips.

At the beginning of 1929, a year that, though we did not know it, was to be momentous for the whole world as well as for ourselves, Mrs. Timmins decided to take the daughters for their Trip Home, to introduce her young fledgelings to the patina of Europe, and herself to renew girlhood memories along the Strand, Norfolk Place and the Inns of Court whither she'd wandered with *her* father a generation before. We all began to get letters from exotic ships, from unbelievable places like Amalfi, or Heidelberg, and with strangely mis-spelt postmarks like *Milano* and *München*, and even notepaper with grotesque statements such as *Warm en Koud water op alle Kamers*.

'Gosh!' I said to Barton, 'they must be having a wonderful time.' Here were we back in dull old Aussie and what's more at school, while they . . .

Then came a long letter from a finishing school at Boulogne-sur-Seine and it breathed such a dolorous litany of disappointments and such a passionate longing for Australia (and incidentally for us) that I thought, despite the implied honour, the girl had gone dotty. I confided in Kevyn (a mistake because he told her sister).

'Ah, she's just crazy about you,' he said. 'That's why she's miserable. You're here and she's there.'

But with the clear-eyed and perhaps admirable naïveté of youth, I replied,

'Oh no, it's Australia she's missing, not me. She wants to come home.'

So indeed it proved. They all came back, but 1930 was a different world from 1929.

Chapter Three

1929

NINETEEN TWENTY-NINE is one of those years, like 1914 or 1066, which in the popular mind slice history with a guillotine blade. An era ends; another begins. In the case of 1929 it is not only the year but the actual date, carrying with it a heavy encrustation of moral unction, Biblical thunders, pride going before a fall and doing as you would be done by. The date is of course October 4, when the New York Stock Exchange transacted what was up to that time its record day of business, and all the American blue chip stocks sank to unprecedented low levels. Millions of investors, we were told, became paupers; paper fortunes vanished overnight. An impenetrable portcullis clashed down between the Roaring Twenties and the Dismal Thirties. We moved from a post-war into a pre-war world; from the Charleston and the Black Bottom to the Rumba and the Bunny Hug; from sunshine to shadow; from the silents to the talkies; from Weimar to the Third Reich; from Prosperity to The Great Depression.

When my children were growing up they often asked me how it was conceivable that I could have really enjoyed my youth. After all, they'd say, it was in the Thirties: that Dead Sea of men's hopes; that abyss of despair; the age of Jarrow and the Hunger Marchers. It was useless to explain to them that the world of the late Twenties and early Thirties was to me a wonderful world simply because I was young. They just did not believe me. But it is true: 1929 was an exciting year because it was my final year at school and I had climbed the heights of authority; 1930 was an equally exciting year because I went up to University and opened the jalousies of my constricted young mind to the heady breezes of learning and controversy. The Twenties merged imperceptibly into the Thirties and both were concerned with the important business of growing up. There is thus for me a continuum between these years, and if they differ from one another at the time or in subsequent recollection, it is the dramatic difference between school and university rather than the great tumble on the New York Stock Exchange. The present is organic with the past and at first 1930 exactly resembled 1929. The sun shone, people went about their business. The farmers and the squatters complained, but then they always did. The waterside workers struck, but that was nothing new. The Thirkell menage had always been poor and the meals skimpy so that there was no change there either. It was only as the Thirties drew on that we began to realize dimly that we were in The Depression, and even then it was hard to feel depressed when the great world was opening up and waiting to be seized and wrung.

Yet the melancholy events in New York did affect us in an unexpected way and one which, while it reflects little credit on us, is an indication of the deeper and truer levels of the human spirit. For our principal reaction to the Stock Market Crash in New York in October, 1929 was one of ill-concealed glee. 'That'll teach the Yanks a thing or two,' we exulted. 'They've been too bloody cocky; this'll take them down a peg.' Wells, the caricaturist of *The Herald*, produced a cartoon labelled 'Humpty Dumpty had a great fall' which accurately expressed our xenophobic and indeed anti-American delight. In our innocence we supposed that the Americans could suffer in isolation and that what went on in the far-off improbable canyons of New York could be of little concern to us—except perhaps to our advantage. Now they wouldn't be competing with us in the production of canned fruit and wheat! It didn't occur to us that they would be unable to buy our wool, and that inexorably we would all be drawn downward in the resultant economic vortex from which would arise, like a willy-willy spiralling upward from the sandy waste of Central Australia, the whirling dervish of Adolf Hitler.

However all this lay in the future. When 1929 opened I saw, with stupefaction and delight, my name among the twelve prefects chosen by the Principal of Scotch College, Dr. W. S. Littlejohn. 'Old Bill' used us to help him keep some kind of order and to deal out, in the best tradition of Dr. Thomas Arnold, some sort of rough justice to the hard core of delinquents in that enormous mass of 1200 boys. To assist us in performing this highly tendentious task we were allotted a private room of our own; we carried a special badge and we had the right to give detentions and to assist when the Captain of the School exercised his right to administer the cane. These were heady privileges.

In the large room itself, the competitive jealousies, as well as the restraining loyalties, of twelve senior boys produced some splendid tensions, and we all vied with one another for the approbation of the Captain of the School, the King Arthur of our knightly table. He was a sober, moderately inarticulate athletic fellow of medium height and unassailable purity. Both his Homeric exploits and his natural modesty put us all to shame. He was a triple blue, Captain of Cricket and Captain of Football as well as being Captain of the School; yet all this eminence failed to keep from his honest face, beneath its thick eaves of tow-coloured hair, a faint form of puzzlement. Perhaps his skill in the field, while matched by his sterling character, somewhat outran his other capacities. Yet such was his overwhelming prestige that we were careful to treat even his limitations with high regard. When the annual medical inspection took place and the prefects had to help in the administrative arrangements, our Captain helpfully pinned on the back of our door a notice listing the equipment that each prefect would require. One item stood out:

Six spatchelors

What was a spatchelor? A cross between a spinster and a bachelor perhaps? Could he conceivably mean 'spatulas'? Or could it be that I was wrong? If a fellow of his character and eminence didn't think it was 'spatulas', was it right for me to hug pridefully to my bosom the correct spelling? I was inferior to the Captain in every way. Ergo, it was I who was wrong and my strong impulse to correct the notice was manfully suppressed.

It was, of course, the Captain who supervised the prescient meetings round the deep oblong table in the prefects' room. These dealt with prospective delinquents who might be subject to caning, and we invested them with ludicrous solemnity. It was generally agreed that the prefects, while having an overall responsibility for the conduct of the boys in school and out of it, would use discretion with their powers. The most heinous crime was undoubtedly smoking, and this was invariably visited with at least six whacks across the seat administered by the Captain whose athletic prowess could not entirely conceal from us his honest distaste at the unwelcome but necessary task forced upon him by the prefect system. Other offences were hiding in the basement of the science block when you were supposed to be taking lessons, or being overheard telling a 'filthy story'.

During my term as prefect we had to deal with the unusual incident of a biology student, who administered chloroform to himself just before the lesson. During the course of the lesson he slowly slid forward under the seat and eventually expired, as it were, on the ground amongst the feet of his companions. The biology mistress, Miss A'Beckett, was highly regarded by us because she drove a small two seater DiDion Bouton with considerable elan, invariably pulling up outside the science block on the mornings when her classes were due, with a fine spurt of gravel. We were therefore shocked as well as amused when her biology lecture was disturbed by deep groans followed by the words 'Oh my guts, oh my bloody guts' emanating from the semi-conscious student. As prefects we had to decide what punishment should be meted out to this ingenious though importunate fellow. The Head let us know that Miss A'Beckett was not taking too tragic a view of the incident and we therefore satisfied ourselves by letting him off with a 'curtain-lecture'.

Walking out with girls during school hours, or during the lunch hour, was not in itself a crime, but if the culprit were detected (or as he would put it, 'spied upon') by a prefect, and was not wearing his school cap, then indeed retribution was swift. The usual procedure was to arraign the culprit before the twelve good men and true and listen to his defence. He was then told to wait outside while we loftily considered what punishment should be administered. There invariably followed, as I suppose there must with juries too, an impassioned debate as to whether he deserved punishment and, if so, what. Such was the power conferred upon us and such, I am sorry to say, our jaunty youthful sadism—sadism with a grin as it were—that all too often we suggested to the Captain that 'six of the best' would be in order. The culprit was summoned back into the presence, usually by the Vice Captain and informed of the verdict. We watched his face with as much interest as the face of a criminal is watched by reporters at the Old Bailey when the Judge dons the black cap. When apprised of his fate the culprit would usually preserve a stoical calm. Asked if he had anything to say in his defence, he invariably preserved, in accordance with the custom of the school, a tightlipped silence. He was then requested to bend over the prefects' long table where in full view of us all the 'six of the best' were administered by the redoubtable Captain. 'You can go now,' and the culprit strode out with no doubt a rich destructive hatred burning brightly inside him.

I did not greatly enjoy these summary drum-head courts martial. Looking back I'm still not sure I think it was a very good idea to give youngsters of 16 and 17 the authority to cane. However, 'Old Bill' was merely following in the hallowed tradition of the great public schools At Home (i.e. England). What they did was bound to be approved by us and so we followed suit. More to my liking were the pains and penalties which lay in the little detention pad of 100 slips with which each prefect was issued upon his appointment. The boys very soon got to know which prefects were 'soft'; which they could treat with impunity and which were savage leviers of detentions. At the end of my year as a prefect I found that I had used only 23 of my 100 detentions and that most of those had been issued, as part of a duty regarded by us all as a bit of a chore, to those boys who arrived late for chapel. Since we ourselves were excused from

46

regular attendance (we were working for final exams), this gave us a rather unfair advantage. Many was the prefect who ought to have been setting a good example by standing at the end of a line of boys in chapel but who instead had taken the twenty minutes grace allowed him in order to arrive late, put his feet up in the prefects' room and read the morning paper.

The most spectacular privilege of all was that of the special badge upon one's cap. This not only indicated to all and sundry in the school, both masters and boys, that one was a weighty fellow; but even more important it became a talisman, a significance of high rank and a status symbol on the tram car going to and from Scotch College. On this tram car rode the girls of the Presbyterian Ladies College and the Methodist Ladies College. These exquisite creatures whose divine lineaments protruded in heavenly glory from pleated skirts, felt hat and black lisle-clad legs caused a great deal of heart thumping among the senior boys. The girls from P.L.C. were supposed to be our sisters in the sense that we had a common religious foundation, and therefore to make eyes at them on the tram car was not necessarily frowned upon. However, such is the unpredictability of life, it was the young ladies from M.L.C., the Methodists, the Wesley Wowsers, whom we sought. In this we were fortunate because the route of the Wesley boys did not lie with our tram car. We possessed it in its entirety except for a small sprinkling of boys bound for Xavier College and, since they were Roman Catholics, obviously they didn't count.

The trick was to board the car at a favourite intersection and weave slowly among the standees and strap hangers towards where the delectable Miss Jones was sitting demurely with downcast eyes folded upon the books which she held on her lap. One hung over her for a moment, egged on by the stares, the nudges and occasionally the whistles of one's fellows, until a propitious moment arrived, at which point one would make some disarming remark about the weather. If the angel felt in an appropriate mood she would raise her eyes and give an appropriate reply. From then on you were in, and could talk to her uninterrupted—this was the rule of the chase—until you had regretfully to touch your cap (with its magnificent prefect's badge in blue enamel on the forepeak) and move slowly and regretfully away, hoping for another rendezvous on next morning's tram. If you couldn't worm your way towards the distantly beloved you could at least cast eyes at her down the length of the car and perhaps pass her a note hurriedly scribbled on the back of a Scholar's Concession Check, though this was a dangerous procedure since it might be intercepted by other boys and folded so as to read 'Scholar's Cock'; and then someone might suggest later on at school that you were not setting the example that was required by a prefect. For the same reason, and since conversation was conducted more or less publicly and indeed at a pitch of voice sufficiently high to impress your fellows with your amorous prowess, it was usually difficult to make a date.

The senior boys who made these conquests on the tram car were the object of much admiration and kidding. They would be given the nick-name of the girl whom they were supposed to be interested in or be asked pointedly 'When is Mrs. So-and-So coming to live with you?' Several of the senior boys were known as Old Mary, Old Jane or Old Betty according to the name of the girl they were dating through their eyelashes (and hers) on the tram car. The girl on whom my heart was set was the daughter of a lumber merchant who lived in the suburb of Oakleigh, miles away from 4 Grace Street. I endeavoured to meet her at movie theatres on a Saturday afternoon, but never succeeded in making contact. Then one day came the staring announcement on the bulletin board of what came to be known as The Broughtons' Balls.

Keith Broughton, a colleague who, while short on paper work was a magnificent footballer, announced that he and his brother were going to give a dance. Sensation! (No doubt also in the breast of Broughton Père.) For this purpose they took the magnificent and all but unattainable clubhouse at the famous Kooyong Tennis courts where the Davis Cup matches were played. To the dance were invited all Broughton's friends and all *their* girl friends and (here you see the stroke of genius that made Broughton the figure he was) any fellow who wanted to have a particular girl asked only had to write down her name in secret and give it to Broughton. He would see that she was invited and the invitor's name would be carefully cloaked in anonymity. Accordingly on the great night I arrived in a high state of nerves together with a borrowed car which a friend and I were entirely unequipped to drive. We had secured this illegal barouche in order to provide a convenient parking place or outdoor couch, if you will, for such spooning as we hopefully believed might be generated by Broughton's dance.

It was the era of those tinkling tinny songs which seemed to have been devoted entirely to dolls or puppets. We sang *Flapperette, Dainty Miss* and *The Wedding of the Painted Doll*. Spurred on by these tinkly tunes and also by the success of a really quite vapid song by our local tunesmith Jack O'Hagan entitled *Josie and Me*, a school chum named Wells and myself decided that we would help out our respective Mothers in these tough times by becoming successful composers of jazz songs. He would do the music and I the lyrics. His initials were H.T. and this was a source of much sardonic amusement to the English master. 'It's a pity it's H.T. and not H.G., eh, Wells?' 'Hoppy' Waller would observe. 'You are aware, of course, Wells, of your more renowned namesake?' and much more in the same vein. Wells led the school orchestra and he certainly knew how to write down a tune; but alas, although we composed between us some seven songs (emulating the young Noël Coward whom we all greatly admired), we sent them rather foolishly to Jack O'Hagan who returned them all with a nice letter.

So the boys and girls cavorted and pranced up and down the hall to the strains of the tinselly tunes rendered by Al Harvey's Hot Licks and I sought out the girl of my dreams. When I asked her for a dance she said, flashing her eyelashes and much to my disconcertment,

'I thought it must've been you that had got me invited.'

Here was a fine dilemma. If I denied the charge I would seem discourteous; if I agreed, she might feel that she had not, as it were, made the grade under her own steam. I therefore contented myself by mysteriously saying nothing and led her out onto the dance floor. After an appropriate time had elapsed I suggested that we might perhaps sit in the car for a little while. She did not demur. We entered the car. To my consternation, and indeed, so puritanical is the male animal, my disgust, no sooner were the doors closed and we were safely ensconced in the back seat of the tobacco-smelling furry little sedan, than she hurled herself at me, reeking of liquorice lollipops. It was the end of a friendship.

*   *   *

The great event of the year for the socially inclined however was less Broughtons' Balls than Monty's Ball, (singular), named in honour of the Misses Montgomery who ran a small dancing academy for determined matrons and their daughters on the fringes of Toorak. It was a great honour to be invited to Monty's Ball though, had we but known it, she was only too anxious to sell the tickets which at thirty bob a pair were out of the reach of most of us. The Ball that year was to be held in the St. Kilda Town Hall. It was in the days of Rudy Vallee with songs like *Deep Night* and *Weary River* and all of us in the prefects' room were determined to be seen not only with the girls of our choice but, and this was most important, in the exquisite egregiousness conferred by wearing a white waistcoat with a black tie and a dinner jacket. After all the Prince of Wales did it, why shouldn't we? The Ball took place shortly after the annual school play in which Broughton and I had leading roles. We were therefore well equipped, as we fondly supposed, to mount onto the platform during the interval and delight our young ladies by a performance on the piano and the drums. But we were stricken with stage fright and when we elected to imitate Rudy Vallee singing *Give me Something to Remember You By* they pelted us with rolls and small cakes from the exiguous buffet which the Misses Montgomery had presented for the evening. Overcome with chagrin we retreated to our own corners and the now tip-tilted noses of our girlfriends.

While I was thus frittering away my last school year in innocent and foolish dalliance a disaster of entirely unforeseen magnitude was about to engulf 4 Grace Street. One effect of the Wall Street crash had been that fewer people in Melbourne could afford to buy cars and this was reflected in a falling demand for the products of my step-father's little engineering works. It might have the magniloquent name of The Australian Metal Equipment Co. (TAMECO for short), but essentially it existed to supply bushes, gudgeon pins, piston rings, bumper bars and radiator caps to the Australian automobile industry which itself was dependent upon imports from abroad.

I spent uncounted hours in the dolorous tedium of 'The Works' for my step-father liked nothing better than to have a youngster at his beck and call. The Works consisted of three high-ceilinged storeys of smoke-grimed once red brick crowned by a small octagonal tower with a domical roof and a flagpole. The whole of the main floor was of beaten earth save where the machines were bedded on cement blocks. Down the middle aisle ran a combined delivery bay and parking lot in which could be found a panel truck from the electro-plater's in Fitzroy, 'our' car (later to become controversial), Harry Haines' Ford and, on occasion, Les Watson's Chrysler Imperial, an exciting maroon with chrome wedges gouged in its hood. Harry was Works Manager and Les Chairman of the Board. Half the space was taken up by the foundry. Here one could see the mouldmaker at work with his neat wooden models of pistons, valves, bushes and gudgeon pins. His name was Eric Fainter and he had an old fashioned paper hat like that worn by the carpenter in the Tenniel illustrations to *Through the Looking Glass*. When I was not being called on to cart empty packing cases into the back yard or to fetch cotton waste to one of the lathes or grinders, I loved to watch Eric at work. His was the one bright spot in the grime and tedium of The Works.

In preparation for a casting, he would place his wooden models in wet sand boxes, each revealing, before they were clamped together, an incredibly neat concave replica of a series of pistons or valves, intimately connected by delicate tunnels and cunningly hollowed fissures. The sand looked and felt damp, tense and elastic. Eric locked his boxes and dug a little gutter from the last one towards the pouring position. This was a space of bare earth, blasted and hardened to adamant by successive 'pours'. Meanwhile the electrical bellows had been building up the heat in the furnace and Don McFadzean, or whoever was in charge of the 'pour', would round up a couple of apprentices and approach the furnace door. A blue bullseye screened the fierce flames within, and Don would squint at the bubbling inferno beyond and raise his hand. An alarm bell sounded and the two apprentices ran an iron bar through the handles of a fireclay pot and held it beneath the outlet. Don pulled firmly but gingerly on an iron chain and the drama began.

From a small hole behind which roared the fires of hell a white-hot river of molten steel scuttled down a spout and slipped like a golden snake into the fireclay pot. As it flowed it glowed and sputtered and sent up a shower of bounding sparks. The two apprentices holding the bar averted their eyes from the glare, and their arm muscles started to bulge and knot with the increasing weight of their molten burden. Don, with a smoked-glass mask before his eyes, reversed the chain; the iron gate clanged down, cutting the golden snake in mid career. A couple of amber gobbets dripped from the spout. The apprentices, urged on by Don, now moved with careful speed towards Eric's sandboxes. The molten metal in the fireclay pot already had a cherry-red scum on its surface and they tipped it slowly forward. Reddish gold, the metal fell from the lip of the tipped pot and rushed into Eric's tunnel whence it disappeared into the sand. Puffs of steam allowed one to follow in the mind's eye its unseen flow through the sinuosities of bush, valve, piston and their connecting galleries. The sand began to harden and crack; the air above the 'pour' shimmered with heat; presently a red button of metal showed at the entrance to the sandbox tunnel. Don lowered his hand and the apprentices eased back the pot and carried it away to cool. Then they extracted the iron bar from the handles and plunged it into the cooling tank with a wonderful crisp sizzle and a great cloud of billowing steam. The ground all about Eric's sandboxes trembled with heat and Don wagged a warning finger.

'Keep off boys; keep right away till tomorrow morning.' No fence was erected but a steel sign on a trestle, which it was sometimes my duty to erect, read 'Danger. Pour. Keep Off.' Next day the job of disinterring the cooled castings from their sandy bed started in earnest. This had to be done with crowbars and sledge hammers, for the sand was now like cement and came away in great jagged slabs. As the dust and rubble settled, the casting was revealed like the vertebrae of some long extinct and improbable reptile. Held aloft by two apprentices the casting resembled a piece of contemporary non-objective sculpture in which one could dimly discern neat rows of barnacled valves or gudgeon pins linked by a network of eroded metal bars : the steel mirror-image in which Eric's tunnels had destroyed themselves. The apprentices took the skeletons off and roughly cut them up, sending the waste—the remains of the tunnels and fissures—back to the furnace, and the valves to the lathes for grinding.

Here the second miracle took place; the dull barnacled valves, dredged up from a sea of sand, seated in the twirling lathe and spun at dazzling speed while the leather belts slapped and whirred. A creamy mixture of oil and water played from a jet and Bill Hilliard whirled his wheel, bringing the cutting tool ever closer. All at once it engaged on the swirling encrusted valve which, as it spun, ejected a curling springy metal, thin as paper but strong as steel. Blue and silver as it twirled, like the skin from the knife of the waiter who peels a whole apple, it fell foaming into the waste box and revealed the glistening beauty and smooth steely torso of the fresh-ground valve. Every so often Bill would check the taper and the width of the valve stem with calipers. When correct to 2/100,000ths of a shining inch, he slipped it off the bed into the out tray and replaced it with another barnacled cousin.

But with the economic uncertainty the demand for even these modest products naturally slackened; profits from TAMECO began to drop, and when the directors cast about in search of a scapegoat they did not have to look very far.

When Dad had become General Manager, TAMECO had bought for the firm, though it was understood that it should be for his use also, a Chrysler 75. In examining the books of the company the accountant found that the car had been used by Dad, to a greater extent than was wise, for his own and family recreation rather than for company business. Accordingly there developed a move among the directors to ease Dad out. The meeting was supposed to take place in the offices of TAMECO located on Jeffcott Street in slatternly West Melbourne next to Sands and McDougall's great printing house and just this side of the railway tracks. It was set for a Sunday morning when the directors might reasonably suppose that Dad would not be there, and would in fact be out disporting himself illegally in the Company car. However, Mother was a great upsetter and putter agley of best laid plans, and she chose that particular Sunday to show the Works to my half-brother, then aged eight, who had not had an opportunity to see the way the family bread was earned.

Accordingly the conspirators—for so Mother regarded them and insisted that we should also—were alarmed to hear Dad's car driving into the machinery bay and to hear his voice and Mother's. They tiptoed hurriedly downstairs into a cellar by a back route and continued their colloquy. They had forgotten, however, that TAMECO operated in the shell of a once vaguely well-to-do mansion in a quarter which had slid severely down the social scale. The old mansion, which now housed turret lathes, millers and grinders, was honeycombed by a series of ancient flues, chimneys and hearths. Their mortal remains printed faint shapes against the mildewed walls in the form of an abstract or tachist composition. Other tunnels conducted air and sound to and from various unsuspected parts of the building. While Mother was showing us over the offices and Dad was gazing abstractedly at some files on his desk, she suddenly heard the whispered colloquy from below stairs. She clutched Dad, sniffed the air, 'pointed' with her ear metaphorically cocked, and then strode to the disused hearth behind the Taylor safe. She bent over for a few moments and then straightened up, her face suffused and wisps of hair falling into her eyes.

'George,' she said, 'Les and Arthur and Harry Haines are down there, and they are plotting against you!'

'Oh, rubbish babe,' he said, 'don't be melodramatic. Plotting!'

'Yes,' she said. 'I heard them quite distinctly, I am going down!'

'I wouldn't bother,' said Dad, ever the easy lackadaisical friendly fellow, but Mother was not to be prevented. Leaving us all in Dad's care she went downstairs.

She had a well developed sense of the theatrical and instead of proceeding down to the cellar by the normal wooden stairway which might have given away her presence by a creaking tread, she went out of a side door, round the back alley, and re-entered the building by a small coal hole in the rear. The 'conspirators' included among them Arthur Dennistoun Wood, lawyer to the Company and a personal friend of both Mother's and Dad's. Wood was also a Tasmanian and knew Dad's family well. His wife was from a well-to-do farming family in the Derwent Valley. Her name was Lowiny and we called her Aunt Lone. Aunt Lone and Uncle Arthur: that curious English habit forced on children of calling friends of their parents Uncle and Aunt. I've encountered it in the most unexpectedly recondite quarters of the former British Empire: in Simla, in Accra, in Jamaica. It sounds just as incongruous from black or brown faces as from pinko-grey. It was on this pair, then, that Mother's wrath was about to descend as she emerged dramatically from the coal-hole.

'So!' said Mother in her best Dickensian manner, 'this is the way you behave when my husband's back is turned?'

The 'conspirators', who were determined at all costs to get rid of Dad, whom they regarded as totally incompetent, were not to be swayed by this appeal. With curt nods and cursory good-days they broke up their meeting and left in good order by the main door. A. Dennistoun Wood, however, was made of less stern stuff. He had the temerity to start to explain to Mother why he was there.

'Angela,' he began piteously, 'I do hope you don't think . . .'

The reckless Denny never got any further. Mother drew herself up to her very commanding height and, observing, 'I do not ever wish to speak to you again, Arthur,' swept out.

Mother of course lived in a world where she was always promising never to speak to people again; but in this case I am inclined to think she was justified. Though Dad was undoubtedly helping to run the company swiftly into the ground, aided by the economic blizzard of The Depression, there's little doubt that because of their friendship Denny ought to have let Mother or at least Dad know in advance that he was going to ally himself with the 'conspiracy'. Mother, however, was this time as good as her word. She left Australia and during the twenty-five years that remained of his life and the thirty of hers she never spoke, wrote to, or mentioned A. Dennistoun Wood.

Not that it made much difference. Within three months Dad was out of TAMECO and his earnings, never very great, had sunk to zero. It was at this time that Mother began to supplement her own small private income by writing articles for Australian newspapers and magazines and by broadcasting for the infant Australian Broadcasting Corporation. It was pretty lean pickings and looking back on it I am full of admiration for the way in which she managed, while caring for an out of work husband and three growing and rowdy boys, to find time to do all this work—and to sell the results. She managed to divide herself into compartments, to shut out what was unnecessary (the obverse, as it were, of never speaking to people again) and, within the quiet eye of the hurricane, she would compose rapidly, skilfully and wittily. During late 1929 and early 1930 she became a regular contributor to *Home* then under the editorship of Kenneth Slessor; she wrote many 'middles' and literary articles for *The Argus*; and she became a regular featured broadcaster on the A.B.C. In those days the rate of pay was a penny a word for *The Argus* and perhaps three guineas for a fifteen minute broadcast over the A.B.C. Mother perforce had to accept these niggardly terms and I can only suppose that it was less the novelty of broadcasting that appealed to her than the absolute necessity for earning extra money.

* * *

These matters were not allowed to weigh unduly on us three boys, but the question of whether I would be able to go to University obviously now depended entirely on myself as there would not now be the money to send me. I worked like an absolute madman in that extraordinary tunnel of exams into which one enters at about the age of fifteen and which one does not really leave until one has a university degree. Fortunately my work was attended by good results. I gained a Scholarship from the State of Victoria worth £40 a year and a Resident Scholarship tenable at Ormond College in the University of Melbourne worth £70 a year. This made a total of £110 a year which, however, even when money was worth perhaps three times what it is now, would not have been sufficient to send me to the University. The *Deus ex machina* proved to be the Shell Oil Company of Australia in the person of O. W. Darch, a very large and formidable man built in the fashion of a rugby player, with a huge head, and a charming American wife with bangs.

The careers masters at Scotch College, who were up to the minute on the latest dodges and wheezes in the scholastic world, brought to the attention of promising lads the existence of this totally new scholarship. It was offered by Shell to a young man proceeding to University and it was in the incredible amount, for those days, of £150 a year. The applicant required certain basic academic qualifications, all of which I had. He must go into residence at the University, and he had to satisfy an oral board consisting of a formidable group of leading citizens. The *quid pro quo* for this scholarship, which was tenable for three years—enough to get the young man through university—was that the applicant should consider joining the Shell Oil Company as a cadet on the executive side upon graduation. The scholarship did not stipulate that he *must* join the Company but only that he should consider the proposition carefully. I thought this was a most unusual and princely gesture. I don't know if Mr. Darch, the head of Shell, was acting on his own initiative or whether he was prompted by London or Amsterdam or New York, or wherever that great octopus had its headquarters in those days. Certainly the idea was in the air that bright young men of academic distinction should enter the business world, and that companies in this fiercely competitive era should be on the look out for such bright young men. But whether the idea was Darch's or not I never found out.

I entered for the scholarship without much hope. I don't think Mother had much hope either although when she learned that her friend Ernest Scott, Professor of History in the University of Melbourne, was on the oral Board her heart may, I suppose, have leaped a little inside her. I was entirely unaware of all this. I went away on a fruitpicking expedition and when I returned to Melbourne I learned much to my surprise that I was one of two lads summoned to an oral Board to be held at the University. We waited eyeing each other uneasily in Registrar Bainbridge's draughty empty room while the Board prepared to receive us. When it was my turn I found myself in a dim room facing the light. Behind desks were a group of men among whom I recognized only Professor Scott and Darch himself. I was asked the usual sort of questions except that particular emphasis was laid on the financial condition of my family and hence of myself. I responded as honestly as I could. The two rivals went out into the sunshine and in a burst of friendship crossed Sydney Road to Johnny Naughton's pub and wrily toasted each other.

In the end the choice fell on me and this meant that my future at University was absolutely assured, because to the £110 in scholarships I already had was now added £150 making a total annual income of £260 which in the year of grace 1930 placed me in a position of positive affluence. When Mother heard the news she flung her arms round my neck and gave me a great big hug. I thought the demonstration excessive but I now see that it must have given her enormous pleasure that one of her children should have succeeded in pulling off such a prize. She insisted that I come with her to the Lyceum Club where she was to read a paper on Virgil; and afterwards she 'showed me off' to her literary, artistic and musical friends. I think she was very proud of me and I was certainly delighted that she should feel proud.

But there was an aspect of the scholarship which escaped me. I did not and perhaps could not know that one of the reasons Mother was so delighted was that my success removed the problem of what to do with 'the grown up son' in the ensuing year. She had already formed within her own mind a decision that if things didn't improve in the business world, if Dad did not get a job, if money didn't start coming in, she would go back to England and live with her parents. Perhaps she had at that time no very clear idea of when she would return, though it seems to me that the possibility of her not returning was always present. The fact that I was now self-supporting removed the final obstacle, and I don't think it's unfair to assume that this knowledge heightened her delight in my modest achievement.

Chapter Four

PEACHES WITHOUT THE CREAM

THE Great Dividing Range, an outlier of the Australian Alps, split our State of Victoria from east to west so that the rivers flowed from the centre of the state south to the Bass Strait and the Southern Ocean, and north into the great river Murray which formed the boundary between Victoria and New South Wales. If you stood on a high hill in Melbourne or even on the top of a reasonably tall building you saw a jagged arc of blue ranges rimming the horizon at a distance of about twenty miles. To escape from this amphitheatre in which Melbourne was placed and get to the north one had to choose one of the 'Gates' through the Great Dividing Range. The nearest to Melbourne was the Kilmore Gate through which the main line to Sydney found its way at an altitude of about 1,200 feet. If you kept on beside the Sydney line you paralleled great mountains to the north-east and eventually reached the Murray which you crossed at Albury and found yourself in New South Wales. If, however, you kept to the left and went due north the hills slowly disappeared and you entered a flat plain which in essence stretched all the way to the Gulf of Carpentaria and the Timor sea almost 2,000 miles to the north. This was the great interior plain of Australia leading eventually to its so-called Dead Heart. This was the route taken by Robert O'Hara Burke and William John Wills in their famous exploratory journey from Melbourne to the Gulf of Carpentaria in the 1860s, of which Alan Moorehead has written so evocatively in *Cooper's Creek*.

The southern reaches of this great plain—those which lay nearest to Melbourne—were fertilized by irrigation canals from the Goulburn River and constituted the great fruit basket of the State of Victoria. From Shepparton, from Nagambie and from the little towns near them came the wonderful peaches, clingstone, and slipstone, the nectarines, the apricots, the currants and the grapes which found their way into canned goods for export or on to the housewife's table in Melbourne. It was thence that we were bound in

57

the desperately hot Christmas of 1929. The only begetter of this exciting excursion was my friend Alister Harvie.

The Harvies lived down on the fringes of Prahran. When I arrived at Scotch, a new boy for the third time, Harvie was one of those told off by the Head to look after me. He kindly invited me to his home where I discovered that there were not one but five Harvie boys, all dependant on the incredible hard work and fierce possessiveness of a tough and compassionate widow. Mrs. Harvie could serve as the prototype of the fighting mother abandoned by fate to a life of toil and rescued by her own extreme toughness and nerve. She'd been widowed when her eldest son was about fourteen and her youngest a baby. Single-handed she brought them all up, and more than that, fulfilled her vow that despite poverty they should attend their father's school.

When I first met Mrs. Harvie she had the concession for the school tuck shop. Later she opened a cash-and-carry store on Glenferrie Road, the first in Malvern. By this time the eldest boy Donald, smitten with polio as a child, had grown up and was working on the construction of the railway the Federal Government was pushing north from Oodnadatta to Alice Springs in Central Australia. The next boy Kenneth had already successfully entered for the navy as a boy cadet and was studying at the Royal Australian Naval College in Jervis Bay.

Next came Malcolm, a born tinkerer and mechanic who could take a motorbike to pieces in his backyard and re-assemble it with the greatest of ease. Fittingly enough he went into the R.A.A.F. Alister was next, my age and my special chum. He was an albino with white hair and pale blue eyes set in pinkish whites and he could not stand being in the sun. But in the shade he was a carefree fellow with a philosophical streak that greatly amused Mother. Once when she half jokingly complained to him about a chore which I had left undone, he shook his head sorrowfully. 'Ah, Mrs. Thirkell, what can you expect? Schoolboys, schoolboys!' He was all of twelve at the time. The youngest, Bruce, like his elder brother Kenneth, joined the R.A.N. This strong and varied brood of five boys Mrs. Harvie raised, fed, clothed and indoctrinated with sound Presbyterian principles all on her own. She was an indomitable woman and much admired by us all.

Alister firmly believed in untold riches to be gained by picking fruit in the hot flatlands north of the Great Divide. If four of us chipped in, the cost of food would be practically nothing. We could take a tent with us and pitch it on a creek bottom, thus ensuring a supply of fresh water and also a swimming hole. You could make as much as £5 or £6 a week picking peaches or apricots, if you were strong and quick with your hands. Living in a tent couldn't possibly cost more than a pound a week—we'd easily net £40 to £50 in a summer's work! But supposing we weren't nippy with our fingers and the pay was less? What about the rail fare to Shepparton and back? Alister threw his shock of white hair out of his pale blue eyes. 'Haven't you any spirit of adventure?' he asked. 'Anyway it's a holiday from Melbourne.'

In the end, loaded down with kitbags and haversacks from Boy Scout days, we took the early morning Goulburn Valley Express. Up ahead in the baggage wagon rode our tentage, cook pots, axes and mattocks; and while the train rattled north from the hills into the flat plains, shimmering in the Christmas heat, Alister regaled us with tales of the sure-fire promises he'd had from a friend of his that there'd be good jobs for us all. We sat, lordly in a smoking compartment, and now that we'd left school puffed daringly, unrebuked; spat expertly into the little brass cuspidor let into the floor and saw, through the hole in its bottom, ballast streaking away behind us to receding Melbourne. As we pounded on northward into the heat, as the train rumbled over wide irrigation canals full of pellucid water from the Goulburn, or trundled through orchards laden with heavy swags of fuzzy peaches, shiny nectarines, golden apricots, grapes and citrus, I allowed myself to be bemused by Alister's adroit yarn-spinning. The train stopped with a jolt at Shepparton Main.

For a whole we stood disconsolate amid a pile of kit with the dust eddying round us and the sun beating down. The train pulled out bound for Echuca, Deniliquin and other mysterious places in New South Wales. Its going removed a wall of friendly solidity and the flat endless landscape streamed in on us from all directions. It seemed to be lurking like a beast of prey at the end of every street we looked down. It turned out that Mr. Murdoch's farm was five miles to westward through the shimmering heat.

'I thought you said it was in Shepparton.'

'Well, five miles isn't much,' said Alister defensively.

'It is if you walk.'

'Walk! With all this dunnage? Not on your life.'

'What do we take, a tramcar or a taxi?'

'Har-de-de-har!'

In the end we found a surly fellow with an underslung jaw who offered to take us and our kit as far as Murdoch's for a pound each in his half-ton truck.

'Daylight robbery!'

'Take it or leave it.'

We piled into the truck. There was room for Jock and me in the cab with the driver. Alister and Herb sat on the tents and kitbags in the bouncy back. The driver headed the truck for a distant shuddering horizon down a ruler-straight road of dusty yellow gravel. There was much gear-changing over washes and dry creek beds. The landscape seemed parched and grey except where irrigation ditches created a riot of foliage, and yellow oranges winked from masses of shiny deep green leaves. I was in the middle and my legs kept getting in the way of the gear shift until the driver told me sourly: 'Keep your legs apart, son; pretend yer a tart in Little Lon.' Finally we reached a five-barred gate in the hot shade of a clump of listless cootamundra.

'Murdoch's,' said the driver.

We seemed to be in the middle of nowhere.

'Where's the house?'

'Bout a mile in.'

'But you said you'd take us to Murdoch's.'

'Ar,' said the surly fellow through his prognathous ill-fitting store teeth, 'You shoulda said the house. Tell you what, take you in for five bob.'

'The lot?'

'Each!'

'Ar, Jesus,' we said. But we paid. He dumped us in front of a yellow-painted, two-storeyed wooden house with a red tin roof. It looked too thin and haughty for its surroundings and stuck out from a nest of scrawny pepper trees like a bandaged neck. Chickens rooted in the dust. The irrigation ditches didn't seem to have reached as far as the homestead. A child with ginger curls and two streams of snot gazed at us abstractedly from an upper window. A yellow collie rounded the corner of the house and kept its distance snarling. Alister mounted slowly and gingerly up three wooden steps and banged on a screen door. The collie growled menacingly. A woman in an apron appeared behind the wire, her tired face dimly visible and seeming to float before us against the inscrutable interior, like a fish in an aquarium. Alister came back.

'Boss is out with the fruit pickers, but the lady says he's expecting us. We can camp on the creek at the bottom of the property.'

'Where's that?' Our eyes sought the shimmering horizon under the wide brims of unaccustomed hats. In the dim distance a meandering line of trees was faintly visible—about five miles off it looked. We started down a rough cart track lugging our kit and sweating profusely. It turned out to be not much more than half a mile and though the creek, when we reached it, proved to be a feeble trickle in a wide bed of gritty sand, at least it was flowing. The water was potable and we foresaw that by judicious damming, a small swimming hole could be created and filled in two or three days. We set to with a will and by mid-afternoon had the tent pitched under a fair-sized white gum, tea boiling in a billy slung from a forked stick and a weir thrown across the creek.

A bit before sundown Murdoch came to visit us. He arrived at the edge of the little cuesta above us, seated on a small shaggy brumby. He surveyed us laconically before he spoke. He was a short thick-set man with a heavy close-cropped black moustache and black hair. When he took his hat off his forehead was pale and fishlike in contrast to his gravelly redbrick face. He cracked his whip and we all ran up the cuesta to greet him. He did not dismount.

'Who's in charge?' he said.

'We all are,' said Alister.

'Then I'll speak to all of you.' He leaned forward slightly on the pommel of his saddle, grasping the short curled-up stockwhip loosely in his hand. The horse bent and nibbled some papery grass.

'Glad to have you here,' he said, 'but don't count on the Scotch College connection. I may be an Old Boy but the terms are the same.' The horse took two steps browsing forward and we followed. 'Pay for fruitpickers is three pounds a week plus a bonus based on bag-weight. You might earn as much as four pounds in a good week but more likely three'll be your limit. Work's seven to four with an hour off for lunch and I expect you to be on time. There's no contract. You're kept on as long as you give satisfaction—and no longer. Report in the fourth field at 6.30 tomorrow and Nugget'll give you ladders and bags.'

He raised himself in the saddle and pulled up the horse's head. The animal cast a ruminative eye in our direction. Murdoch gestured towards our tent with the stockwhip.

'You fixed up all right here?'

We nodded.

'Don't start any fires then. And no funny business with chickens either. The neighbours have shot-guns and not much sense of humour.' He sketched a half salute with the whip, twitched the horse's reins and was off through the bush, his battered hat framed in the sunset. We looked at each other glumly.

'Sounds tough.'

'Not much money in it either.'

'And we've spent a fiver getting here in that damned truck.'

'Ar, come on, buck up,' said Alister. 'It may be no picnic, but we'll still make on it. Anyway it's better than hanging around town.' We nodded sagely, cooked ourselves some damper in the hot ashes of the fire, rolled up in our blankets and went to sleep.

* * *

Alister's alarm clock roared fiendishly in the grey dawn and we tottered from our fusty bedrolls, gulped scalding tea and started off for the fourth field. Jock stayed behind to cook and clean up camp. We planned to have one man do this each day on a roster; it seemed the only way the rest of us would ever get to work on time. Our long morning shadows scurried thinly through the scrub, and the dust was held by the faintest of dews. But the sun was already a huge blood orange above the eastern horizon and it promised a suffocating day. We crossed the main canal from the Goulburn, running cool and green amid the dusty levees; then we followed a small irrigation ditch fringed with bull rushes and reeds. On both sides spread the dusty-green peach trees, their heavily freighted boughs propped up with stringybark saplings. Whichever way you looked there was a neat geometrical tunnel with a base of hard grey clods and a ceiling of soft crinkly grey-green leaves. The ditch at our side narrowed to a wooden sluice box from which a tiny stream of life-giving water gurgled out at right angles. We followed it between two rows of trees.

Eventually we came to a spot where a huge knobbly fellow in a grey sleeveless flannel shirt and dungarees was turning the stream down each row of trees with a single massive twisting thrust of his spade. We watched him admiringly. His shoulders were rippled and knotted in great muscles; sweat streamed down his temples and neck and forehead, even at seven in the morning, from beneath the crown of a battered old velours hat, its brim trimmed save for a peak fore and aft. He looked like a tar stripped for action in a Napoleonic naval battle and we watched him in wonder while the clock crept on. A hand bell jangled violently nearby and the giant paused.

'Seven o'clock,' he said. 'Time for a smoke-oh.'

Fear mounting in our throats we ran as fast as we could, stumbling over the hard grey clods. We came out in a small clearing in the trees where a great surge of fifty to sixty men were grabbing three legged ladders and canvas bags and staggering off into the leafy depths. Seated behind an upended packing case next to a long wire-mesh sorting table was a tough chunky little man with dark black hair, a blue chin and eyes like pistol points. This must be Nugget.

'Okay,' he said. 'Here's ya slips. Hang on to them come pay day. Get yourself a ladder and a bag and vamoose. Ya late already. Peaches today and don't pick 'em too green.'

I reached for the great canvas bag, threw it apron-like over my head and clipped it with toggles at the side. It opened at the bottom and made me feel like an anonymous citizen in the crowd scene of a Shakespearean play. I grabbed the nearest ladder and hoisted it on to my shoulder. It was a three-legged monster with ten steps and it weighed about two tons. I started awkwardly by banging it against an overhanging branch thus dislodging a shower of green peaches which thudded alarmingly to earth. Would Murdoch hear? Would I be sacked out of hand?

Nugget called out 'Clum-see!' but then goodnaturedly helped me balance the contraption on my shoulder.

'I didn't see you that time. Get it? But watch out you don't do it again, son. Else old man Skinflint'll take it off ya pay Friday.'

I thanked him and staggered off over the rough clods in search of a 'free tree'. I eventually reached it sweating generously. Poking the prop of my ladder well in under the branches, I managed to get the steps conveniently placed and started to climb.

'Hey snowy, what's the big idea?' An angry face beneath a stained stetson peered down at me from the leafy jungle above. 'Me and me mates are workin' this tree. Hop it! Get yourself another tree.'

I apologized hurriedly. The face seemed mollified and I lurched off to the next tree. There the same thing happened and when I finally reached a tree that seemed to be free I found that I was further from the sorting table than anyone else. I decided I must make up for lost time. Positioning the ladder as best I could, I swarmed up it and soon had my bag filled with big firm peaches— thirty pounds of them. I stumbled back along the lumpy grey furrows to the sorting table, undid the clasps on my bag and emptied it proudly and thumpingly. One of the men sorting looked at me as if I were a dangerous lunatic.

'What's the game? Greenies! Hey Nugget, this kid's ringin in a lot of floggin' greenies.'

'Now then, whatsa trouble,' said Nugget striding up chunky and bandy-legged.

'The kid's ringin in greenies,' repeated the sorter surveying my pile in great disgust. 'What'm I s'posed to do with 'em?'

'Stuff 'em,' said Nugget. 'Kid's green himself. Shove'm under the table, John-o, and the Old Man can use 'em for cattle feed.' He turned to me. 'Here, son, don't be a dope all ya life eh?' He picked out a large peach, firm yet with a faint blush staining its green virginity. 'Take this along as a sample, eh? Pick 'em firm but not green eh? Watch for the flush.'

'Gee thanks, Nugget.'

'What about me tally?' complained John-o. 'How do I make that up?'

'Ar put a sock in it,' said Nugget, 'can't you see the kid's green? Give him a chance.'

My heart bursting with love for Nugget I almost ran back to my tree with the empty bag flapping round my knees. I'd show him I was worthy of his trust. When I reached the tree my ladder was gone. I thought I spied it under a nearby tree but when I reached it a pair of boots protruded at the level of my head. I spoke to the anonymous boots up in the bosky leaves.

'I think you have my ladder.'

There was no reply.

'That's my ladder you have,' I called again, at the same time giving the leg a jerk. I was rewarded by a blow on the head. My unseen antagonist had hurled a green peach at me with startling force. Blinded with rage I seized one leg of the ladder and jerked it with all my strength. Down came a canvas bag, a shower of peaches and a tall thickset fellow with dark curly hair, thick lips and a John Gilbert hairline moustache.

'You young barstid' he said in an English accent. 'I'm going to do for you. Come on. Put up yer dooks.'

I backed away. He put up his fists and so, very reluctantly, did I. As we pranced round each other, from absolutely nowhere half a dozen men appeared and formed a ring. I was no fighter and was looking desperately for an avenue of escape. This took my mind off my opponent who suddenly let fly a tremendous kick in the general direction of my groin. If his boot had connected this story would have come to a rapid end, but by luck I just happened to turn at the moment of impact and his boot grazed my hip bone and one cheek of my bum. A low growl went up from the ring.

'Foul !'

'Kick a man in the balls !'

'Pommy barstid.'

'Leave the kid alone.'

My mustachioed opponent was squaring off for another attack when Nugget burst into the ring.

'You crazy galoots !' he shouted. 'You wanna lose your jobs? Old Man Skinflint's on his way down. You all wanna get the sack? O.K. This is the way to do it.'

'Let im try.'

'Who'll pick his floggin fruit for im?'

'O.K. O.K. Back to work.'

My opponent stood clasping and unclasping his hands which hung loosely at his side. Nugget turned to him.

'One more word outa you George Rose, you Pommy barstid, and you're out. You take the kid's ladder?'

'I didn't know it was his,' said Rose with an oily smirk.

'I know it by the mark on the fifth rung,' I said. Nugget scowled.

'Keep quiet. George, take the ladder for today. You, kid, come and help me on the sorting table. Yer too much trouble outa me sight.'

Rose smirked. 'Soft job, eh?' he said. He rubbed the palms of his hands down his corduroy pants. 'Might see you later,' he said to me in an oily threatening voice. I walked up to him and put out my hand.

'I've no quarrel with you,' I said. 'Shake.'

'A eddicated fella!' said someone.

Rose gave me a strange look, but he put out his hand. It was moist and feline in curious contrast to his powerful frame and the general air of sweat and dust in which we were both enveloped. 'Okay,' he said.

'Come on, kid,' called Nugget impatiently. The little crowd walked away and I followed him obediently to the sorting table. Here the work was certainly easier. Instead of clambering up and down the ladder with an increasingly cumbersome burden of fruit, reaching over your head to twist off the greeny-rose peaches, and then staggering a hundred yards down the grey clods to the table, you just stood and sorted. If you were tired you could even lean up against the table though this action, if detected, usually generated the ribald query,

'Givin yerself a thrill, mate?'

You had to be quick with your fingers though, learn to spot the 'greenies' and sift the large from the small. At the far end of the table stood the packers; very skilled men who filled a narrow divided box fast and deftly without bruising the fruit and covered it with a sheet of plain newsprint. At the very end stood the finisher who nailed up the lidded box with two-inch nails, and toted it to a growing pile. Once every half hour a one-ton truck would back in and load up the boxes. This job was very exhausting in the hot sun and was performed by a couple of aborigine youths whose jet black skins shone in the harsh sun with the sweat of their exertion. I used to feel sorry for them manhandling the heavy boxes up there in the heat while the white driver sat snoozing or smoking in the cab just waiting for them to finish. I said so to Nugget.

'Don't you believe it,' he said, 'the "abos" are used to the sunshine. They like it. Why up in the Northern Territory they go around with nothin on but a jockstrap.'

'But they don't have to work as hard.'

'Ar, they're lazy buggers. Only reason they work here is because they want a coupla pots at the end of the day.'

It was not only easier at the sorting table; it was cooler and the atmosphere was more comradely. Out in the orchard you were alone with your ladder and your bag unless you and a mate agreed to 'work' a certain tree. There was no one to talk to and if you tried to rest for a bit there was always the chance that you'd see, peering sourly up at you through the grey-green crinkly leaves, the Boss's suspicious face. He used to tread quietly around among the trees checking on the hired help, and anyone that he caught loafing he'd pay off at the end of the week. But at the sorting table you could chat and work at the same time. Provided your fingers were nimble enough and the flow of boxes kept coming to the truck, Murdoch didn't mind if you talked. The sorters were a tough, friendly, intolerant bunch of men. They hated the bosses, the Italians (Dagoes) and the police (the bloody Johns); they had a goodnatured contempt for women and 'abos' and their conversation consisted largely of re-telling their exploits in Little Lonsdale Street, or 'Little Lon', the then famous red light district of Melbourne. These were cast in a Homeric mould.

'Just wait'll I get down to Melbn,' said the ace sorter known to us as Hairy Joe. 'I'll be borin right through the mattress.'

'What's wrong with the sheilas around here?' asked Nugget.

'Ar, these girls up the country are no good, I tell you. Got no bounce!'

'Maybe they just won't look at ya.'

'Yeah? They *look* all right! Why they pray for a fella like me,' said Hairy Joe. As he sorted he grunted and the fellows sometimes grunted in unison to kid him. 'Trying to get me goat, the barstids,' he'd say. One morning when he was chopping wood for his camp before going on to the sorting table a group of men surrounded him and began to grunt in unison with each blow of the axe. Eventually Hairy Joe got mad and hurled the axe at his tormentors. Fortunately the head flew off at the start of the trajectory, but the handle whirled through the air and caught one fellow across the shoulder blades. This man, whose name was Peter Latta, rushed up and closed with Hairy Joe in a wrestler's grip. They were both writhing on the ground in a cloud of dust, and fearful carnage impended, when the Boss came up on his horse and separated them with one crack of his stockwhip.

'Any more o' that,' he said, 'and you both get the order of the D.C.M.'

'What's that?' I whispered to Nugget.

'Don't Come Monday.'

But round the sorting table Hairy Joe's temper was less touchy.

'Jeeze, I had a bonzer tart the last time I was down, Nugget,' he said.

'Uhuh,' said Nugget, who'd heard all this before.

'Know what she says when its over? Joe, she says—'

'Didn't she say Hairy Joe?'

'She says "Ya rode a good race", she says. "I should back ya at Flemington", she says. You know what I says? I says—"Yeah, me for the Derby and you for the Oaks." I says! Har Har!'

'Trouble with some people,' said Nugget. 'They can't keep outa trouble.'

'Watcher mean?' said Hairy Joe suspiciously.

'Mean ya gonna get yerself a dose o' the clap.'

Hairy Joe snorted in great contempt.

'Me? Not in your life. Always use the old letter.'

'Personally give me Shepparton every time,' said a small man with piggy eyes named Rafferty. 'Gimme the old Shepp of a Sarry arvo. With me pay. That'll do me.'

'All you ever do with your pay is get shickered,' observed Nugget sagely. We went on with the sorting.

At the end of my first week I'd spent two days picking, three days on the sorting table and a day turning prunes and apricots on the drying racks—slow and very tedious but restful work. But when I lined up with the others on Friday evening outside the back stoop of Murdoch's house I was chagrined to see that my pay only came to £2 15s. I compared notes with Alister and Jock, both of whom had been on straight picking. One had £3 5s. and the other £3 7s. I considered myself very ill used and went to complain to Mr. Murdoch. He looked at me as if I were a poisonous insect.

'You've been on the table?'

'Yes.'

'Well the table pays 1s. 6d. a day less than the trees. You don't expect to get extra for the cushy jobs, do you?'

I pocketed my money and slunk away. After a while I cheered up. We could all go into Shepp, visit the movie and drink beer and perhaps, who knows. . . ? When I arrived back in our camp Alister, Jock and Herb were drawn up with their backs to the tent. Facing them and looking belligerent were Rose and a pal, lean, gristly and empty-eyed. I smelled trouble.

'Here he is—at last,' said Rose.

I advanced slowly and with some trepidation. 'What do they want?' I said, addressing Alister.

Rose gave an unpleasant laugh and clenched and unclenched the hands hanging loosely at the side of his corduroy trousers, just as I'd seen him do on the first day.

'What do we want, Vic?' he said looking at me but speaking to his lean companion.

'Whatever you say, George.' His face was cold, locked away,

impossible to read. He looked like Dan Duryea in a gangland movie.

'You know what we want Vic,' said Rose, wrapping his lips around the words as they oozed out. 'We want this skinny young runt that said I pinched his ladder.' I remained silent. Rose took one step forward, seized the ridge pole and pulled down our tent.

'You bloody floggin barstid,' cried Alister, launching himself at Rose like a windmill. Rose stood his ground, a sardonic expression on his face. As soon as Alister was within punching distance he gave him a short sharp terrible uppercut. It sounded like hitting stones in a bag with a hammer. Alister fell soundlessly to the ground and lay there, out cold. We all paled.

'George was middle-weight champion of Nottingham before he came out here,' said Vic tonelessly. 'Best not to try conclusions.'

Valour was not my strong point, but I had at least the gift of the gab. I foresaw that we would have somehow to live with these two fellows, and that none of us would have any chance against an ex-champ. Almost before I'd formulated any strategy I heard myself saying.

'You don't need to knock down a fellow to show how strong you are. We believe you. If I'd known you were an ex-champ I'd never have bothered about the ladder either. Obviously. There's four of us to two of you; that doesn't mean we're going to try conclusions. It might even mean we've some things you'd like to share.'

Rose looked contemptuous. 'Such as?'

'My Mum and Dad are coming up next weekend from Melbourne with a hamper. Maybe you'd like to join the party?'

'I might,' said Rose. He walked over to our fire and very slowly and deliberately pissed in it. The fire did not go out but a boiling of steam and ashes arose and with it a fearful stink. 'I just might,' he repeated.

'Then help us get the tent up,' I said, 'and put Alister inside. You've hurt him badly.'

Vic bent over Alister. He looked vaguely troubled.

'George, you don't know your own stren'th. You hadn't ought to be so ready with your fists. This boy's hit hard.'

Rose growled 'Serve him bloody well right'; but he helped us re-erect the tent and get Alister inside. We laved his face with cold water and he came to. He felt his jaw gingerly; then looked up at Rose with a mingled expression of hatred and fear. He said nothing.

'Are you all right Alister?' He nodded.

'You better stay in the tent for the rest of the day.'

Our cold silent helpless fury was burgeoning like marsh gas. At last even Rose felt it.

'Well,' he said, 'too bad this had to happen. I'll see it doesn't again. But take note,' he whirled on me menacingly 'that I have me own rules about ladders, and about everything else. And I don't like interference, see!'

He thrust his face close to mine.

'I see,' I said. 'But why be a bully all your life? We'll do as you say.'

Vic pulled his sleeve. 'Come on, George. Give the kids a chance.'

'Okay,' said Rose grumblingly. They walked away together, followed by our hostile immovable stares.

*   *   *

It turned out that Alister, though in pain and resentful, had no bones broken. In the end he decided that he'd come with us into Shepparton for the Saturday evening spree. We thumbed a ride on the back of a truck loaded with bagged wheat and at dusk the four of us stood in the wide main street of The Shepp watching the dust settle gently into the tired earth, and a great moon rise over the flatlands as the town came to life. It was before the days of neon, but coloured electric lights were festooned over the fronts of the little stores set deep behind verandahs covering the entire broad sidewalk, like eye sockets in a skull. Kerosene lamps strung on wires across the streets swayed a little in the evening breeze now whispering through the parched town. From the open doors of pubs came the deafening noise of the 'six o'clock swill'. Beyond the fringes of the town, in the dark thick bush along the edge of the Goulburn, we could hear dimly raucous catcalls and an occasional snatch of a concertina or ukelele from the men who lived in shanty town.

'A rotten mob,' said Nugget. 'Just a lot of bludgers. Never do a day's work in their life.'

It may have been true, but by this time they were as likely to be the earliest victims of The Depression.

Occasionally the air would be rent by a curse or the inane cackle of a fellow drunk on 'plonk'. In town, as in all towns, the pubs closed at six and the only way to do any serious drinking was to either register in an hotel as an out of town visitor or else to stock up on 'plonk'. The former procedure was tricky because if the cops came and found that you weren't from twenty-five miles away they could run you in. The latter method was rough only on the membranes of the gut. 'Plonk' was cheap red Australian wine, usually heavily fortified to the consistency of a sweet port. It was also known as 'Nelson's Blood' and 'Block and Tackle'. It cost 1s. 6d. a bottle and could, and did, make you raving stinko in about half an hour. Truck loads of fruit pickers used to come roaring into camp at two and three o'clock of a Sunday morning blind drunk from 'plonk' and ready to bash up the poor voluble helpless Italians, who grew and sold vegetables from a lovingly tended stretch of creek bed.

On this particular night we drank a lot of beer and then very innocently went to an early talkie with Monte Blue and Louise Dresser. When we reached the corner where the truck was supposed to pick us up to take us home, there were George Rose and Vic. We eyed them warily. Vic gave a pale grin. Rose said,

'Hitching a ride? Mind if we come along. Always did like company.'

When the truck arrived the driver protested at the extra passengers. Rose flourished a fist under the driver's nose and we all got aboard. But the driver was concocting a stratagem of his own as we bowled along in the sultry moonlit night. Presently we crossed the main canal from the Goulburn and he pulled over to the side.

'What's wrong?' someone called.

'Ar, Jesus it's hot. You blokes feel like a dip?'

'Bonzer idea,' we all cried. We were full of beer and sweat and dust, and the cool waters of the great canal, here running in a concrete channel thirty feet wide and six feet deep, seemed unbelievably inviting. Yodelling and cackling like idiots we started to peel off our clothes and dived in. When we surfaced the truck had disappeared. Vic was annoyed.

'It's your own bloody fault, George. You're too free with your fists.'

To our surprise Rose took it in good part. 'I might've known,' he said. 'I might've known. How far have we to go?' We stood there in the starlit darkness pulling on our sweaty clothes.

'Not too far,' said Vic. 'I can see the lights of Beckford's farm.'

'Let's go and pull the dagoes out of bed,' said Rose. You could see his wet lip and moustachios curl in the night.

'You're barmy,' said Vic. 'What we need is a coupla nice fat pullets.'

'Right you are, Captain Cook.'

'Are you boys game for a little roost-robbing?' said Rose. 'I'm by way of being a bit of an expert and can maybe make it up to you for earlier this arvo.'

'I don't mind,' said Alister. We all realized we hadn't much choice; Rose was determined to spread the responsibility by implicating us. He wasn't going to run the risk of tattle-taleing and we couldn't argue with his fists. Though still half tipsy he was prancing about delicately on the balls of his feet at the edge of the starlit canal, making expert throttling gestures with his hand.

'A quick approach,' he said. 'A fast grab in the dark, hand round the neck and—scrrrk!'

'Beckford's got a dog.'

'Who says we're going to rob Beckford's roost? I owe old man Murdoch a thing or two!'

'We want to keep our jobs,' I said.

'Don't worry about your little job, little man. You're in the hands of an expert,' said George Rose. 'Come on, vamoose.'

I must say his dispositions for this highly exciting and totally inexcusable raid were excellent. He posted Jock and me as lookouts towards the house, Alister and Herb as lookouts towards the road. Then he and Vic approached the hen roost crouching silently and swiftly. All we heard was a faint click then a low mildly anxious cackle instantly suppressed, and there were Rose and Vic each with a big fat Black Orpington hanging head-down held by the claws. Their necks had already been wrung and they were quite dead.

When we'd put three hundred yards between us and the chicken roost by hard running down the dirt track towards the river, Rose called a halt while we listened for sounds of pursuit. There were none, only the bush sounds: the furtive scratching of a wombat, the tinkly call of the night-jar, the gurgle of the canal and, very far off, the rumble of a distant train as it crossed the Goulburn, high on a reverberating girder bridge.

'There's your share,' said Rose handing me a great warm cushion of feathers in the dark. 'We'll take ours over to our camp. Call it quits, eh?'

'Okay,' I said without enthusiasm.

'Watch when you cook it,' said Vic. 'Do it at night and burn all the feathers from plucking. Murdoch'll be smelling around. It's good today's Sunday.'

Amen to that, I thought smitten with guilt for the night's folly. Before going to bed we plucked and singed the bird, burned the feathers, burned the claws and head, wrapped the bird in cheese cloth and newspaper and put it in our meat safe at the base of a red gum. The dingoes got at it during the rest of the night. They ate the cheese cloth, the newspaper, one wing and one leg. But we stewed and ate the rest. We were not going to be deprived of our ill-gotten gains by a couple of dingoes.

From this time on we lived a two-faced and lawless life. We joined hands with our former enemies to work hard by day but to live the life of Reilly by night on stolen goods. The successful chicken raid on Murdoch was followed by similar raids on Beckford, Casoni, Laidlaw and McTague. We took maize and egg plant from the Italians; tomatoes and cucumbers from McTague and Casoni, and of course we regarded all fruit—be it peaches, pears, apricots or nectarines—as ours by right. Weren't we being paid to pick? We even essayed to make a gallon of apricot brandy, but when we gave to George Rose the honour of drinking the first glass he spat it out with the cry

'Kee-rist! Take the skin off a man's dingle-dongle.'

I was affronted as it was I who had kept watch over the sizzling fermenting mess, skimmed it, strained it and produced this elixir of life. But I swallowed my resentment for word had reached me from far-off Melbourne that Mother and Dad were at last coming up for the weekend, and I knew Mother just loved apricot brandy. I filled a ten-pound MacRobertson's Maxmint tin with the stuff, and buried it under water in the bed of the creek. When the parents finally arrived they brought my kid brother and my girl friend. I was beside myself with nerves and exasperation, particularly as, at the precise moment when Dad gunned the car into silence among the blue gums and the willows, George Rose and Vic appeared to spend the day.

But I needn't have worried, because George and my Mum took an immediate shine to one another. He recognized in her crisp Kensingtonian accent the voice of authority; she, in his Notts inversions and glottal diphthongs, a member of the genuine English Lower Orders to whom she could lay down the law because he was not Australian and therefore biddable. Mother and George Rose retired to the tent to discuss, in the foetid suffocating heat, life amid the alien corn and the difficulty of keeping up standards. Their conversation was punctuated by genteel sips of my *soi-disant* apricot brandy, now a sulphurous bubbling mess in the Maxmint tin. Dad took himself off up to the homestead to drink beer and reminisce over the battles of the Somme and the Ancre. Vic took my companions over to his tent and I—miraculous to say—was left alone with my girl friend. We couldn't use the tent as we'd hoped to, but we used the banks of the creek and it was almost as wonderful.

With the cool of the evening Dad decided to return to Melbourne, driving the 130 miles in the dark. He'd hoped to stay the night but the invitation hadn't been forthcoming. I gave them as a farewell present a case of pears for which old Beckford had charged me £2, no doubt with some notion of recouping his losses on the chicken roost and in the cornfield. It was worth about fifteen bob. The girl friend and I clung to each other behind a coolibah tree, and eventually the jolting sedan bore them all away into the red dust-filled gloaming.

George Rose and Vic remained behind, Vic because he liked

company, Rose to hug to his bosom the memories of his afternoon in a cultural heaven with my Mum. He positively mooned.

'Ah,' he kept repeating, 'your Mother's a real lady, Graham, a real lady. Such a wonderful turn of phrase. Promised to send me one of her articles from the *Cornhill* magazine; really did, you know. I'd value that, believe me. It's a touch of Old England.'

From this time forth George Rose and Vic were our devoted friends. They haunted our camp; they didn't insist that we follow them on all their raiding expeditions so long as we kept mum about them. We were now earning between £3 and £3 10s. a week and we were on top of the world. Then one day Murdoch came down to our camp with a policeman from Shepparton and a trooper from Dookie, the nearby seat of the Agricultural College.

'Sergeant would like to talk to you boys,' said Murdoch. He sat morosely on his horse at the top of the cuesta above us while the police-man from Shepparton came down into the camp and asked us a lot of searching questions about thieving in the neighbourhood. I could see that despite our best efforts the questions were tending to incriminate Rose and Vic. It was up to us to warn them. I tipped the wink to Jock who asked the trooper if he could go into the bushes to relieve himself. The trooper was wearing a tight-fitting blue serge tunic with a high collar and it was slowly choking him. We offered him some apricot brandy out of the Maxmint tin. He didn't like it much but he undid his collar and became a bit more human, and under cover of this relaxment Jock ran like the wind up the creek and warned the boxer and his mate.

'You'd better take us to see these pals of yours,' said the trooper. We assented dutifully and offered to guide them, but when we reached Rose's and Vic's hideout we were suitably astounded to find camp hurriedly struck and the birds flown. Murdoch couldn't con-ceal his annoyance. I think it must have been he who put the cops on to us in the first place. They all went back to the homestead with a very ill grace. We didn't see Rose and Vic again until after we all returned to Melbourne, though this was sooner than we expected because two days later when we reported for work Murdoch handed all four of us pay slips and the money owing us.

'What's the big idea?' we said. We'd become men in the inter-vening six weeks and could now talk tough.

'Haven't any work for you,' said Murdoch shortly, twitching his heavy thick black moustache under his battered wideawake. We looked very glum.

'Crop's tailing off,' he said. 'Sorry,' and he turned on his heel.

I went to see Nugget at the sorting table. I just couldn't believe we were no longer required. There was still lots of fruit to be picked. I was sure Murdoch had fired us because he suspected us of collusion with Rose and Vic (in which of course he was entirely right). Nugget looked sage.

'Tell you, Turkey,' he said, 'when the boss says he don't want you he don't want you. Aint no real use argyin about it unless you're with the Union. You ain't with the Union are ya? Paid ya dues?'

I shook my head.

'Best accept it then. Hell, you'll be back next season. What d'you kids want with dough anyway? You've all got families in Melbourne. Oodles o' boodle.'

We shook hands all round. When it came to Hairy Joe's turn he grabbed my hand in a crushing grip, gave me a broad wink and shouted so that the rest of the sorters could hear,

'Off ya go kid, an ride a good race for me down in Little Lon. Har har!'

* . * *

Back in Melbourne news greeted me that I'd been successful in securing the Shell Scholarship. This, and the fact that despite the low pay, the deduction, the expenses and the lousy living conditions, I had managed to save eighteen pounds fruit picking seemed to call for a celebration. The summer had been crowned with success. I rang up the girl friend and asked her if she would like to come for a drive.

'But you haven't a car.'

'I'll get one.'

'But you haven't a licence.'

'Why do you want to be such a wet blanket?'

'It's just that . . .'

'Will you come or not?'

'Of course.'

'I'll pick you up at three o'clock.'

Of course I didn't have a car; of course I didn't have a licence. But I was eighteen (almost); lots of fellows of eighteen had licences. Why should I (just because I didn't happen to have one) be deprived of the pleasure of taking the girl friend for a spin? I got on a tramcar and went down to Armadale where there was a man (well-known to daring unlicensed senior schoolboys) who would hire you a car and no questions asked. The sum was quite absurd of course and an appalling racket: £5 for the afternoon plus the cost of gasoline. However, no doubt the poor fellow had to pay stiff insurance premiums, and while, if there was any trouble, he could always claim that the renter was a licensed driver or accuse him of lying about his age or his licensed condition, no doubt the police would make things nasty for him. Perhaps even in pious Melbourne he might have to grease someone's palm. Anyway I paid the monstrous sum, engaged the clutch, bounded forward like an antelope, stalled, flooded the carburettor, started again after considerable waggery on the part of the garage hands, moved jerkily forward to the gate and set out in a series of voluptuous curves in the general direction of the intersection of Toorak and Orrong Roads.

The car was a very early version of the De Soto and it coughed and spluttered a good deal, but perhaps that was due to my driving. I pulled up with a jerk and some trepidation outside the residence of the grandfather. Out came the girl friend looking divine in a pleated skirt and a bandeau. She climbed in beside me and with immense pride I engaged the gears. We shot backwards at a fearsome pace. I managed to correct this and we zoomed forward, accidentally shifting from low to high in a single movement. I accelerated sharply. We breathed a high exhilarating air and sped perilously down Orrong Road. Our ecstasy was short-lived. At the intersection with Toorak Road a car bore down from the right. I became flummoxed and forgot that I had to give way. Both cars took avoiding action and escaped damage by the merest hair's-breadth. But as I braked to a nervous standstill there was an ominous tinkle on the road. My rival, a portly elderly gent in a black Homburg hat was minus the hub cap of his right rear wheel. Mercifully the dreaded John Hops were not in sight. I dismounted trembling (fortunately remembering to switch the motor off while the girl friend put on the handbrake); my face proclaimed my guilt and consternation.

'And what do you think *you're* doing, young man?'

'I'm very sorry, sir. I'll pay for it.'

'I should hope so. What's your name.'

I gave it. A look of puzzlement came over his face.

'Surely you're George Thirkell's boy?'

'Yes, sir.'

'Shouldn't have thought you were old enough to drive a car.'

I remained silent. He sighed windily and said 'Well, I don't want to get you into trouble but it's going to cost me a pound to get that hubcap fixed, so it's going to cost *you* a pound to enable me to fix it, isn't it?'

I gulped. I'd spent all my money on the hire of the illegal demon chariot.

'I'm afraid I haven't a pound, sir.' Visions of prison, of cops, of Mother's extreme displeasure—don't know which was the worst—arose before me. Suddenly I had a brain wave: Dad, good old Dad, my stepfather, always good for a touch. He'd be at the Naval and

Military Club now—always was on a Saturday afternoon. And my opponent knew him.

'Sir,' I said, 'if you'll give me a chance to phone my Dad, I know he'll lend me the money.'

'Am I to wait here while you phone your Dad?'

'Yes, sir. I mean no, sir. Well . . .'

He fumbled in his fob pocket. 'Here's my card. Bring the money round as soon as you can get it.'

'Yes, sir.' It read Mr. Justice Higgins.

He mounted his car and rode majestically off, leaving the hubcap winking merrily in the middle of the road. At this point I became aware of a cop surveying us from the far side of the street. He began to saunter slowly over, his tall black patent leather helmet gleaming in the sunlight. I decided to leave the hubcap where it was and went back to the car. My girl friend was at the wheel and I was much put out by this. Did she have no trust in me at all? But she gave me such a quick conspiratorial look that I went round to the offside of the car to open the passenger door. As I did so the cop picked up the hubcap, examined it suspiciously and moved slowly over to where we sat. It seemed to take forever in the warm empty Saturday afternoon heat. At last he arrived and put his big boot up heavily on the footboard.

'Afternoon, lady, and what's this supposed to be?' He brandished the hubcap.

'I don't know, officer, I'm sure' said the girl friend. I said nothing, sitting glumly in the passenger seat and waiting in a sweat of apprehension to be unmasked as the unlicensed driver of a rented car.

'Looks like a hubcap,' said the cop.

We nodded brightly.

'Wouldn't be off this De Soto, would it?' He walked slowly round the car. 'Naow, it must be some other car.'

We remained silent. The cop ran a thumb over his chin stubble. 'Any idea whose car it might be?'

The girl friend shook her head, 'No officer.'

'What about you, son, let's see yer licence.'

'It's my grandfather's car' said my angel quickly, 'and I'm just taking this friend of mine round the corner to his house.'

The cop looked extremely sceptical.

'And who might this grandfather be, Miss?'

'Mr. Justice Higgins,' she said with freezing hauteur.

The cop was visibly impressed. Though not a snob, and able to scent, like all Melbourne cops, the very faintest trace of 'pull', he knew who Higgins was. He took his foot off the running board and straightened up.

'Yerss,' he said. 'Ah, yerss. A very fine type of gentleman. Well, get along and go slow.'

'Oh yes, officer, I will,' said my girl.

She drove a block and a half to her grandfather's house, parked the car very carefully at the kerbside, put her face in her hands and burst into tears. I was too ashamed myself even to try to comfort her.

Chapter Five

THE DIGGER HAT

BEFORE I could enter University or even sort out my tangled loves, I had to complete compulsory military service. Australia had not imposed conscription during the First World War. The effort to do so had rent the country politically, with the bantam Prime Minister W. M. 'Billy' Hughes and the Anglo-Saxons on one side, and the Roman Catholic Archbishop of Melbourne, the Rev. Daniel Mannix D.D., and the Irish on the other. In the end it was more important to keep the ship of state afloat than to impose conscription. But once the war was over a basically conservative minded government introduced and maintained a system of compulsory military training.

To a boy, once he had reached his seventeenth birthday, this took the form of a 'bluey' instructing him in the name of King George V to report to the nearest Drill Hall on pain of severe penalties, and to prepare for two years training in each year of which he would perform not less than thirty 2½-hour drill periods and spend not less than ten days under canvas in a military camp. I was still at school so this was easy, indeed a bit of a lark, because it meant Wednesday afternoon off to parade at the Hawthorn Drill Hall under the eye of the inevitable, grumpy and exasperated C.S.M. i/c trg., who, though he vented stentorian sarcasm on us we ploughed through our square-bashing, has also a rich fund of Anzac tales. This was no hardship, though a bit of a chore, and when we actually got our issue uniforms and put them on, the world was excitingly if briefly changed.

My stepfather, an unscathed (except for a bit of shrapnel in one leg) veteran of Gallipoli, the Somme and Villers-Brettoneux took an erratic maudlin interest in my approaching military career. It stirred his memories of the dear dead days and there was nothing for it but that I must be an artilleryman—a gunner, not simply a member of the P.B.I. As a sapper, he'd spent the war with the P.B.I. and knew what a wonderful time, by contrast, the gunners had had, tearing through the Flanders mud on the limber of a 25-pounder field gun while the poor infantry bastards were stuck in the trenches 'up to their necks in shit and slime' as described in *Mademoiselle from Armentières*. What he had missed I should now achieve. He foresaw the younger generation—if not exactly his own flesh and blood, then at any rate the son of the woman he'd married—roaring on to success where he had failed. So he spoke to his crony, Col. H. O. ('Oz') Caddy, V.D., at the Naval and Military Club, and Oz spoke to Johnny Gates who spoke to Pip Watson who spoke to the C.S.M. i/c trg. at the Hawthorn Drill Hall with the result that one day the following conversation ensured.

'Taylor!'

'Please, sir, he's ill, sir.'

'Sick is 'e? Thirkell!'

'Sir!'

'See me after drill.'

'Yes, sir.'

'Thomas!'

'Sir!'

and after a dreary afternoon of 'Form Fours!' 'Form Two Deep!' 'By the right quiiiiiick *MUH*!!' etc. I stood to attention in the C.S.M.'s little cubbyhole.

'Stand at ease.'

'Yes, sir.'

'Yer Dad wants you to be a gunner.'

'Yes, sir.'

'A bit awkward because we got no issue of britches or leggings here. All infantry.'

'Yes, sir.'

'You really want to be in the artillery?' He cast a ruminative eye at me from a face as pocked and pitted as any Flanders Field.

'My Dad . . .'

'Ner mind yer Dad!' he roared. 'I arst *you*!'

'Yes, sir.'

He sighed windily, clutched up his belt and looked at his huge black broken fingernails as if he'd never seen them before, as if they were spades to till recalcitrant recruiting soil.

'Orright then!' he barked. 'Take this chitty down to the Prahran Drill Hall and they'll give you britches and leggings; the rest you can get here. And mind you get a receipt! This is Australian Government property.'

'Yes, sir.' I saluted and went out.

Next day I took the uniform home and surveyed it with wonder in the privacy of my own room. I even stood before Will Longstaff's picture of *Menin Gate* and brushed my cheeks with the rough honourable serge of my new breeks. In total the uniform comprised :

a floppy tunic of khaki serge buttoning up to the neck and cinched with a belt;
a pair of khaki serge breeks with the inside of the seat and thighs reinforced with leather;
a pair of brown leather leggings;
a pair of brown leather boots with huge squared bulbous toes, soles about an inch thick and hobnails which announced the wearer's presence at least three blocks away;
the 'Digger' hat—a really wonderful piece of headgear of stiffened felt with a wide brim, turned flaring upward at one side.

I dressed carefully and adjusted the hat. I looked like one of the Diggers at Suvla Bay or Gaba Tepe or Anzac Cove. I wasn't yet allowed to wear the rising sun badge of the A.I.F.—no recruit was; but somehow the wearing of the Digger hat—the Anzac hat—made me one with the heroic tradition. Despite the growing pacifist or perhaps anti-war feeling at school, I felt the simple pride of belonging, which is presumably the soldier's greatest strength. When I emerged from my room into the bosom of the family and even more when I ventured out into the street there came pride of another sort. My younger brothers gaped in admiration, my Mother said I looked very handsome and even Dad, a genuine Anzac, said I didn't look all *that* bad.

On the street and above all in the tramcar those restrained plaudits became real 'ohs' and 'ahs' of adulatory admiration. On drill days we wore our uniforms to school, and despite competition from colleagues similarly clad, the discomfort of the hobnailed boots and the self-consciousness induced by the newness of everything, there was no doubt that there's something about a soldier that is fine, fine, fine. If not, then why did all the girls on the tramcar flutter their eyelashes and twitter together like starlings; why were unattainable demi-goddesses suddenly all smiles; why did the girls from the Presbyterian Ladies College daringly indulge in forbidden carmine lipstick and even a touch of eye shadow; why did some of them, contrary to strict school rules, remove their hats the better to shake their glossy locks at us? Oh, it was great to be a soldier !

At least it was great on Wednesday morning, but not quite so great on Friday evenings; and when we were told that we had to give up the best part of two weeks of the precious long vacation to live (and work—'Don't forget you're in the Army now; no time for slackers !') under canvas, the outlook was distinctly bleak. However,

King George V had spoken and there was nothing for it but to obey.
We were loaded standing in one ton trucks with our kitbags and
haversacks, and rolled northward to the Army Camp at Broadmeadows.

Rarely has a place been less aptly named. It conjured up a vision
of a meandering creek fringed with willows, of fat cattle grazing in
deep grass starred with buttercups. The reality was a gently undulating dry and almost treeless plain seared by the hot 'brickfielder'
that roared down from the Mallee in summer, and blasted by the
southerly buster that came whooshing up from Antarctica in the
winter. There is also a dreadful sameness about military camps no
matter where they are located, and Broadmeadows with its duckboard
sidewalks, its 'temporary' weatherboard and tarpaper hutments
(erected in 1914-15) and its dusty alleys signed Kitchener Road,
Monash Street, Foch Street, was certainly no exception.

Upon arrival we were decanted, our kit hurled out in a great pile
by the unsympathetic driver, and faced the immediate task of erecting a bell-tent. Scouting had given me some inkling of how to guy a
tent, but ours were modest 8' × 12' affairs. This was an enormous
brown canvas parachute 18 feet in diameter with a huge centre-pole
and a complex system of guy ropes which entangled us in their
tricky skeins. Metal tent-pegs had to be banged home with mallets,
and shifted and re-shifted to satisfy the critical eye of the Permanent
Force lance-jack who'd been put in charge of us. Eventually it was done;
we disentangled our own kit, secured our own straw palliasse and
trooped over to the mess hut. There at least was an improvement
over scouting days. Instead of boiled potatoes and onions and bread
and jam, there was a great steaming dixie of beef stew, big hunks of
cheese, plum duff, scalding tea and oceans of tomato sauce. The meal
was eaten in silence and with incredible rapidity, in perhaps five
minutes; though an inveterate gobbler I was left far behind. We re-
repaired to the canteen, where beer was served, and until lights out
I secured for myself a precarious popularity by 'shouting' interminable rounds of Foster's Lager.

After the tedium of drill, and the chores of camp house-keep-
ing, came the boredom of the sand table and the mapping
classes.

'Now what do you see on the chart, Murphy?'

'I see a gum tree, sir!'

'In the army we have only two trees: pine trees and bushy trees.
Unless you want to find yourself up a gum tree, bear that in
mind!'

'Yes, sir! I see a—a—' (what *was* a gum tree? It certainly wasn't
a pine tree. Were there any in Australia except the Christmassy

Norfolk Island Pine or the imported *pinis insignis* of suburban wood-lots? A gum tree wasn't 'bushy' either; it soared straight and true and thin) '—a—a bushy tree sir!'

'Right!'

'What do you see, Taylor?'

'On the left I see a hedge, sir!'

'One moment! In the Army we don't call a hedge a hedge, we call it a hedgerow, otherwise you might confuse it with a hedge like the hedge of this here board.'

We droned on in the stifling dusty heat and then at last magically it was time to harness the horses and limber up the 25-pounders. This was real fun and we learned a lot; and here my country farm-boy training with Nell and Basil Hall came in handy. I could ride passably well, knew how to saddle and bridle a pony and, what was more important, how to harness a team of horses to pull a wagon: bridle and bit in the mouth and over the head; breeching and girth strap neatly adjusted; crupper under the horse's tail; back slowly into the shafts; affix the traces; bring the reins back through the saddle thongs and there you were.

But at Broadmeadows each man was in charge of two horses and they were no ponies, but contumacious old Army hacks with leathern mouths and mean dispositions. And they didn't know us. It took all our journeyman skill and patience to get the beasts fed, watered and harnessed, let alone hitch them up to the limber and guns. They had a dreadful habit of leaning on you, threatening to crush you between the great heaving body and the stall. They refused to open their mouths to take the bit; they laid back their ears and showed the whites of their eyes in a most fearsome and provocative manner. They twisted around in the stall and entangled the harness until the corporal had to come round and sort you out with many a head-shaking cluck and what was the Army coming to, and Jesus, this was the worst bunch of recruits he'd seen since 1920 and that was saying a lot, by Jesus.

But at last they were ready and we led the horses away to back them into the limber. Each gun had three pairs of horses in tandem with one gunner to each pair, riding the outside horse. The single leg shaft from the limber ran down between the horses and you wore a steel leg guard like a big knife which you slipped down the inside of your left legging to protect you from being bruised or crushed by the shaft. You guided your own animal with the reins and you had a small whip to keep your rider-less companion horse under control. In point of fact since these animals were used entirely for training they could do all the manoeuvres blind-fold and once the corporal had made it clear to them that if they played any more monkeyshines with the recruits they'd have *him* to reckon with, they became much more docile and co-operative.

I didn't have much to do because I was never on the lead horse and once the limber was hitched to the team, and the gun hitched pointing backwards to the limber, there came the tempestuous canter, sometimes almost a gallop into 'action'. Riding with a team of six fiery horses, the wind in your teeth, the flaring Digger hat firmly anchored by your chinstrap, with flying traces, jangling harness and clanking wheels and chains, it was wonderfully exhilarating to race across the great dry Broadmeadows downs in full career. All else subsequent to this was really a chore and an anti-climax : reining in the team, unhitching the gun from the limber, manhandling it into position on the plate, taking up gun stations and turning away in a crouch with thumbs in ears when the actual 25-pounder was fired— only blanks of course in peace-time. By the end of the camp we could perform all these manoeuvres tolerably well and it was decided that we were now smart enough—just—to return to the artillery barracks in Melbourne with our guns rather than in a one ton truck. They had that much confidence in us.

We sat up half the night rubbing dubbin into the harness and the saddles and into our own boots, and after lunch next day we set off. It was about eleven miles to the barracks and once we got off the paddocks and on to suburban streets we could no longer gallop or canter; and even the admiring looks of girls at intersections couldn't make up for the tedium of waiting at traffic lights and having to manoeuvre the gun and the limber so that the wheels didn't get caught in the tramcar tracks. But at last we entered the long deep canyon of Swanston Street, Melbourne's main thoroughfare, and here the sense of being on a parade bucked us up no end. The traffic was stopped; tramcars were immobilized in the midst of the city's great wide 99-foot streets as we lumbered and jangled by. Flags were out. What did this mean? Could it be for us? *Us?* Impossible. Yet as we came abreast of the Town Hall we heard the cry of 'Eyes Left', and there at the top of the steps leading up to the portico was a wooden dais covered with the Southern Cross and the Union Jack, and taking the salute with his eagle beak beneath a staff officer's cap, and resplendent in red tabs, was Colonel H. O. (Oz) Caddy, V.D., D.S.O. At his side—and I was so astonished that I almost fell off the horse—was Dad in his own uniform, slightly moth-eaten and tight across the pot, of an A.I.F. Captain. I was consumed with military pride and fervour as we clattered by and when later, on the Domain in front of Government House, we gave a display before proceeding to barracks and my team was personally congratulated by Oz and I saw Dad wink at me in the background, I felt that my military career would now burgeon splendidly and that I would climb to great heights.

*   *   *

But at this point was heard the siren voice of Greg Spencer the same lad who had chloroformed himself during Miss A'Beckett's biology lecture. He was going to Walhalla and he wanted me to come with him. Deep in a woolly cleft of the Baw Baw mountains, accessible only by a narrow gauge railway which wriggled its way through steep gorges, lay this Australian version of the home of the Nordic Gods. One imagines Valhalla among beetling crags and torn strips of wispy mist, somewhere up near Ultima Thule beyond the voyage of Othere, the Old Sea Captain. Aussie Walhalla, a derelict goldmining town, resembled its Nordic counterpart only in its inaccessibility.

Eighty or so miles east of Melbourne you abandoned the Gippsland Express, crossed the platform to a toy 2 feet 6 inches railway line and chugged north into hills behind a woodburning Garratt double-headed tank engine. The train normally consisted of a rake of ten or twelve open freight cars loading gypsum and gravel, at the end of which was a single passenger coach. Most passengers preferred to sit on their kitbags in the rattling gypsum cars. This was worth doing not because of comfort but because of companionship with the tough leather-faced men in battered and frayed wideawake hats who dropped quietly off at the way stations or clambered silently aboard preceded by a well-aimed kitbag. It was eminently worth it when the little train, having slowed panting up the hills, enclosed in a clanking tunnel of hot tindery bush, suddenly breasted the skyline and Australia Felix was revealed in all its grandeur. From the little gamboge-painted weatherboard station at Erica, lost in an immensity of olive-grey bush, a great vista of tangled purple mountains opened up, their topmost ridges flecked with snow. The sky seemed enormous and the huge declivities that yawned at your feet gave an exhilarating sense of power and glory. As Kenneth Slessor has written:

> 'The monstrous continent of air floats back
> Coloured with rotting sunlight and the black
> Bruised flesh of thunderstorms . . .'

Far below lay contorted bony hills covered with a hairy growth of eucalyptus and even deeper down, in a gorge as narrow and secret as an armpit, lay Stringer's Creek and the derelict town. Slowly the train began to inch downhill, flanges whining on the sharp narrow curves, iron brake-shoes squeaking on the tire-rims. After an interminable descent through dust-filled air into the super-heated gorges the train halted at the edge of a great greeny-brown river, a hundred yards wide. At the entrance to the plate girder bridge was a sign-board *Thomson*, the river's unromantic name and the last flag-halt before the train wormed its way up Stringer's Creek past the melancholy grass-grown tailings of abandoned mines into the little town that was one street wide, like a snake caught in a drain.

Here, miles from anywhere, was where Spencer wanted me to come with him. We'd camp alone, he said; be our own bosses. We'd grow vestigial beards, wear filthy old pants, catch fish, pan for alluvial gold, and drink beer with the fettlers along the railway. Better than Broadmeadows, eh? We would be free as air; no reveilles, no parades, no cleaning harness and boots; no tedious housekeeping chores, no map and sandtable work; no R.S.M. to bash your ears. I slipped quietly out of my Anzac hat and my leggings, slid into grey flannel pants and an old bashed-in grey fedora of Dad's and followed Spencer into the bush—into the true Australia of the romantically inclined who can never forgive its people for clustering in the five enormous cities round the seaward edge of the great grey saucer.

I already knew something of this magical land, for I had earlier attended an institution known as Abu's Camp. This was run for a small group of senior boys by Mr. Adams the English master known, because of his monstrous brood, as Abu (Ben Adhem, may his tribe increase). It was a week's good fun and swimming on the banks of the Thomson ending, for a select and hardy few, in the famous hike across the Baw Baw mountains from Walhalla to Warburton over the ranges that lay between the sources of the Latrobe and the Yarra. Because of the risible sound of the name Baw Baw and because it was associated in people's minds with a rather sickly type of sweet biscuit, the magnificence of these great hills was likely to be underestimated. But in a continent whose highest peak is not much over 7000 feet, mountains of over 5000 were counted as—and were—majestic. They reared their great woolly shoulders up into the rare, for Australia, region of annual snowfalls. Their upper slopes were covered with strange mosses and lichens, with dwarf gums, wan and ashen in the antipodean winter dawn. Those who took the five-day hike, carrying all their food, clothing and equipment on their backs, never forgot the high thin air, the blessedness of being both bone-tired and well-fed, and the exhilarating vistas of Australia's roof, the Alps, Mount Bogong and the Dargo High Plains. What gallop across the dun fields could compare with that, even with a limber and gun in tow?

Greg Spencer and I set up our headquarters in an abandoned saw-mill on the edge of the Thomson, here running in a cleft some 400 feet deep, and next to the bridge carrying the narrow gauge track to Walhalla. Our neighbours were a dour contractor who was erecting a new road bridge over the Thomson, and an aged and eccentric recluse who panned alluvial gold. The contractor spent most of his time with one foot up on a log staring sourly at the excessively slow progress his men were making with a steam-operated pile-driver down below.

'Who'd be a contractor?' he used to say, sucking noisily on his pipe, gripped upside down between great stained yellow teeth. 'Always get the thin end of the stick! Look at those blokes down there! Takin' their time they are. Just hangin' around. Ar, I'll never make any money out of this job.'

'Buck up,' we'd say, 'course you will!'

'Naow,' and he'd shake his head gloomily. 'There's a penalty clause, see? Every week over the contract date and they start slapping the penalty on you. Daylight robbery, that's what it is.'

'But supposing you finish ahead of time?'

He looked at us as if we were mad.

'You blokes need yer heads read. How 'm I ever gonna finish *ahead* of time, with *that* mob? Just look at 'em.'

'Maybe you should hire better men.'

'Ar, it's easy to say that. Try and get 'em though. All they want is their three squares, they tell you—until it's knock off time or time for a smoke-oh, or pay day, and off they go into Walhalla and you're lucky if they turn up at all for Monday morning, let alone sober.'

'Who's going into Walhalla, eh?' It was the recluse with his wispy white snatches of beard and his wild blue eyes rimmed with red. His faded khaki shirt was open at his gravelly old turkey-cock's throat and spouted a great fountain of white fuzz. 'Ya goin' into Walhalla? Tell you something. You could get a ride in on the fettler's hand trolley. A lot faster than walkin'.'

'Which fettler?' said the contractor morosely.

'Jack Motta. The Italian lad. I seen him. I tell you he's goin' in.'

'Where'd you see him?'

'Down by the river. Down where I'm panning. Oh, I see him all the time . . . I see 'em all.'

The recluse rolled his eyes and muttered and cackled to himself. We all thought him crazy and in fact he had once been in a mental home and if you ever let him get started it was a compulsive non-stop monologue:

'. . . an then the sister says, Albert she says, ya too rough. Ya gettin' too rough, she says, we gotta give you the office. You know what they do? They jab you in the arse with a great needle. And then one time the needle wasn't enough an I was kickin' up a row, see, and the Doctor comes in. I don't like me food, I says. Wots up with you? he says. Wots wrong with it? he says. Albert, he says, we gotta give ya the office again only this time, he says, this time it's gonna be the parallahide ya gonna get. Oooh, that parallahide, that's awful stuff . . .'

And he'd roll his scary eyes and suck his unkempt wispy moustache into the inside of his mouth. 'Awful stuff. You boys ever had parallahide?'

'Show us your pannings, old un', we'd say. He loved that. He'd take us down to the little bark humpy where he lived on one of the creeks that flowed into the Thomson and show us his gold. In those days gold and gold dust was worth about £12 an ounce and, with the onset of the Depression, many a lonely man had gone back into the bush panning for gold to make a precarious but self-respecting livelihood. The recluse was one of these. His equipment was minimal. He had no sluice box or cradle or high-pressure hose. All he had was a small shovel and a pan. He dug alluvial gravel out of the creek bed, chucked it into the pan and simply pushed the pan with both hands down into the creek until it filled with water. Then, squatting on his hams at the water's edge, he slowly began to tilt and swirl the pan, adding water from a billycan and patiently slopping out the gravel. He worked with intense concentration, his red-rimmed eyes never leaving the pan, and presently there would remain swirling slowly on the bottom, like tea leaves in a pot, a small deposit of gold dust and even one or two minute nuggets, the size of a pin's head. The gold was mixed up with flakes of mica or mundic, 'fool's gold'. To separate this out he poured the contents of the pan onto his one piece of professional equipment, a sheet of smooth chamois leather spread on top of an empty wooden packing case. With a pair of ordinary manicurist's tweezers he would separate the gold from the fool's gold and pour it into a small medicine bottle. He used to pan about half an ounce a week, but he'd usually wait until he had a couple of ounces before walking three miles up the railroad track into Walhalla to hand it in at the government assay office. We used to ask him if he wasn't afraid of being robbed, because, whenever we went to see him, there was the little medicine bottle in an upended whisky case with an old piece of dirty towelling hanging in front of it.

'If I'm robbed I'm robbed,' he'd say with admirable simplicity. 'But don't worry, boys, no one's getting to rob an old fella like me. I'm past it, boys, and what's in it for them? Anyone can pan gold around here.'

This was true enough. Though the main vein in the Stringer's Creek valley had long since been worked out there was still enough in the creek beds to keep the townsfolk in pocket money. Walhalla itself had shrunk from a brisk mining town of two thousand people, for which it had been worth building a railway, to a husk of perhaps two hundred inhabitants. Yet there was enough panning to make it worth the government's while to have an assay office there instead of moving it down to the main line at Moe, twenty-five miles away.

Saturday night in Walhalla was a sobering occasion. We used to walk in by the very rough cart road and return, if we were lucky, on Jack Motta's hand trolley along the railway track. After you passed the huge grey mounds of tailings and the little round-house for the narrow gauge locomotive, the town was a single street with every second or third house abandoned, sagging just a little, its weather-board scurfy with age and neglect, hitching posts starting to split, and old signs and billboards faded into X-ray shadows of once power-fully beckoning displays: STRINGER'S CREEK EMPORIUM; WAL-HALLA SADDLERY AND HARNESS; WALHALLA-ABERFELDY STAGE COACH. At night the single street was lit with kerosene lamps at odd intervals and, since the only pub in town shut at six, lost revellers on the lookout for a bottle of 'plonk' from the bootlegger would drift through the darkness between the grey wooden false-fronted buildings like melancholy ghosts. Above the little township the hill rose steep and hairy, shutting out light and life.

The Public Library and Mechanics' Institute stayed open until nine and the recluse, having handed in his gold dust at the assay office and filled his belly with beer, would sometimes ask us to read aloud to him, for as he touchingly announced: 'Boys I never had the time to con me letters and ye'll just have to put me to sleep.' He didn't mind what we read him: news a week old from Melbourne; old newspapers; Dickens or Dumas; a railway timetable or a seed cata-logue. Most of all, though, he liked extracts from *The Blue Lagoon* by H. de Vere Stacpoole, and before he finally dozed off with his wispy beard on his chest and the librarian—an elderly spinster—started to make clucking noises with her teeth, he'd say,

'Oh, boys. That was the life. Why didn't I find meself a desert island instead of all that parallahide? Now why didn't I?'

Then he'd start snoring and it was time for us to wake him up and walk him between us down to the fettler's hut at the engine shed to see if Jack Motta was prepared to take us back to Thomson on his hand trolley. It was downhill on a gentle slope all the way from Wal-halla to the river, so the little handle whipped itself backward and forward without our aid as the warm night wind whistled in our faces and a cool and distant moon peered down from the woolly hills. One night Jack, a swart chunky fellow with a chin like a cleaver, who per-formed this service for the sheer joy of it, greeted us at the fettler's hut weaving on his feet and brandishing a bottle of 'plonk' in the air.

'Goin' into Moe tonight,' he said thickly. 'Right down to the main line!'

'You'll never get up the hill,' said Greg. The line climbed about a thousand feet between the Thomson crossing and Erica.

'Who says so?' said Jack belligerently, taking a great swig at the bottle. 'Ya wanta come along?'

'Sure we want to come along?'

'Then get the trolley on the line. Here's the key.'

He chucked the key which described a silvery arc through the night and landed at my feet among the cinders and clinkers at the edge of the track. We dumped the recluse on a white-painted concrete mile-post, liberally bespattered with weed-killer, and manhandled the trolley out of its little tin shed and on to the line. It weighed about three hundred pounds and we were both puffing by the time we had it chocked on the incline. The moon shone cold and silvery on the curving tracks and the inner edges of the guard-rails.

'Come on, Jack!'

'Orright, orright.'

He stuffed the bottle of 'plonk' into his hip pocket and climbed aboard. We hauled up the recluse.

'Kind of tight fit tonight,' said Jack. 'You'll have to cuddle up a bit!'

He roared with boozy laughter, removed the chock and off we trundled into the night. By the time we'd cleared the yard we were doing twenty, and at the first bridge we were hitting thirty. The handle was flying back and forth like a weaver's shuttle and we crouched clinging to the stanchions to avoid its fuzzy lethal arc. We hurtled round the curves, roared over culverts and the bush swished by at breakneck speed. There were no trains on the line at night, but I began to think we stood a very good chance of sailing off a curve into oblivion with a good old-fashioned smash-up. I shouted against the roar and rattle in Jack's ear.

'Hey, slow down a bit, you'll have us off the track.'

His reply froze the blood.

'Can't hold 'er now. She's goin' too fast. Got to give her her head. Ha—ha—ha!' He reached for his hip, took out the 'plonk', wiped the mouth of the bottle with the palm of his hand, and swigged.

We clung on for dear life, jerked violently to left and right at each tight curve. The flanges squeaked and squealed. Thank God for guard-rails, I thought. The recluse had me in a death-grip, his eyes closed, his lips moving. We twisted and turned in a mounting roar of sound, and at last emerged on to the straight-away leading to the Thomson bridge. Useless to attempt to stop the trolley. We flew over the bridge barely touching the rails and roared half a mile up the hill towards Erica before coming to a stop. I shook Jack but he was dead to the world. I yelled to Greg.

'For God's sake chock it before we go back down the hill!'

But it was too late. Backward now we rolled though mercifully at somewhat reduced speed. We rounded the final corner in fine style, roared on to the Thomson bridge and came to a stop above the middle of the stream. Once again we tried to shake Jack awake.

'Wassa blurry matter?' he said.

'You've got to get back to Walhalla.'

'Where are we?'

'Thomson Bridge.'

'I'll go back in the morning,' and he nodded off again.

Despite our best efforts we couldn't move him. The recluse suggested we leave him to sleep it off and as there were no trains on Sundays we agreed. But first we pushed the trolley with Jack on it off the bridge and on to the near side of the river, and chocked it with stones. There we left him snoring peacefully.

Next morning both Jack and the trolley were gone. The trolley to our great consternation was shortly seen protruding from the bed of the river. With throbbing temples we bolted a breakfast of flapjacks and hot tea heavy with the horrid metallic taste of regurgitated plonk, and began to search for the body. I mounted the bridge while Greg waded in the shallows. No trace of Jack. Poor bastard, we thought, washed away in the flood. We repaired to the recluse's bark humpy to enlist his support. He and Jack were playing two-handed pontoon, and so deep was their concentration that we stood there resentful and open-mouthed for some minutes before they noticed us.

Finally, 'Ar there boys,' said Jack.

'We've been looking for you all morning. What happened?'

'Draggin' the river, eh?' said Jack thumbing his early morning bristles. The recluse's eyes were smoke-blue tunnels in their red rims.

'What he needs is parallahide,' he said.

Jack laughed. 'Sorry to scare you,' he said. 'I clean forgot Snowy Fraser was comin' down last night on the put-put from Erica. He scared the pants off me. Just had time to jump before he hit me. Reckon the trolley's a write off. Ar well. Can't be right all the time, can ya? Bastard wouldn't even gimme a lift into Walhalla, he was so sore at me. Come on, old un? You gonna see me or bust?'

*   *   *

At the end of four blissful weeks we took the little train back to Moe and the Gippsland express into Melbourne. We'd helped the recluse do a little panning and each had an unexpected bonus of about £8 in our pants pockets. At home I found another bluey awaiting me from King George V. I was reminded that I'd missed four parades, and that I'd better present myself at the drill hall where an explanation would be required. But I also noted that during our absence the Bruce–Page Conservative-Country Party government of the Commonwealth of Australia had been swingeingly defeated. The new Government was that of the Australian Labour Party led by Joe Scullin, and it was committed to put an end to compulsory military training. I pondered deeply on this as I donned my uniform in preparation for the ordeal of explanation that would follow my reappearance at the Drill Hall.

To my surprise the atmosphere was entirely different. The C.S.M. nodded at me offhandedly. There was no 'And where have *you* been?' On the notice board was a large poster announcing the abandonment of compulsory military training and expressing what seemed to me the rather guarded hope that those who wished to do so would volunteer for re-enlistment in order to keep up the fine tradition of the Australian Imperial Forces. I detected the fine Irish hand of Joe Scullin, Ted Theodore, Eddie Ward and other members of the anti-Empire and pacifist Australian Labour Party. Good old A.L.P. No more galloping across the tawny Broadmeadows acres on my foam-flecked steed; no more rattle and clash of limber and gun. No more I mind the day my old Shako when first you graced my head; what time I wore my sabretache, my spurs and jacket red. Heigh ho, that would indeed be many a year ago now, My old Shako, my old Digger hat. For me the woolly clefts of Stringer's Creek, the high thin air of the Baw Baws, the plashing of the new born Yarra at Wood's Point and the frosted roof of Australia in the dim distance. When parade was over I went to see the C.S.M.

'Yes!' he barked without looking up.

'Sir, I've read the notice.'

He cocked a rheumy eye. 'Want to re-enlist eh?'

'Not exactly, sir.'

He didn't seem terribly disappointed.

'You want to get out? Is that it.'

'Well, sir, yes.'

'Don't say I blame you. Army's outa fashion now. But it'll come back into fashion. There'll always be wars,' he added sombrely gazing grisly-faced at the sepia photograph of anonymous automatons trudging through the Flanders mud. Only the hats to identify them, to distinguish them from Briton, German, French or Slav. 'And there'll always be soldiers. All right! You keep your britches and your boots. Return your leggings and tunic to Q.M. Stores.' He bent again over his papers.

'What about the hat, sir?'

'Return that too.'

'Yes, sir.' The disappointment in my voice made him raise his head.

'You want to keep it?'

'Yes, sir.'

'All you young fellers are the same,' he said with melancholy satisfaction. 'You all want to keep the hat. Want to leave the Army but keep the hat. Want to have your cake and eat it. Well I suppose that's what they call the New Deal! O.K. then, keep the hat.'

'Gee, sir. Thanks!'

'Nuffa that,' he growled. 'We'll say it got spoiled in the wearin'. Wasn't worth calling in. Damaged goods, eh?'

He looked up sharply, sensing my discomfiture.

'Don't want to change ya mind, eh?'

'No, sir—not really.'

'Off you go then.'

He gave a nod of genial dismissal and I went out of his little cubbyhole and clumped across the wooden floor and out into the sunny dusty suburban street. My military career was over. I was a free man. But somehow just at the moment I didn't quite know what to do with my freedom, for it had brought with it an unaccountable sense of loss.

Chapter Six

ET NOVA ET VETERA

THE bony didactic fingers of the Scots dominies reached out far beyond the confines of the secondary schools and fastened their talons on the State's only institution of higher learning: The University of Melbourne. The Vice-Chancellor in the year that I went up was Sir John MacFarland and he in turn was ex-Master of Ormond College, the residential Presbyterian foundation into whose sandstone portals I walked with some trepidation, carrying my Revelation suitcases.

'Scum!'

I heard the contemptuous monosyllable cracked out down the length of the linoleum-floored corridor. What did it mean, I wondered.

'Yes, you!' repeated the voice. 'Come here.'

From a half-open door midway down the passage an angry face, topped by a thatch of black hair, peered towards me. I dropped the bags and began to walk down the corridor.

'Run, scum.'

I did so and came abreast of the face. On it was a barely perceptible grin.

'Remember me, scum?'

It was Nairn the demon footballer who had been my 'husband' in a school play aeons ago. 'Yes,' I said. He looked displeased.

'Yes, who?' he bellowed.

'Yes—sir!'

'That's better. What are you doing inside the portals of this great seat of learning, scum? Why do you even exist? Eh, scum? He thrust a mottled face close to mine and I drew back. 'From now on you're to be my batman, you understand?' 'Yes, sir.'

'Tea at seven o'clock in the morning and see that my shoes are well-shined. Don't forget! Frank will show you your cell.'

'My study?'

'Scum don't have studies! Crawl back into your cheese, and let me not see you until seven tomorrow morning.'

He shut the door in my face and I went back up the corridor to find standing by my suitcases a tiny wizened gnome of a man, with a bald head, a hooked nose and a pair of deep-sunk watery blue eyes.

'Are you Frank?'

'Yes, sir. You'll be one of the new men, won't you, sir? Let me see, I believe you have been allotted one of the Tower Studies, sir. It's rather a long way up, the third floor in fact, sir, but let me help you with your bags.'

'Thank you.' It seemed monstrous that this little man should tote my bags while I, a hulking freshman six foot two, should walk empty-handed. But Frank, who had been the College porter for over thirty years, was all gristle and tendon. In a flash he had my bags on his shoulders and was pounding nimbly up the stone stairs. After four flights we found ourselves at the bottom of a steep narrow wooden ladder leading up into blackness. A tough manila rope served as banister. Frank clambered nimbly ahead with the suitcases while I followed panting in the rear. The stair gave on to a large empty floor with an enormously high pyramidal ceiling. Up one wall crawled another stairway. We were clearly in the base of the clock tower which, modelled by Scots exiles on the gothic crenellations of Kelvingrove, could be seen for miles around. Above the floor on which we now paused was the actual chamber containing the clock. You stood inside the four faces looking out through the huge roman numerals at half Melbourne spread out frighteningly far below. Students who had invited young ladies to tea would often arrange to take them up the tower into the clock chamber immediately before the great bell struck the hour. This event was preceded by such an alarming series of whirrs and clacks, as of a giant making up his mind whether or not to sneeze, that the tension as well as the un-expected noise was known to drive girls right into the arms of their escorts. Above the clock chamber a perilous ladder soared up to a trapdoor leading to a small balcony at the top of the tower. Some-times ladies could be coaxed up this ladder, provided the escort gripped the ladder round the girl's body, thus providing a pleasing sense of measurable danger.

Once you were up on the tiny balcony all Melbourne lay spread out below, the streets running like arrows down to The Bay and in the northern distance the horizon rimmed by a long blue line of hummocky hills ending in the great camel-back of Mount Dande-nong. From here too, on Commencement Day, daring students harangued imaginary mobs through loud-hailers, and here was staged the Homeric battle between two students which ended with one of the bodies hurtling down on to the tiling of the steep-pitched mansard roof and thence, after an appalling crunch, to the ground below. The Master's relief when the body was discovered to be a tailor's dummy was matched by his annoyance at having been duped by a freshman's jape.

The master was D. K. Picken—David Kennedy to be precise— with a burr as granitic as that of any Scots dominie, and a moral fervour as rigid and unyielding as that of any fire and brimstone pastor who ever thundered from St. Giles. He was not in fact in orders; but this was an accident. He was a lay preacher, a staunch pillar of the Presbyterian Church and an inflexible stickler for all college disciplines. He habitually wore both gown and mortar-board and his approach in swift, purposeful and evidently *urgent* stride, no matter what the object of his progress, created a very uneasy feeling in the breasts of undergraduate bystanders. What had they done? Being Men now—and so addressed—their conduct was of course to be judged by other standards than those of the schoolroom whence they had so recently departed. But still, you never knew. The hurrying figure would suddenly pause and remove the mortar-board, revealing a forehead of bulging yet vaguely Jovian proportions, topped by a boiling of wiry black hair. Thick horn-rimmed glasses rose above a knuckle of nose between which and a long bleak mouth was the most enormous moustache. Though clipped close it covered such a vast area that it appeared almost as a deformity, a smear. From beneath it would crack with startling suddenness some crisp but elliptical observation touching on your behaviour, delivered in rugged Scots.

'Ahve not noticed ye in chapel lately, Bairnard. You Men should be aware that sairrtain standarrds are now requairred of ye.'

'Yes, Master.'

'Wurrking hard?'

'Oh yes, Master—er—sir.'

'No excuse for neglecting the releegious side howeverr. Good day.'

Back would go the mortar board and away he went with the same grim purposeful lope to scare the daylights out of the next 'Man'. He was at his most fearsome and tedious at chapel which, during our first year, we were required to attend four days a week. After reading the lesson he would note with a grim smile that for the umpteenth time the hymn selected by the students was *Abide with me*. They could not forgo the pleasure of listening to D. K. Picken singing the line

> 'Change and decay in all around I see'.

Then after a pause would come the explosion:

'Men, Ah'm sorry to have to obsairve that once again The Sairpent has raised its ugly head in the College. I'll not tolerrate it and will make an example of those men who desairve it. . . .' The Sairpent was booze. Ormond was a dry college; that is to say, drink was not allowed inside the building. (How we envied the relaxed Anglicans at Trinity College next door who had their own buttery in the Oxford and Cambridge manner.) Furthermore, though drinking outside the college was not forbidden, undergraduates were expected to show a decent sense of decorum in Hall during meals. If they failed to do so, Old Digger (on the cockney punned rhyming analogy of Picken— pick-an' shovel—digger) would invariably make his nightly sermon the occasion of a lecture on The Sairpent.

Digger had been twice married and had six daughters, but no sons, and was hence the object of much pious sympathy and covert ribaldry among the students. He was alleged to be always digging for dates for his daughters among the student body and the fact that The Sairpent was not allowed to be seen (or smelled) in Digger's house—The Master's Lodge where all the girls lived—was of course a cogent reason for not dating them. Another was their very plentifulness. At college dances, of which there was one each term, fellows who had neglected to make arrangements for a partner, or who were at odds, or at outs, with the current girl friend, could ungallantly say at the last moment 'Guess I'll take one of the Picken girls'. Digger had the heavy-handed avuncular touch of a many-daughtered father. He let you know by forced geniality that he approved of your taking out his daughter, but by an equally crisp jocoseness that you'd better not get it into your head that this was going to change his stern attitude towards you and your wurrk.

In my case the attitude was, to begin with, particularly stern, and with reason. Ormond had attached to it a Presbyterian Theological College and though it had been founded as a lay institution by Francis Ormond, a wealthy Western District squatter, its Presbyterian flavour had always been strong and the possibility of its becoming, in effect, a Calvinist theological seminary had always existed. When another pious benefactor named Wyselaskie died and left some thousands of pounds, what more natural, then, that Wyselaskie Hall should be attached to the college complete with three theological professors? During my time at Ormond the theological students in residence numbered almost a quarter of the total student body. We didn't really like them because, though they strove hard to be regular fellows, they carried about them not so much the aura of holiness as of censoriousness. Their lips often seemed to be pursed, or else they were looking at you over their spectacles; and as a number of them had received 'the call' at the advanced age of twenty-five to thirty they had the bulk of the much younger student body at a disadvantage. They could and did boast of sin and redemption, of errors and mended ways, while we, almost beardless 'Men' of eighteen and nineteen, couldn't compete except by being combatively bawdy or scatological. They then looked pained and retired to their studies to discuss over innumerable cups of strong tea the finer points of O. T. Exegesis. But though we scorned them we felt that they had a secret weapon that was denied to us in our rollicking fleshpots: direct access to You Know Who.

Occasionally some rural hobbledehoy thrown into contact with big city ways would Have Doubts. Digger and the other theologs talked him out of them. Or even worse, philosophical converse with other lads, or even gossiping with them and listening to their uneasy talk about pubs and girls and horses and excursions in fast cars down to the bayside beaches, would cause a tremor to pass over an other-wise glazed and inward- (or Upward-) looking eye. Worst of all would be the theolog who, during the course of studying the English and History, the Logic and Ethics preparatory to his more serious religious instruction, would have his mind opened to the possibilities of alternative explanations of man's fate. The Church of Scotland, whether Wee Free or U. P., might be wrong? At the least, there existed the possibility of doubt. We Godless men worked on these chaps with real zeal and there were two or three spectacular falls from grace during my years at Ormond. All was not roses for such fellows, for most of them had come from poor families and were on theological scholarships which they had to give up when and if they decided they might have been mistaken about their 'Call'.

With this background and all that it implied I should clearly have been on my guard against flipness or irreligion right from the beginning. But inflated with my own success in having secured a resi-dent bursary I importunately dared to insert in the entrance form under the question 'Is it your intention to qualify for the Ministry?' the word 'No' with an exclamation mark. My room mate, an aspiring medical student, and myself, had filled in the forms together in the anteroom in the Master's Lodge. We were about to take our leave when Picken—Digger already to us—burst from the study brandish-ing the form.

'What prrecaisely is the meaning of this?' His tone was icy, his lips a thin line under the enormous smear of Groucho Marx mous-tache, and his eyes were boring through my precarious carapace of self-possession. I temporized.

'The meaning of what, sir?'

'Thiss!' He shoved the offending form under my nose, his knotted stubby finger trembling above the daring word. I gulped convul-sively. Suddenly I saw—perhaps at this distance I can even say that I suddenly had the sense to see—that my future hung in the balance.

The gristly finger trembled before my nose. I summoned up my best school debating club manner and dropped my voice humbly.

'It has no meaning, sir, except that I wished to convey as forcibly and respectfully as I could, that I have no intention whatever, at present, of entering the Ministry.'

There was a pregnant pause. Digger cleared his throat.

'That is not the impression which it conveys to me.'

'I'm sorry, sir.'

'It conveys to me an impression of frivolity!'

'I greatly regret that, sir.'

'You had better be most careful in future as to how you express yourself. I shall have my eye on you.'

'Yes, sir.'

'You may go.'

Had I but known it, a debating club air was the one least likely to arouse Digger's sympathy because he was resolutely opposed to debating. He regarded it as immoral for a man to defend a cause in which he did not passionately believe. Debating societies were frivolous bodies which set cynical young men at each other's (verbal) throats in immoral abandon. Debating might encourage the specious rhetoric of the advocate, but not the moral fervour of the Presbyterian. For this reason he would never allow an Ormond debating team to compete officially with Trinity, Queen's or Newman, our sister colleges. An unofficial team, with no standing of any kind, might accept an offer from the suave Trinity man for beer and battle in wordy conclave; but the Master turned his back, as also, in honour bound, did the Warden of Trinity, Dr. J. C. V. Behan.

Of all this however I was happily unaware as I trembled for my future and bent my neck and doubled my back to pass beneath the series of Caudine Forks which I was sure Digger would erect for me, during my first year. In point of fact by dint of very hard work, carefully disguised after the fashion of the epoch, I was able to do well, though towards the end of my year even first class honours barely averted the wrath of the Digger's deputy, the Vice-Master, H. W. Allen.

Allen, known as 'Barney' after a famous local bookie, was the perfect foil for Digger. He was one of those men who because of a dry sense of humour and a mild scepticism seem born to be deputies. As someone wrote of him in a Valedictory Dinner menu:

> I am the Vice-master of my fate
> I am the Vice-captain of my soul (W. E. Henley, alt)

While Digger ruled with an iron hand and with Divine Intercession Barney, though he could be just as tough when the occasion arose, believed in the velvet glove. He paid us the compliment of assuming we knew how to behave ourselves, that we were indeed Men of Ormond. Digger was never quite sure. He was always ready to point a moral and adorn a tale, to level a finger, to view with alarm and to express the hope—in which he clearly did not believe—that we would be worthy of the great good fortune which had befallen us in being selected to come into residence at Ormond College. Barney on the other hand ruled with a relaxed hand and with the mild cynicism befitting a classics man (he was tutor in Latin and Greek as well as performing his other duties). Digger was a Leader, Barney a persuader; Digger an inspirer, Barney an administrator. The contrast between them was epitomized in the grace which each asked from High Table in Hall:

Digger: for these and all thy manifold gifts, Oh Lorrd, we render grateful thanks, Amen.

Barney: Benedictus benedicat.

—followed in either case by an immense gargantuan scraping (later eliminated by 'domes of silence') as 124 undergraduates sat down to dinner.

Barney Allen had a long proboscis, a head of thin rumpled sandy hair, pale blue eyes and a mouth around which played incessantly the ghost of a smile. Digger, you felt, had been born fully adult; it was inconceivable that he had ever been an undergraduate. Barney on the other hand quite obviously had been one. On the walls of his study hung faded sepia photographs of the cast of Aristophanes' *The Birds* and *The Frogs* produced in bygone days by the undergraduates of Ormond. In these portraits Barney's humorous proboscis stuck out a mile. Furthermore he lived in an atmosphere of rumple and acrid pipe tobacco in two rooms in the College. He was the archetype bachelor don who shambles fitfully from bedroom to study to Hall to tutorial with the faint nod of one who might possibly share with you some recondite joke. He was ruthless but kept the twinkle behind his severity. So too did his gown, a tattered remnant green with age, the wearing of which somehow symbolized a secret bond between him and us whose gowns, whether from poverty, laziness or importunity were similarly tattered and torn. Digger's gown appeared in Hall and in Chapel as neat and black and freshly pleated as the day it was made.

Barney also endeared himself to us by watching all our important games. Digger would put in a brief routine appearance at an intercollegiate football or cricket match, duck his head with an air of hurried embarrassment at one or two of the senior men and their girl friends, and move off at his purposeful lope. Barney would materialize silently on the sidelines in a haze of tobacco-smoke and an hour later you would still find him there engrossed in the state of play. He himself was an amateur skater of note and we all took great pride in his biennial trips to Europe where his lean figure, complete with knitted toque, smoking pipe and wool-mitted hands clasped behind his back, could be seen cutting exquisite if cautious curves on the ice at Davos or Mürren. Melbourne was of course far too warm a city for skating and the only place where this graceful art could be performed was at The Glaciarium, just across Prince's Bridge behind the big illuminated 'Aspro' sign.

Most of us went to 'The Glacie' to meet girls. Barney did not grace the portals of this emporium, but bided his time for the biennial visit to Switzerland and of course to England Home and Beauty; for although among the most Aussie of Aussies he shared the common illusion of the times. This made him highly acceptable in Mother's eyes because it linked him with her passionately longed-for and never-forgotten homeland; and Barney's interest in Home and the classics (the Mackail network again) resigned her to my residence in Ormond. The Mackail heritage might mean a love of Scots education and raw winds and porridge and chilblains and dry-walling and addressing exiled Caledonians as 'We Scotsmen, sir'; but Mother could never quite stomach D. K. Picken. She found him bleak and unresponsive. Also I think she secretly despised him because, in her view, he was really one of the Lower Orders, barely rescued from indecent oblivion by his Scottishness. Barney however was clearly a gent, a classics man and an anglophile and generally O.K.

Barney went off to Switzerland and those of us who were hopelessly mired in Latin Part I found ourselves unexpectedly sitting at the feet of Father Murphy, S.J., Rector of Newman College, who had agreed to fill in during Barney's absence. This bubbly rubicund Irish priest with his honeyed blarney and his soft Dublin voice made Latin suddenly seem fun, and, because fun, comprehensible. Much to my surprise and certainly to Barney's I got my year. It was as well that I did so for towards its close I had committed an act of stupidity such as only a really good year could recoup and which drew down on my head Barney's naked wrath.

A first year is of course always one for student japes and ours was no exception. Looking back they seem fairly harmless and pretty dull: filling the main cistern with two gross of Reckitt's Bag Blue ('The Blue in the whitest Wash') so that all the showers and toilets ran a rich ultramarine for an hour or so; jamming the college organ so that a discordant ninth or seventh blared arrestingly in the midst of Vespers or their Presbyterian equivalent. But Barney put his foot down firmly when he found us dressing up the college sheep in Trinity colours, and over the affair of 'the leads' he was both wrathful and severe.

The Tower study, to which I'd been shown by old bent wizened Frank soon after my arrival, remained our home during my first year. But towards the end of that year it became plain that my room-mate would fail his year and thus forfeit the residential Free Place to which, as a son of the Manse, he had been entitled. Across the corridor in the other Tower study, an engineering student from Tasmania found himself similarly placed. We therefore agreed to join forces and to apply for our second year for a study with a fireplace. Ormond, Gothic and draughty, was of course entirely unheated, and the studies with fireplaces were havens of warmth in the brief but chilly Melbourne winter. Here you could stretch your legs easefully before a blazing log fire and even entertain your friends to hot buttered toast of a winter's evening.

The pact signed, we both departed for our first long vac; but in the heady pause of happy exhaustion which followed the completion of our final exams, we decided to clean house. My new mate, departing by the *S.S. Oonah* for Tasmania and the mining community of Mount Lyell, left me to dispose of the mess. What more natural than for me to dispose of all our surplus paper by having a little bonfire? The best place would be the roof, easily reached by a door from the Tower study, and, safe behind a parapet of corbelled greeny-yellow sandstone. The fire blazed merrily and when all was consumed, or charred as I thought beyond recognition, I bolted the door onto the roof and made my way gaily into Town, leaving Ormond behind until the next year when I would no longer be a freshman but proudly a Second Year Man. The ash would blow away, the tiles were fireproof; I'd forgotten about the leads.

Barney's telephone call came to me at 4 Grace Street whither I had gone to bid farewell to my stepfather and to pack some kind of kit for a camping trip in the bush.

'I shall want to see you immediately. How soon can you get up to the College.'

'In about an hour, sir. Why?' I was still mystified. Incredible as it may seen, it had not yet dawned.

'I think you know why. I shall expect you in an hour.'

Riding up the Sydney Road in a cable car the truth suddenly hit me hard in the pit of the stomach. I walked up the curving drive to the friendly Gothic battlements and the tiled mansard roof and the tall spindly clock-tower, and they too looked bleak. Barney's barked 'Come in' to my tentative knock reverberated menacingly through the empty college.

He was seated behind his large scuffed old desk surrounded by his sepia photographs and his skating trophies and his bust of Virgil and high on the wall behind him a couple of trophy oars. He looked extremely forbidding. Without offering his hand or asking me to sit down he said

'This is an act of the most obtuse and egregious folly. What is your explanation?'

'There isn't one, sir.'

Incredulity blurred the cool anger in his face.

'Am I to believe that?'

'What I mean, sir, is—well, we—I didn't think.'

'Evidently.'

'It was the end of term, sir, and we had all the papers to get rid of and—I know it sounds very stupid now, sir, but at the time we thought it best to burn them.'

'Thereby doing extensive damage to the fabric of the College?'

'I'm afraid we didn't think of that, sir.'

'We—who else is implicated with you in this venture?'

'I, sir. It was me.'

'It did not apparently occur to you that lead has a low melting point? No? Well it has, and your bonfire was sufficient to melt some eight or nine pounds of lead which then ran down the inside of the wall causing a fire which, but for Tobin's alertness might have burned down the College. You could be charged with arson.'

'Oh, sir! But it wasn't deliberate, sir—at least not in that sense, I mean.'

It sounded incredibly foolish. Barney's tone shifted imperceptibly from hardness toward a faintly discernible tinge of compassion.

'Were you out of your senses?'

'I must have been, sir.'

Barney looked at me as if I were a mess on the floor.

'You will consider yourself under suspension until the examination results come out. On them will depend our decision as to whether you return next year. Let us hope for your sake that they are good. You will of course be sent a bill for the damages. I am told that it will amount to approximately £35.'

I gulped at this. 'Yes, sir.'

'That is all.' He nodded curtly and I went out into a very sobered world.

Much later I learned that Barney had written about me to Mother expressing grave doubts as to whether someone so feckless should undertake a serious University career. She replied in a pleading fashion exercising all her wiles of composition and wit on my behalf, and presumably this had its effect. However, my exam results must have helped too. At any rate one hot January day when I was helping to put out a real bushfire in the Walhalla hills I was greatly relieved to receive a letter from Barney briefly congratulating me on my results and wishing me 'a more successful second year so far as the College is concerned'. I felt like a man reprieved from the scaffold.

Even this tenuous hold on college life was reached by a long and arduous route. The senior who had yelled 'Scum!' when I first entered the college forebore to tell me that, for the first month until the Easter break, we would all be subject to the horrors of initiation ceremonies into the cult of the great god Kai-pokai. With visions of Aztec bestialities we trembled as we made tea for our new masters, cleaned their shoes, bought their cigarettes and jumped at the sound of their commands.

Not for us, as yet, the joys of hurling a water bag in through the window of a colleague's study, nor the ecstatic pleasure of lowering on a rope a large chamber-pot in which was a ringing alarm-clock, the whole apparatus timed to appear outside the study window of a colleague who was entertaining a young lady. Not for us, as yet, the committee work on the various student bodies that ran the college: Hall, sports, Valete Dinner, Ormond Ball, the Play. Nor, above all, the proud right to wear (when duly purchased) the Ormond tie or the Ormond blazer.

No. We were scum. All thirty-six of us. We were the biggest freshman entry in seven years and had we but known it the seniors were apprehensive lest we might revolt under some beardless Spartacus and slay them all in their beds. But we didn't know this, and so each morning we were all up betimes to bring hot tea, biscuits and shaving water to our particular master. Then the rush down to an early breakfast in Hall; porridge followed by the sour query from one or other of the elderly crones who waited on table, 'Choppasteak?' No eggs or sausages or bacon or other delicacies; we were to be reared as Men. Then the dash along the cinder track beside the playing field, across the lugubrious lane lined with corrugated iron, and known as Tin Alley, and thence to our lectures.

But it was during the evenings that hell really broke loose for us. After we had served supper to our masters we were ordered to parade in pyjamas and bathrobe with an identification card hung round our neck while our tormentors stood about fully dressed and flicked or belted us with knotted towels when we failed to perform impossible errands or answer complicated questions on the history and structure of the College. We swam on our back the length of the polished common room floor; we recited, back to the wall and hands above the head, the biography of Francis Ormond; we composed, under sharp duress, brochures bound with pink ribbon on such subjects as 'The relative advantages of beards above and below the belt'; we performed, under similar duress, nonsensical public acts which sorely tried the patience of the Melbourne citizenry.

The final initiation was less jocose and more tribal. Stripped to our underpants, our bodies daubed with foul-smelling castor oil, we were forced to parade by candlelight in a crocodile round the dimly lit corridors of Ormond, singing an asinine and dolorous chant entitled 'The worms crawl in and the worms crawl out'. What a falling off was there from the pinnacles of schoolboy achievement! Ex school Captains, prefects, prominent schoolboy oarsmen, footballers, cricketers, debaters, actors, editors of the school magazine and just plain swots: all became part of an almost naked oily line of towel-flicked neophytes swaying in the ghostly gloom. All, too, went through the ritual of being forced to eat the worm (actually a string of cold spaghetti); and finally, all were admitted to the glorious confraternity of Ormond Men, whose god, Kai-pokai, was a symbol of excessive virility.

At once, as by a miracle, the shackles were off; the lights blazed up, our one-time torturers handed us our dressing gowns, and half an hour later there we were sitting on *their* sofas in *their* studies being handed hot buttered toast and tea by *them*. Our eyes wet with gratitude, we stumbled off to bed and awoke next morning to the cameraderie of Ormond. No longer were we 'Scum'; no longer were we forced to address arts students as Professor, and medical students as Doctor. The morrow broke with a feeling of indescribable pride and relief. We were greeted by our christian names, answered joyfully and shyly back in kind, and were free now to take more detached stock of our tutors.

With Barney to ram us through Latin, a quadrumvirate of instructors made our academic life more intimate and perhaps more meaningful. Our spiritual needs were ably met by Digger and, since attendance at Chapel was compulsory, he had a captive audience. He was not a good preacher or reader in biblical matters. But on the subject of morals as affecting the College he was very good indeed. Across the broad palm-lined expanse of the Sydney Road was Johnny Naughton's pub, and here we repaired after football games or for other celebrations with the result that entry into Hall in the evening would be marred by loud voices and rowdy behaviour. At chapel the next night Digger would give out: 'Men! I regret very much to have to tell you that The Sairrpent has once again raised its ugly head . . .' Chastened, we decided to mend our ways—until the next intercollegiate football match.

Though no women were allowed in the college, except on weekday afternoons from three to five where they might be entertained at tea by an ambitious or smitten young man, Digger endeavoured to arrange a release for our pent-up energies by sanctioning and indeed attending our Common Room dances. These were a wonderful mixture of the exciting and the lugubrious. Exciting because, having dated the girl, you then arranged her entire programme with conniving friends, so that you could have the first dance, the last dance and of course the supper dance. Incredibly this was still the era of pasteboard programmes to which a tiny pencil was attached by a baby blue silken thread. These had the advantage that they warned a girl what to expect, and if she saw that, for example, she had two dances running with her swain she could be pretty certain that this would mean a visit to the swain's study (sole tenancy ensured by prior agreement) and could make her dispositions accordingly.

The lugubrious part was attendance on the Pickens—Master and Mistress. Chairs were set for them on a small carpet in one corner of the Common Room and they 'received' students and their girls between dances, enduring in the intervals the strains of a combo led by Colin Keon-Cohen, a local amateur jazzbo whose style at the piano included stomping his feet and raising his rear end from the stool on the off beat. A saxophonist and a drummer accompanied him. Digger took this appalling noise in good part, but it must have seemed to him like an invitation to The Sairrpent.

When girls were presented Digger was polite, guarded and stiff; Mrs. Picken, a motherly woman in silvery blue brocade and grey hair in a bun, was tired, kindly and more flexible. An especial chore fell on the President and Officers of the Committee who had to have The Master and Mrs. Picken to supper. Though they strove hard to be genial their presence inevitably had a dampening effect. Sharp at eleven all merriment ceased and students escorted their girls home, many of them secretly glad of an early night for very few of us indeed had cars, and taxis were far beyond the student pocket except in an extreme emergency, or when a girl had indicated she would like it that way. Most of us were delighted to be able to take the last train or last tram, sitting sedately in our evening clothes among boozy Lodge members, tired Mums with kids and baskets, and the occasional serious elderly student returning from night school. Then soberly—and singly—to bed.

But the Common Room Dance was the exception rather than the rule. Most of our social activities were all-male. There was the Annual Dinner, the Ormond Ball and the Valete dinner to say good-bye to those about to leave, with its wonderful song intoned as we all stood (full of beer secured at Johnny Naughton's):

Humping My Bluey

Vos defuncti spatio
Socii salvete.
Hora praeterit ludorum
Venit aetas seriorium
Socii, Valete!

Even as a freshman one felt the poignancy of departure—'Forty Years On' all over again—and at the same time the thrill of comradely unity, of belonging, of *esprit de corps*. More frivolous were drinking parties over at the pub, and a swimming gymkhana organized in the College pool at which a senior theolog delighted us all by diving into the water clad solely in an Ormond tie knotted around his privities. We felt there was hope yet for those destined to the Ministry.

While all this was going on I suddenly received the electrifying news that (provided I paid my own way) I was invited to accompany the Melbourne University Athletic Team, as a non-playing member, on its visit to Adelaide for the Inter-Varsity Sports meet. My ability to turn a phrase had been noted, and I would be expected to work my passage by reporting events for *Farrago*, the University students' weekly. Frantic with delight I bought my ticket and prepared to board the magical Overland Express.

Chapter Seven

WHO SPAT THERE?

OUR school chaplain used to tell us it was so hot in Adelaide that you could fry an egg on the steps of the Town Hall *in the shade*. Certainly Adelaide lay much further north than Melbourne; and the State of which it was the capital, South Australia, was so enormous that little Victoria clung like a poor relation to the bottom of its immense doorway, stretching up the 141st parallel of E longitude far past the Queensland border. Most of S.A. we were told to bolster up our Victorian morale, was desert, Certainly much of the country that you crossed on the way from Melbourne to Adelaide was not much more than that. But Adelaide itself lay in the well-watered south-east corner of the State and was supposed to be a sub-tropical garden. In any case mid-winter would hardly be the time to fry eggs.

What was the folklore about Adelaide (unvisited)? Well, we poked fun at the citizens because their 'river' (the Torrens) had been created by a dam and was no more than a synthetic watercourse, whereas our own noble Yarra—well, of course! Adelaide was also supposed to be more 'holy' in the pejorative sense, than Melbourne. It was reported that the Presbyterians and Methodists were in full control and even the local C. of E. apt to be blue ribbon and intolerant. I enquired regarding this piece of folklore from Ginger Davidson, son of the Manse and athlete extraordinary, to whom I owed in part the invitation to accompany the team.

'It's a lot of bollix' was Ginger's curt summary. 'Just you see what kind of a time the Adelaide fellows show us—specially after the games.'

I nodded sagely. Ginger was an expert high jumper, 100, 200 and 440 yarder, and footballer to boot. It ill became me to contradict him.

Anyway a journey of 500 miles was in itself so exciting and improbable to a home-bound Melburnian that I didn't really mind what lay at the end of it. I wrote to my very distant, indeed possibly courtesy, cousins, the J. C. McKails who lived in the suburb of Walkerville—a bleak entry into S.A. I thought—and asked if they could put me up. That way I could save some money. I figured that the relationship, which had been discovered when my grandfather came to Australia on his lecture tour seven years earlier, would be good for bed and board for his grandson. So indeed it proved. I bought a second class return ticket—no sleepers for the young naturally—and with a high sense of adventure attached myself to the group of chattering undergrads and their girl friends who stood all decked out with rosettes and ribbons for the occasion, clotted round the enormous panting behemoth that drew the Overland Express.

The train left sharp on time at five p.m. and a couple of hours later, with eight of us crammed in our small second class compartment, it was struggling double-headed up to the Ballarat plateau. The names of well remembered childhood villages and townships swam past in the dark, like lighted ships riding at anchor in the night: Ballan, Warrenheip, Bungaree. For this was where we used to spend our schoolboy vacations with Nell and Basil Hall. Yet to glimpse the familiar names in the strange context of a continental journey hinted at a vast unknown Australia lying at the back of my timorous childhood ventures out of the city.

The train stopped for half an hour at Ballarat and we wolfed unsuitable cold meat pies, scones, apple dumplings and tepid coffee at the station buffet, complete with steaming urn, crosspatch dirty waitresses in stained uniforms, and the dead buns under glass so dear to the hearts of their English cousins. It was late autumn and up on the plateau inclined to be chilly. We returned to the compartment bundled up in a good fug. Pretty soon the windows misted over, but so full of adventure were we that at each major stop— Ararat, Horsham, Stawell—we leaped nimbly to the platform, peering for arresting differences and new sights in these essentially identical gamboge and chocolate coloured barns, empty and desolate in the windswept night.

We roared on through the Wimmera, leaving the hills behind us, and emerged on to the great flat open plains. It began to get really cold. For this purpose the Victorian Railways had provided chemical footwarmers. These were small oval tanks covered with rough canvas. If violently agitated they would generate a quite surprising warmth which, however, soon subsided leaving the luckless passenger to be jerked to chilly wakefulness and the vision of a hostile moon riding the telegraph wires as the train rounded a bend, bellowing mournfully.

We huddled together in our overcoats. Some ingenious fellow had thought of placing the card table between the seats and on top of

three well shaken footwarmers. We took turns in cramped foetal
positions on this makeshift bed while the train rattled on over the
dark and mournful plains. Strange names swam by in the gloom:
Nhill, Kaniva, Dimboola, and then the train ground to what proved
to be an unconscionably long halt. We heard voices calling 'Service-
ton!' and there was much clanging and shouting. This was the
magic name of the last station on the Victorian side. We shared
with South Australia in those days the unique distinction of being
the only two states without a break of rail gauge at the frontier.
Within a few minutes we'd picked up steam and, just before cramp-
ing myself down for another fitful doze, I smeared a hole in the
window fug with the heel of my palm and saw the name 'Border-
town' roll majestically by. South Australia. Onward in the dark
night and over the black windy plain we slept in sheer exhaustion.

Dramatically it was daylight. The train was stopped and an
enormous river, the biggest I had seen in my life, lay in a great
curve to our left. The Murray! Australia's Nile, here at Tailem
Bend on the last stretch of its 1,600 mile course from the far off
Australian Alps to the great pattern of shifting sand bars which
ultimately blocked its full and majestic escape into the Southern
Ocean. Half an hour later we rattled across the noble river on a high
truss bridge. The explorer Sturt's words came to mind, as he discovered the river in 1829:

'At 3 p.m. . . . we were hurried into a broad and noble river . . .
The boats were allowed to drift along at pleasure and such was
the force with which we had been shot out of the Murrumbidgee
that we were carried nearly to the bank opposite its embouchure,
whilst we continued to gaze in silent astonishment on the capa-
cious channel we had entered . . .'

'Murray Bridge. Twenty minutes for refreshments!' bawled the
conductor and we tumbled out into the chilly morning air to join
in the frantic struggle at the buffet counter for hot tea and a warmed
up sausage roll with tomato sauce. How the Aussies loved to make
themselves uncomfortable.

Drawn now by an enormous 4-8-2 giant of the S.A. Railways,
clearly patterned on an American cousin, we pulled smartly away
from Murray Bridge, but, owing to the sheer perversity of the
Australian topography, soon slowed to a heaving crawl. Old mother
nature, who placed the mountains round Australia's edge so that
most of the rivers ran inland to the desert, dwindling as they flowed
further from their source; who made a native cherry with its stone
stuck on the outside of the fruit; who created black swans and
the duck-billed platypus; here chose to interpose the long thin barrier

of the Mount Lofty ranges between the mouth of the Murray and St. Vincent's Gulf. While this presented an incomparable site for a new city nestling against the foothills, it raised a formidable obstacle for the railway which, after traversing plains of an apparently endless monotony for the best part of 300 miles, suddenly had to climb a wall 2,000 feet high. At last the summit was reached and there, lying on the seaward plain below, was Adelaide, the city of our dreams, laid out in pristine rectangles by the fervent followers of Edward Gibbon Wakefield who had believed that 'squatting' on crown land would cease automatically if it were sold at 'a sufficient price'.

Under the guidance of Colonel Light the faithful few had disembarked in 1836 and a new colony without the stain and stigma of convictism was established. Seen from the train snaking down the Mount Lofty hills it seemed as if Light's and Wakefield's neat squares had become a trifle lopsided in the inevitable real-estate scrambles of the nineteenth century. Nevertheless we found the city upon arrival much cleaner than Melbourne (though smaller, of course) and the people even more purse-proud and censorious. There is an Adelaide tale based on three of the city's principal monuments, which serves as a wry reminder by the citizens themselves of their own idiosyncrasies. Queen Victoria, seated in regal glory on King William Street with her patrician nose twitching in the air, is supposed to be saying

'What vulgar person spat on this pavement?'

The explorer Charles Sturt, his wideawake hat pushed back and his hand shading his eyes against the desert sun asks, 'Where?'

Colonel Light, his right index finger pointing down rigidly at the future city, replies, 'Here!'

11 Redmond Street, Walkerville, turned out to be a small stucco bungalow in the suburbs. I was given a camp bed in one corner of the dining-room and introduced to 'Aunt' Mary, kindly, talkative and opinionated, 'Uncle' Jack, wry, taciturn and moody, and two female 'cousins' in their early teens with whom, since I was a lordly University undergraduate, I secured easy triumphs by dint of much specious loquacity.

Our friendly rivals at Adelaide University couldn't do enough for us. We had free tickets to movie shows, girls galore and even some rachitic transport organized by an energetic and resourceful fellow named Bob McKay who was my opposite number on attachment to the Adelaide team: that is, a reporter, organizer and general hanger-on. In these ancient jalopies we wheezed up to the top of Mount Lofty and there saw an arresting vista across the sea-plain and the broad silent waters of St. Vincent's Gulf with a hint of a further shore fifty miles away. We roared down to Brighton and Glenelg with our girls, and danced, fuelled on illicit hip flasks, in various Alhambras and Palladiums along the despondent seashore. We visited the sombre smoky factories at Port Adelaide and the dreary flat wastes of Outer Harbour where the ocean liners called on their way 'Home' from Sydney and Melbourne.

We whined up into the hills to attend a party in our honour at which the hostess—who fancied herself as a contralto—was unwise enough to attempt to call a halt to the festivities, while she sang Joyce Kilmer's *Trees* to the accompaniment of a reedy grand piano. Alas, the sound of revelry intruded and in the pregnant interval following the phrase 'Poems are made by fools like me,' a loud sotto voce 'Amen to that!' was heard.

We were entertained at tea by C. R. Jury, the classics don, a middle-aged exquisite in a tweed coat and a blue flannel shirt. We were given a sumptuous lunch by Professor Sir Archibald Strong, Dean of the English school, whose lively green eyes and hair like a scrubbing brush made his formidable scholarship a good deal less intimidating. And every day there were track and field events which Bob McKay and I would dutifully write up and report to our respective undergraduate papers. As the points piled up tension rose, but in the end Sydney won and the hatchet was buried in a tremendous Inter-Varsity dinner at which everybody broke training and caution was thrown to the winds, out of the window and over the balcony.

It was one of those magnificent period Australian hotels, all verandah and hitching posts and iron lace work. Normally these may be seen in the outback and are familiar through the paintings of Sidney Nolan and Russell Drysdale; but this one was slap in the middle of downtown Adelaide. After the dinner and the speeches the beer went on flowing and the party oozed out on to the upper balcony eventually engulfing it in deafening boozy talk. An elderly gent in plaid checks did an impromptu gaelic sword dance between two carving knives. His watch bounced out of his fob pocket, slid beneath the balcony railings and down into the street where it fell with a sobering tinkle. A couple of Queensland hurdlers tried to slither after it down the hitching posts to the ground. A Tasmanian was discovered relieving himself over the edge of the balcony into a nearby vacant lot. The upper balconies were crowded with men waving pint pots and the noise could be heard several blocks away when a police prowl car dashed up with a squeak of rubber and started to bang on the door. We retired in good order to a large dance hall on North Terrace where the patient girls were by now none too patiently awaiting us.

I was feeling no pain. I strode along the sidewalk arm-in-arm with a giant long-jumper from Western Australia and a shot-putter from Sydney. Up ahead, Ginger Davidson, hero of the Melbourne team, who had almost won the intervarsity challenge shield, weaved splendidly to and fro supported by stalwarts from Melbourne. Inside the dance hall the orchestra was blazing away—the Duke Ellington arrangement of *Three Little Words*. Marvellous. The floor seethed with couples. Elegant ladies awaited our pleasure in rustic seats of varnished raffia and sea-grass adorned with plastic rosettes. From the centre of the roof hung an enormous sphere covered with hundreds of mirrors. As it revolved slowly limes and kliegs played on it from hidden corners and the entire dance hall was bathed in whirling scintillating patches of red and yellow and blue and green and purple. This must be paradise.

I bowed carefully, jerked a willing girl to her feet and insensibly we melted into each other's arms and into the moving surging crowd of dancers. Our feet did not belong to us. They executed daring and impossible steps. Friendly or dreamy faces swam at us from all directions. The music rushed forward through the gaudy night; the lights changed from red to sultry purple. The girls clung; the men gripped; taffeta and silk and crepe-de-chine rustled by. Couples hummed snatches of old tunes; the saxophones melted in a maze of honey-buzzing rhythm and the staccato trumpet pierced the night with a sharp red flame. Paradise.

A wave of nausea surged up from the pit of my stomach. My partner looked vague, apprehensive, then greenish. The room, as well as the lights, started to spin. I found myself, dry throated but salivating richly, alone among the rustic seagrass seats at the edge of the throng. Bob McKay materialized out of nothing. He gripped me by the arm and half-guided, half-supported, me into the men's lavatory.

'Just put your head between your knees. You'll be okay in a few minutes.'

He went out shutting the door behind him. *Three Little Words* drifted in over the transom as from a great way off. That was the last I knew.

It was dark and silent. No lights filtering in from the ballroom; no noise of *Three Little Words*. No word at all in fact. I groped with my hands and felt the zinc-lined walls of my little stall. I tried to rise but the top of my head came off and my stomach rose up to my chin. I rested for a while and then tried again. Better this time. I fumbled around, treading with extreme unction like a very frail old man, and found the door. Locked. I tried to unlock it. No go. I rattled and shook it but the effort exhausted me, the door remained closed and no one came. I sat down again and waited for a long time; then I slowly stood up and rattled the door. After a while a voice outside the building said,

'What's wrong, mate?'

'What time is it?' I croaked.

'Quarter to four.'

'Are you the night watchman?'

'That's right.'

'I'm locked in. Can you let me out?'

'Wait a minute.'

I sat down again and found myself shivering quite uncontrollably. Where had they all gone? I'd been abandoned, that much was clear. But why had I been locked in the lavatory? Where was Bob McKay? A flashlight wavered through a chink and after a lot more rattling the door opened and the flashlight shone in my face.

'Christ, mate, you're in a mess,' said the voice behind it. 'Where d'you live?'

'Out in Walkerville.'

He clucked sympathetically. 'Last tram went hours ago,' he said, 'and it's a couple hours to the workers' early special. You better come round to my little cubbyhole and we'll try and get you a taxi.'

I thanked him and staggered out behind him into the cold night air. Though this sobered me sharply I sat huddled in misery in his little wooden box, racked by waves of nausea and remorse until he finally located an all-night cab. Then he guided me in the darkness through the empty ballroom toward North Terrace. The place was cavernous and smelled vaguely of stale cosmetics. The great crystal ball was motionless, but the flashlight struck sparks from it which lit up odd corners of the ballroom: an up-ended plastic seat; a pile of paper streamers on the floor; the hooded string-base standing like a brooding pin-headed sentinel over the darkened and deserted dance floor.

The cab cruised up. I pressed a ten bob note into my benefactor's hand, and fell into the rear seat. Mercifully the hackie was taciturn. I begged him to cut the motor as we entered Redmond Street and to let me off some doors away. The place was silent as the grave. I fumbled my borrowed latch key, stripped hurriedly in the dark and fell into bed.

*   *   *

Aunt Mary was staring down at me with a cup of steaming tea in her hand and it was broad daylight. The teenage cousins hovered expectantly in the background.

'So you're awake.'

'What time is it,' I rasped.

'Half past ten.'

'Struth!'

'Now dear . . .' Aunt Mary was a daughter of the manse. Uncle Jack came in.

'How do you feel?'

'Terrible.'

He turned to his wife. 'It's Sunday. I think we'd better get him up to Nuriootpa to your brother's place.'

She nodded. 'He may as well stay there and get some good country air,' she said with a brisk efficient nod.

'Maybe stay a couple of days,' said Jack.

'I've nothing to do,' I said. 'The party's over.'

'Some party.'

'I just want to crawl into a corner.'

'We'll leave you alone.' They drew solicitous curtains and tiptoed out. I took one look at the cup of tea and turned my face to the wall.

Later that day I was just able to board the diesel railway coach, named after the Minister of Railways, the Barwell Bull, and with Uncle Jack beside me we set off for the Barossa Ranges some fifty miles north of Adelaide. As we neared the hills, truck gardens and orchards gave way to neatly planted rows of vines, bare now in the antipodean winter with their gnarled black fists and fingers receding in parallel lines into the distance, like crows on a telegraph wire.

Mary's brother, tall, ginger-haired and gangly, met us at the station with a Model T Ford. By this time I was able to sit up and take notice as we slid on long sandy wheel tracks among the winter vines and at last pulled up in a patch of white slithery sand a mile from nowhere with sad pine-trees and dwarf casuarina marking a two room wooden shack where our host lived—himself a viticulturist in a small way and a notable recluse. On the deal table were a couple of bottles of red wine and a bottle of white. I didn't think I could look them in the face but by the time scarves of appetizing odours began to streak through the room from the brother's beef stew, my appetite was back. We emptied the three bottles between us and during the rest of that weekend we floated in a beneficent haze of the best Australian wine.

We had hock for breakfast, claret for lunch, burgundy for dinner, champagne for elevenses and as a nightcap. There were always a couple of bottles of wine on the table and we kept a flagon of 'loose' wine by the bedside. We drank no water, milk, tea, coffee, whisky or gin. By the end of two days, we were all as *bien arrosés* as any

Who Spat There?

Norman farmer tanked up on Calvados. And yet the ill effects were absolutely zero. The clear dry wine, nourished and brought to perfection by the sturdy descendants of the German immigrants who had first settled the Barossa Valley fifty years earlier, left our heads clear, our tongues uncoated, our feet steady and our brains stimulated for wordy intellectual battles. We tackled and solved all the problems of the Universe in those days and not *ambulando* either. And yet we found time to visit the 'capital' of the Valley, Angaston, to climb the hills behind, and to spend most of one morning being shown over Hardy Brothers' Château Tanunda and the cellars of the famous Seppelt family.

I returned to Adelaide clear of head, true of hand, straight of eye, steady and aglow, to find that the athletes had all departed and that having filed my copy there was nothing else for me to do. I mooned about the afternoon movie houses on Rundle Street and King William Street. I went to the races at Woodville and lost five pounds. I received decorously an explanation from Bob McKay for my Walpurgisnacht: 'I wasn't in very good shape myself.' I went surf-fishing unsuccessfully with Uncle Jack at places with unlikely names such as Aldinga, Noarlunga, and even Dingabledinga. Clearly I was getting bored with Adelaide, yet the McKails' hospitality appeared unbounded, and besides I couldn't go back to Ormond College while the vacation was still on, for it stood empty and untenanted.

In a last desperate bid to fend off *ennui* I convinced myself I was in love with a shingled redhead who lived in the far off suburb of Thebarton. After winning with her a foxtrot competition at a Grand Euchre Party and Dance held in the local church hall, I prepared to plight my troth. She spurned me—silly girl—and in high dudgeon I caught the Overland Express for Melbourne on the following day. The McKails and Bob McKay came down to the station to see me off and were soon deep in Adelaide gossip while I stood disconsolately on one leg meditating on the perfidy of women. At last the train pulled out and started the long twisting climb up Mount Lofty. We roared our 500 miles through the night and about noon next day reached dear, dusty old Spencer Street Station. Back in Melbourne Town! Well, it might be a bit drab, but it was big, wasn't too censorious, wasn't small-town gossiping, wasn't above all—I twitched my sensitive undergraduate nose—suburban. After all: 'Million-peopled cities with a European environment'. That's what Melbourne (and of course Sydney) was. Wasn't it? Well, the Australian National Travel Association posters said so anyway.

Chapter Eight

POSTERA CRESCAM LAUDE

ORACE was a great success with the exiles from the groves of academe who strove to build a new Oxbridge in Aussie's grey and cryptic land. By the time the University of Melbourne came to be founded in 1855, someone had already pinched *vivit post funera virtus* and *non omnis moriar*, so it was left to U. of M., 'the shop' as we irreverently called it, to pick *postera crescam laude*. We were never quite arrogant enough to think that it could apply to us. We would never grow by the praise of after ages, though the university might. We preferred the students' song, which more accurately described us; though its coy correctitude and archaic slang were perhaps Victorian rather than Georgian:

> We're Varsity students all
> Sir John he is our father
> We throng the Wilson Hall
> And we love the ladies—rather!
> Toujours, toujours,
> Pour Bacchus et les amours.

Beer and girls, like all students. And certainly, to a new undergraduate, the first things that struck him were his unfettered access to Bacchus and to les amours. The opening up of the doors of the mind came later.

Bacchus meant variously Johnny Naughton's pub on the Sydney Road, or the right to be seen (and to see) in any of the big City pubs, unrebuked. The favourite was Young and Jackson's at the corner of Flinders and Swanston Streets, well placed between the suburban line railway station and the Anglican cathedral, and surmounted by a sign in gilt letters advertising complete dentures and painless 'twilight sleep' of Messrs. F. & G. Turner. This pub tasted doubly of forbidden fruit because its chief, indeed its splendid, feature was an oil painting of a nude of luscious proportions named Chloe who reclined above the principal public bar.

At first blush the M.U. campus seemed to be literally overflowing with women. After years of sexless segregation, after observing the young ladies of St. Catherine's and Merton Hall from a distance and entrenched behind black lisle stockings, serge tunics and squished down shapeless felt hats, one now saw these goddesses emerge in their glory, and actually sit amongst us in the lecture rooms, rustling their silks and satins and sending out great waves of heady perfume. Even those in bobbed hair and tweeds seemed inordinately exciting. Their presence was most disturbing to those men who wanted to study and to learn, and of course some of the girls did come not so much to study and to learn as to pursue the course known to the male undergraduate as 'Arts for Matrimony'. The professors were well aware of the searing effect of some of these beauties, and the redoubtable Professor Scott, who held the chair of History and who (though clearly susceptible since twice married) preserved the illusion that he was a misogynist, once rounded on one of these young women in a tutorial for which she had palpably not undertaken any preparation with her essay. With his formidable lisp he bared his professorial teeth at her.

'You don't appeaw to have taken much twouble with this papew, Miss X.'

'I'm sorry, sir. I did my best.'

'I should think you might be bettew employed puwsuing awts for matwimony wather than histowy.'

'Yes, professor?' said the imperturbable lass. 'Would you recommend Part I, sir, or Part II?'

Scotty was a remarkable institution. When we sat at his feet in the early 1930s he was two years away from retirement but as vivid and bludgeoning as ever. He was rather like a caricature of H. G. Wells: short, plump and balding with a quiff of what had once been auburn hair, and an auburn (and tobacco-stained) untidy don's moustache. But in no other way was he untidy. Though a former newspaperman, he was a natty dresser with a taste in dark blue suits with a white chalk stripe, polka dotted bow ties and wing collars. Scotty lacked higher education, yet he was already a historian in his own right when appointed to the Chair. He had lived as a Hansard reporter through all the exciting and frustrating times attendant on the birth of the Commonwealth in 1901 and had been a personal friend of such legendary giants as Edmund Barton and Alfred Deakin. Scotty's *Short History of Australia*, though now out of fashion and its judgements questioned, was the bible of two generations, and just before I went up to the University he had published two massive collections of original documents on Australian discovery by land and sea. All three volumes were of course 'set books'; this was part of the normal way in which Universities then, as now, helped professors to eke out their meagre salaries.

We students didn't object to buying Scotty's books a bit, but, such is human nature or the basic snobbery of young men, that we did resent having to buy, as a 'set book', Milton's *Paradise Lost*, edited by Professor Cowling, head of the English Department.

This had nothing whatever to do with the merits of the works in question. It was rather that while Scotty was a *bon vivant* who invited students to Sunday supper at his house in Brighton where he dripped cigar ash on his ample waistcoat and told endless anecdotes about the early days of Federation, Cowling was from Yorkshire, had the 'wrong' English accent and lived in one of the professors' dreary liver-coloured brick houses on the campus. Scotty had a rich wife who was an accomplished musician, and a brother-in-law who was a mysterious financier with an Imperial. Scotty fingered a glass of Madeira in his immense library with books from knee height to ceiling. There was no catalogue, but he could place his finger unerringly on the correct volume glimpsed through a shroud of satisfying cigar smoke. Cowling's wife was kindly but 'professorial' and her rented house was academic-spartan. Scotty had no degree and was therefore regarded by us as unorthodox and daring. Cowling had an M.A., but it was from Leeds. Though Leeds resembled Melbourne far more than either of them resembled Oxford or Cambridge we hated to think so. For us there were only four universities in the world: Melbourne, Oxford, Cambridge and Sydney, in that order. We imagined ourselves an antipodean Oxbridge, and sneered at an M.A. from Leeds.

But the real reason I think why we all worshipped Scotty and only tolerated Cowling was that Scotty had a powerful personality and was a born lecturer and tutor, whereas Cowling was diffident and apologetic. It was easy to associate Scotty with the stylish phrases, unorthodox views and rather naughty sallies that poured in a coruscating cataract from the lisping lips beneath the stained moustache. But it was not easy to believe that the impassioned devotee of Milton, as revealed in his critique of *Paradise Lost*, and Professor George Herbert Cowling, the good grey lecturer, were one and the same man.

Scotty was in some ways bad for undergraduates for he nursed prejudices, loved to make outrageous pronouncements and was not without a secret desire to *épater le bourgeois*. There were a number of pious nuns and paunchy priests in the lecture theatre and he delighted in flaunting an anti-catholic bias which included a straight-faced lecture on 'Pope Joan'. In British History B he was quite openly a Cavalier, and Clarendon was his favourite historian of the period of the Civil War. In Australian history he was a debunker of John MacArthur and of the explorers Burke and Wills—still local heroes in Melbourne. On the other hand in his tutorials where, alone with him you read out your essay and discussed it with him, he could be sharp and terrifying. 'What do you mean by that?' 'What is youw authowity for saying that?'

Once in my not so innocent innocence I invented a source which I had the temerity to quote in support of a view that I was advancing.

'Whewe did you find that?'

'It was referred to in another source book, sir.'

'But you didn't wead it youwself?'

'No, sir.'

'Continue.'

I thought I was safely over the hurdle but at the end of the tutorial he said

'A workmanlike essay. By the way, that source you wefewred to. Always identify your source vewy pwecisely; otherwise people might be tempted to suppose you had invented it. Good day.'

There was more kick in this than in listening to Cowling intone: 'Thrones dominations princedoms virtues powers.'

Cowling was assisted by Enid Derham, another good grey type, a spinster who was herself a poet in a modest way, but whose passion was Shelley who sometimes has this effect on middle-aged ladies of virtue. She would recite and then give us the critical exegesis on long passages from *Epipsychidion* and *Alastor*, reading out the verse in a thrilling and reverent voice. We felt she had fallen for the young god with the open-necked shirt, the staring eyes and the starry hair, and we resented it. Why pretend it was the poetry when really all the time you had a crush on the fellow? If it had to be Shelley, let it be *Ode to the West Wind* and such sturdy stuff as that (even if he did say 'I fall among the thorns of life I bleed'— who doesn't, we asked?).

We kidded her with the singular unfeeling obtuseness of youth. She withstood it stoically. She even presided at a meeting of the Literary Club at which the son of a well-known brewer read a paper on the works of a fictitious American negro poet whose principal verses seemed to be aimed against Shelley. We assumed in our self-assurance that Miss Derham was taken in; of course she wasn't but she listened with forbearance and refrained from comment. Later she invited the brazen lad to coffee and rock-cakes along with two other anti-Shelleyites, one of whom had based himself on Matthew Arnold's disdainful comment and the other of whom had quoted at length from a virulently anti-Shelley essay by Aldous Huxley. She tolerated us all, smiling gravely and holding court among the empty coffee cups. While the iconoclastic undergraduate talk swirled about her she was at one with Shelley—though resenting Mary Godwin a bit, we thought.

These men and women were driving us slowly into the narrow funnel (there should have been a sign like those on the F.D.R. Parkway entering New York: SQUEEZE RIGHT) that led to the enormous exam factory in Wilson Hall. Here in this tall mid-nineteenth century high-Gothic barn we sat and scribbled for three hours on each subject and emerged dazed and befuddled into the hot midday December sun to compare notes and speculate on results. Wilson Hall was the centrepiece of our University, and was in its way distinguished, in the High-Victorian-St. Pancras Railway Station tradition (though based on King's College Chapel, Cambridge). The other buildings were more commonplace, ranging from the Gothic of the old quad through the mock Tudor of the yellow sandstone Arts Building (opened in 1929) to the severe red brick of the Medical School and the Edwardian baroque of the Teachers' Training College. Our campus was strangely crowded for a new University in a new continent of supposedly endless space, and during my time it was still cluttered up by the wooden and tin 'temporary' buildings of World War I. The Residential Colleges were set in more generous grounds, but 'The Shop' itself always seemed a little confined and higgledy piggledy.

Wilson Hall was the focus of our corporate life in its grander manifestations. The students might meet in the Clubhouse, along with the Melbourne University Rifles and a tiny women's annexe, much frowned on by misogynists. But the really big shows were put on in the Hall. It was here that our collective *persona* was on view. Here we held the annual Convocation when the dais was packed with academic dignitaries strutting and pouting like venerable macaws and peacocks in their gorgeous robes. Here the new students were welcomed by the President of the Students' Representative Council; and here, during commencement exercises, we held our *bal masqué*. Wilson Hall was later consumed by fire and in its place was erected a lean and hungry edifice of glass and steel and brick from whose northern wall an enormous non-objective composition gazes with the unwinking and baleful impassivity of a lizard. But to those of the generation of the early thirties Wilson Hall will always be associated with Commencement revels.

The Lord Mayor and Corporation of the City of Melbourne were kind enough to allow these revels to slop over into the city on the final Saturday. We never ceased to marvel at their forbearance and that of the citizenry as a whole, even though our antics were performed in aid of charity. Dressed in every conceivable guise—swaggies, blackamoors, topsies, soldiers, footballers, judges, politicians—

we descended on 'The Block', the heart of Melbourne, in a series of open drays hired from two local breweries; and for a couple of hours on that Saturday morning were allowed a quite unbelievable licence in plying our trade. In order to sell copies of the Commencement magazine (proceeds to charity) we stopped honest citizens in the middle of their promenading; waylaid hurrying businessmen and lawyers on the sidewalks; held up private cars and importuned the occupants; swarmed all over tramcars and buses rattling our tin cans; invaded shops and stores, danced on the counters and fleeced clerk and customer alike. By one o'clock an uneasy calm descended on the shattered town. The streets emptied of larking students and the pubs opened their doors to them. The sour old john hops who had unwillingly turned a blind eye, under orders from higher up of which they mightily disapproved, now proceeded to issue with grim relish their customary warnings and fines.

Back at The Shop, the clubs and societies flourished, embryo organisms for the production of future lawyers, doctors, engineers, artists and businessmen. All clubs and societies were under the general direction of the Students' Representative Council, and the competition was keen for office on this august body and its Presidency, whose incumbent was in effect the senior student of the university. Elections were contested with fury and passion as the electors endeavoured to avoid the Scylla of the Great Athlete and the Charybdis of the Great Swot. During my time the office was held by a genial and extrovert Anglican theolog; by a commerce student named 'Happy' Taylor whose disposition shines from his nickname; and by Chester Wilmot. People like me ran for office, but were never elected because we were regarded as too frothy or too 'clever'.

The S.R.C. controlled the weekly students' newspaper *Farrago*, which being the natural outlet for students' exuberance was always getting into trouble. Our printers, Brown, Prior & Co., were in a fearful sweat over possible libel actions. As 'Chief of Staff' of *Farrago*, in charge of reporting assignments, it was my job to make the weekly trip down to Little Collins Street and confer with the nervous Mr. Brown and Mr. Prior. They sat in a small cobwebby office above the din of the flat-bed presses with a dusty skylight giving on to higher buildings. They used to greet my arrival to check the galleys with a sort of comic resignation. While I was checking for typos, they would point out with trembling finger some particularly violent or scurrilous attack on a well-known public figure.

'They'll sue us for certain. And it's all right for you young fellows. You haven't any money.'

'And you have, Mr. Prior?'

'Well . . .'

'Then, how about giving us a special rate on the print job?'

'Arrr, you'll be the finish of us yet. Look at this phrase "Who is lining his pockets at the expense of the student body?" You just can't say that.'

'But isn't it true?'

'Oh, it *may* be; but you mustn't *say* it.'

'Okay. We'll put that aside for consideration later. Now, let's look at the next galley.'

The general rule was: say what you like about students or even in most cases the faculty, but be wary of public figures outside the University. Usually I would give in on these, or in special cases call up the Editors (if I could get hold of them) and get a ruling. Anything to have the paper out on time.

The Dramatic Society, as such societies in Anglo-Saxon institutions tend to be, was the preserve of intense or busty young women and effeminate young men. It was divided into two factions: those who preferred traditional favourites such as *She Stoops to Conquer* and light creaking drawing-room comedies such as *His Excellency the Governor*; and those who preferred the more 'daring' playwrights like O'Neill, Elmer Rice and Noel Coward—the latter two being equated as equally daring in 1930 (this was the post-*Vortex* but pre-*Private Lives* era). In the tussle, an exquisite fellow who affected an opera cloak lined with magenta silk, acted as a fluttery-handed go-between for the two factions, persuading the busty woman producer to take on 'Something eighteenth C. my dear', and the grave young Eng. Lit. student—also a member of the Labour Club—to include J. M. Barrie in his series of one act plays. In the end we put on Goldsmith's *The Good Natured Man*, with a sheeny brilliantined black beauty in the female lead (her sheen appropriately covered in a powdered periwig) and a popular debater-footballer in the role of Honest Jarvis. Later however, the avant garde section gained control and produced Elmer Rice's *The Adding Machine* for which they had the temerity to hire the Princess Theatre downtown with a seating capacity of 1,800, instead of the much more modest local hall. One hundred and fifty of the faithful turned up and from a waste of empty seats applauded ardently almost half their number on stage. The deficit was redeemed by a well-to-do and stage-struck law student.

Finally, an intense commerce student who had surprised us all by marrying a first year philosophy girl with, as one fellow put it, 'the biggest knockers north of Little Lon', captured the Society and forced it to put on a series of—to us—recondite plays by people called Chekhov and Ibsen. The treasurer said this would ruin the

Society, that it was far-out stuff that nobody would come to see. Give them *A Cuckoo in the Nest* or *Charley's Aunt* every time. However, since the student and his wife both acted in all the plays, the undergraduate body rallied round in large numbers to see the knockers, and this resulted in a most gratifying diminution of the perennial deficit.

The medical students were a group very much to themselves. Their concern, especially after second year, with bodily functions led them to an interminable emphasis on the gut which was at least a change from the normal student bawdry, by now rather dull around the edges. They staged at Commencement each year a show called *Medical Medleys* with much emphasis on bums, water closets and other Chaucerian wheezes; but in the end their scatology became as dull as our bawdry and we considered them a pretty dreary crew with one-track minds, save for the romantic Charlie Hopkins who played a mournful violin in his study and was deemed by us all to be beyond the baser bodily necessities.

A group almost as inward looking, and speaking, moreover, its own arcane tongue, was the Labour Club. Though it had less than fifty members it was periodically rent by the most crashing internal schisms: between Trotskyists and Leninists; Trotskyists and Stalinists; the followers of Bakunin vs. those of Gorky; and on the fringes the good old socialists—from Webb gradualism through Marxism and direct action to the Labour Party's overt appeal to the wrongs of the Irish. All vainly strove to gain, and, harder, to keep control of, the Club. But it was a brilliant and hirsute tutor in law at Ormond who was responsible for getting the Labour Club its biggest visiting star attraction: Dr. Herbert Vere Evatt.

It was one of the rare meetings of the Labour Club attended by more than forty persons. Instead of the modest back room at the Clubhouse the secretary boldly booked the enormous lecture hall in the Arts Building, normally filled only by the Public Questions Society or the student shenanigans during the annual Commencement week. He was not disappointed. The hall was crammed to capacity and scores stood in the corridors outside (before the days of sound systems) to hear the fiery 'Doc' Evatt denounce 'Honest Joe' Lyons, the ex-Labour Prime Minister who had 'ratted', joined the capitalists and formed a 'National' government to 'beat the slump'.

If the Labour Party lived to be rent asunder, then the freshly formed Australian Party never even got off the ground. Along with one or two friends I was there to see it falter and flop. The Australian Party was the single-handed creation of the Rt. Hon. William Morris ('Billy') Hughes, Australia's wartime Prime Minister and perennial member for North Sydney. Billy Hughes, the nation's idol for his tough, cantankerous behaviour at the Versailles Peace Conference, had been rejected by the electors and ever since had been trying unsuccessfully to make a come-back through a series of bewildering alliances and independent initiatives. Hughes had become a cross-bencher and, as the economic crisis deepened, he saw a future for himself as a national leader. He formed the Australian Party with one member, himself, and proceeded to stump the country to gain support. He was at this time in his early seventies and totally deaf; but he was not a man to be under-rated. A politician to his finger-tips, he would go anywhere and address any meeting, to propagate the gospel of the Australian Party, i.e. Trust me and all will be well.

It happened that Hughes had an admirer in none other than the Hon. J. Hume-Cook of the Australian Industries Protection League. Hume-Cook slipped the word to young Kevyn and lo and behold we were in the political business. We formed ourselves into a committee of three for the propagation of the gospel of the A.P., wrote a polite letter to Billy Hughes who accepted with alacrity, put a notice on the bulletin board and rented the great P.Q.S. Hall—the same one so recently filled by Doc. Evatt. The Hon. J. Hume-Cook came through with a cheque for £5 for lunch and we figured that with a little care we might save something over for a celebration at Johnny Naughton's pub once the Great Man had left. We awaited Billy's arrival in high fettle and were convinced that with a little luck we would be playing, like the Labour Club, to S.R.O.

But the undergraduate has as sharp a nose for the mountebank as the next man. Billy arrived in a rented sedan. He proved to be a formidably testy old gent about the size of a gnome. Like many deaf people he spoke in a loud monotonous bray, and was also a non-stop and highly egocentric talker. The lunch was a brazen monologue and when we entered the hall it was to find in all that enormous expanse of rising circular tiers just seventeen people, three of whom were there as professional hecklers from the Labour Club. It was a most painful occasion for us, but Billy didn't seem to mind. Rapidly sizing up the situation he cut his speech to ten minutes, gave a ringing denunciation of 'Honest Joe' Lyons, dealt briefly with the hecklers and was outside beaming like a friendly gargoyle at the door of his rented sedan before we could either lose our composure or regain it. The aftermath in print proved a salutary lesson for us all. *Farrago*, read by 1,400 students, reported the meeting as a flop but the *Argus*, having received an advance copy of Billy's speech, gave the old boy a column and a half with a picture.

By now the students were thoroughly aroused and a great monster meeting was planned at which the Nationalists, A.L.P., Liberals, Country Party and even Communists and Lang-Labour from N.S.W. (supporters of Premier J. T. Lang) could meet and fight it out. Rival supporters clashed and pandemonium broke loose, in the midst of which Sam White, now the revered Paris correspondent of the *Evening Standard*, but then a young Labour hothead, arose and made a defiant speech in favour of the Workers of the World. Bully boys from Trinity College closed in on Sam who was dumped into 'The Lake', a sheet of ornamental water about three feet deep. Collective fines were imposed for this disgraceful fracas and the President of the Professorial Board read the riot act to us. We simmered down, but not for long, for now the Inter-Varsity debates were in the air.

I got a place on the Melbourne team partly because the debates were being held in Tasmania and it was known that I had more than a nodding acquaintance with the island. Anyway there was my name on the bulletin board along with those of Chester Wilmot and others. Chester was leader of the team: sturdy, ebullient, booming and utter incorruptible. He was even then excelling at the type of tough flexible argumentation and passionate curiosity to get at the facts which was to land him in trouble with General Blamey in New Guinea during World War II and later to earn him world-wide fame as a B.B.C. war correspondent, and some degree of immortality as the author of *The Struggle for Europe*. He organized us all and kept us working.

Our second man was a disputatious and articulate ex-theological student. Tendentious arguments and effective hair-splitting were his debating armoury and it was inviolable. Finally there was an engineer whose exploits, as it turned out, were to dominate our entire visit to Tasmania. For though we did not shine in debate, being outwitted by a bright lass from Western Australia who later became a Federal senator, our progress through the island state caused something of a sensation and not a little annoyance.

The engineer was of Dutch origin and, because of his courtliness in a democratic Australia, was nicknamed ironically 'The Baron'. Someone conceived the bright idea that the Melbourne debating team could gain much-needed publicity by presenting him to the world as a genuine Baron—in fact an aristocratic envoy from the early Hitler Germany. As student japes will, the proposal took fire and when the debating team sailed for Tasmania on the *Loongana* a large crowd of students, including many co-eds, was on hand to see 'The Baron' off. We entered into the spirit of the thing with a will and the engineer himself, whose bearing (if not his debating) was impeccable, moved with courtly formality along the dock, clicking his heels, bowing from the waist and barking 'Gewiss! Gewiss!' As he walked stiffly up the gangway the assemblage, by prior arrangement, broke into a spirited rendering of *Deutschland Uber Alles.*

It worked all too well. When we got down to our cabins there was a note inviting 'The Baron' to visit the bridge, and when we arrived at Launceston next morning the press of Tasmania were there to interview 'The Baron' whose supporters, (i.e. the M.U. Debating team) dutifully sang *Deutschland Uber Alles.* From then on we were stuck with the legend and paid more attention to keeping it alive than we did to preparing for our debate against Western Australia. 'The Baron' was received at the Town Hall by the Mayor, at Government House by the Governor, at the House by the Speaker; and a luncheon was given for him by a distinguished member of the legal profession. The engineer behaved perfectly throughout, bowing, clicking, expressing banal views on international politics in a bortschy English and, when at an apparent loss, lapsing into German which he spoke well enough. The deception was kept up during our entire ten days on the island and it really is an extraordinary testimony to the gullibility of human nature that it was not found out.

Towards the end of the visit 'The Baron' became heartily fed up with his role and longed to relax. But his fellow team members were too deeply committed to the legend and the impersonation to allow him to do so. We dogged his footsteps day and night and made sure that he was never alone. But on the last week-end three of us went up the Derwent Valley as guests of a well-to-do hop farmer, leaving 'The Baron' to his own devices in Hobart. Longing to be himself, he drifted to a pub and was there discovered by the local stringer for *Smith's Weekly*, the Australian equivalent of *The News of the World.*

Fortunately for our hides *Smith's Weekly* was published in Sydney and the storm therefore did not break while we were still enjoying the Tasmanians' hospitality. But a week after we returned to Melbourne, break it did; and hideous was the wrath of the outraged islanders, whom the story made to seem a great deal more foolish than they really were. There was a duel by telegram across the Bass Strait and since we, as members of the official University team, had been party to the deception, the S.R.C. ruled that a written apology was required. This mollified the Tasmanians, but the rest of us turned on the poor bemused befuddled engineer. Why had he blown the gaff? His explanation, piteous in its lachrymose utterance and assuredly symbolic of the Depression, was unanswerable: 'I needed the money.'

Chapter Nine

THE GOLDEN VALLEY

FACETIOUSLY known as Tassy, The Speck or Tatt's-mania (because Tattersall's had its headquarters there) Australia's smallest state offered a sharp contrast to the Mainland. It was a small, coolish, green and mountainous island as opposed to the large, hot, grey and flattish continent. It was the most southerly as well as by far the smallest of the states of the Commonwealth, lying about 200 miles off the south point of the Continent, whipped by the Southerly Busters, and slap in the middle of the Roaring Forties. It seemed miraculous to us that the Dutch Navigator, Abel Janszoon Tasman, should have hit on it—and only on it—out of a waste of seas one morning in 1642 on his way from Java into the unknown. Why hadn't he gone on to discover the rest of Australia? Why had he blundered on across the sea that now bore his name to discover and baptize New Zealand (Te-ika-a-Maui to the Maoris), and then fetched an enormous circle back to Batavia, passing through Torres Strait, yet leaving the immense 1,500-mile-long fertile eastern coast of Australia to be discovered 130 years later by the immortal Captain Cook?

Why, above all, had he called this new island Van Diemen's Land? He had done so presumably, as good civil servants will, out of an understandable desire to please the boss, in this case Antony Van Diemen, Governor of the Dutch East Indies. And of course he couldn't have foreseen that Van Diemen's Land would become a vast prison holding convicts transported for life and that eventually the very name Van Diemen's Land would carry with it such connotations of bleakness and misery and desperation that the English, who had corrupted his patron's name by their considered cruelties, would in the end atone by re-naming the island in honour of its discoverer. Abel Tasman, most unlucky of navigators, who missed the great prize of Australia for his Dutch masters, giving them instead a lonely rock-girt island on the edge of the great Southern Ocean and two other larger islands filled with Polynesian cannibals. Yet a lucky man, too, who left to posterity not only the Tasman Sea but Tasmania, thus joining Amerigo Vespucci and Christopher Columbus in that small company of explorers with the rare distinction of having had a country named after them.

What was this country like? The Tasmanians called it 'Scotland of the South' and it was of about the same size and the same ruggedness; but the climate was sunnier and clearer, beset with rude west winds rather than Midlothian fogs. And there was about the mountains (Ben Lomond, Tasmania, being some 500 feet taller than Ben Nevis, Scotland) an equivocal withdrawn quality absent in Caledonian crags, a feeling of indescribable oldness as of the worn-down wisdom teeth of a Genesis creation. Beside the enigmatic tors and grey olive-clad rocks of Tasmania the black stones and rough moorland of Scotland seemed a shade *parvenu*. And like Greece in relation to Europe, Tasmania, though small, was carved in the grand manner, cast in a majestic mould with great empty vistas and burnished distances. In the fertile valleys were shiny red apples, fat yellow pears, papery hops and plums with soft empurpled powdery skins. Along the estuaries were bright little wooden farmhouses, busy ferry steamers, smoking factories and chugging trains. On the central plains were rolling fields of wheat, sleepy rural rivers and century-old stone bridges lichened by time. But get up on top of any one of the ludicrously accessible mountain peaks and you saw Tasmania for what it really was: little ribbons of closely settled fertile ground overborne and overwhelmed by a great craggy sea of old and tumbled hills clothed from foot to crown in the woolly hair of the cryptic Australian bush: old, tired and listless, yet aware.

The Tasmanians who crowded the valleys and estuaries of their beautiful island were proud of their Dutch discoverer. Tasman, shortened to 'Tas', was a popular boy's name. Dutch memories were preserved in Mount Heemskirck and Mount Zeehan (named for the two ships of Tasmania's first expedition of 1642). They were reminders, as are Cape Leeuwin, Groote Eylandt and Houtman's Abrolhos still today, of a time when the whole of the western portion of Australia from Cape Keer Weer on the Gulf of Carpentaria to Dirk Hartog's Island at the extreme western point was known—and claimed—as New Holland.

But though now it was Tasmania, the memory of Van Diemen's Land still persisted. When the harsh winter winds blew up from the icy Antarctic, or when the Roaring Forties sent sheets of rain cascading down on to the already drenched west coast with its storm bound sandbars, fluted cliffs and queer horizontal scrub, then indeed murderous memories of mutual savagery among convict, settler and aboriginal black man rose very near to the surface of the communal mind. Grimmest relic of all was Port Arthur, now a tourist attraction, but one only too well able to strike horror into the breast of the tourist

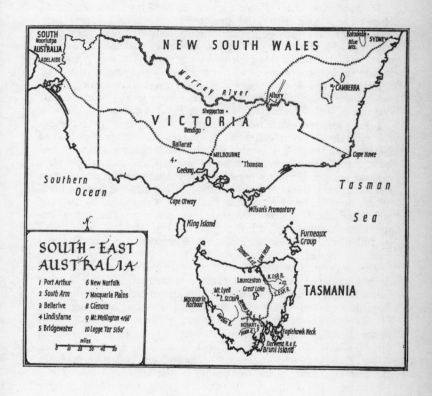

SOUTH
Nooriutpa
AUSTRALIA
ADELAIDE

NEW SOUTH WALES

Karoombo
Blue
Mts.
SYDNEY

Murray River

Albury
CANBERRA

VICTORIA

Shepparton

Bendigo

Ballarat

MELBOURNE

Geelong

Thomson

Cape Howe

Southern
Ocean

Cape Otway

Wilson's Promontory

Tasman

Sea

King Island

Furneaux
Group

N.

SOUTH - EAST
AUSTRALIA

1 Port Arthur   6 New Norfolk
2 South Arm   7 Macquarie Plains
3 Bellerive   8 Glenora
4 Lindisfarne   9 Mt. Wellington 4166'
5 Bridgewater   10 Legge Tor 5160'

miles
0 10 20 30 40 50

Tamar R. & E.   Low Head

Launceston
Great Lake
N. Esk R.
S. Esk R.

Mt. Lyell
L. St. Clair

TASMANIA

Macquarie
Harbour

Gordon R.

HOBART
Huon R.

Eaglehawk Neck

Derwent R. & E.
Bruni Island

even on a bright summer's day. The gutted Gothic Revival church and the ruins of the cells, the flogging posts and the scaffolds, rose on a storm-bound peninsula dangling from the main island by an isthmus less than a hundred yards wide: Eaglehawk Neck. Here savage half-starved hounds kept watch for escaping convicts while sharks cruised the sinister waters on either shore.

My stepfather was a Tasmanian and so were my numerous brood of step-aunts, step-uncles and step-cousins. I cannot say that they seemed to be as oppressed by their environment as I was. They were frightened by other things: the red skull and crossbones at the base of the pylons that carried high tension wires; or the stories I would read aloud to them from Poe's *Tales of Mystery and Imagination*. The little Doric temple in memory of Franklin of the Arctic, which nestled unexpectedly in a bushy gully overhung by the striated basalt crags of Mount Wellington, also made them profoundly uneasy.

I don't know whether it was the process of growing up or the discovery of the Derwent Valley that for me removed this fearful cloak of Nessus from the grim Tasmanian landscape. Perhaps it was a little of both. At any rate from the moment when, alone in a second class carriage on the narrow gauge line, I probed up river past Mount Dromedary and the little town of New Norfolk into the snug orchard-filled amphitheatre of Macquarie Plains and was greeted by teen-age girls miraculously transformed from prim dancing partners into conspiratorial adventurers with flying golden hair, the sun came out in its full glory, Van Diemen's Land was permanently exorcized and Tasmania smiled.

The Derwent was a really noble river. It rose in Lake St. Clair, a deep mysterious pool of Turneresque romanticism filling a cleft below Mount Ossa and Mount Pelion. It almost seemed as if the early English explorers—military men having a Victorian's aggressive familiarity with the classics—should have deliberately wished to prefigure the impossible association between Australia and the Aegean out of which the Anzac legend was born. Ossa, Pelion, Olympus, Athos, Campaspe and Meander all appeared on Australian maps. In the case of Lake St. Clair the quality of the light, and the uncompromising crags lifting in the clear sky, certainly fostered Attic echoes. Debouching from the Lake on the 170 mile journey to its tortuously convoluted estuary, the Derwent foamed green and cool down from the eucalypt-clad mountains, and eventually became a stream of long placid reaches overhung with willows planted by the homesick exiles. Beneath The Dromedary it reached tide-water where mussels and whelks rather than slime and pond-weed festooned the wharfs, and the air smelt of salt rather than of sedge. Most of the way down to its placid reaches the Derwent was green and turbulent but about half way on its course it spread out to irrigate a large amphitheatre some ten miles in diameter. When people down in Hobart said they were going up the Derwent Valley, this was the part they meant, and this was where I now came.

The Valley was crammed to overflowing with soft fuzzy peaches, bright shiny apples, Jonathan and five crown, and big crinkly tobacco-leaves, all intersected by gurgling flumes. Most dramatic of all were the hop-fields hanging down in great curtains of lustrous green. As you entered them the cool gurgle of the Derwent sank into silence and you were engulfed in a solid weight of heat welling up from the baked ground and the soupy irrigation runnels. The dregs of the afternoon hung soggy in the air and not a leaf moved. You couldn't cut diagonally across the field because of the curtains of hops, hung like furry green washing out to dry in the sun. You had to walk along the edge watching the curtains of green move by in stately rows, and then dive down a green canyon with your bare feet sucking and singing in the rich red mud between the rows of hops. You stumbled onward past the edges of the great green curtains, every ten feet or so stepping neatly over a guy wire, one of a pattern of diagonals straining to anchor in cement blocks the great waterfalls of hops before they should all come tumbling down in a green ruin. Sweat fell into your eyes from the aquarium heat of the hanging forest and you blinked. You were at the bottom of a large green crevasse and at the end of it something black swam and dodged: perhaps a person far away crossing the ends of the curtains; or something that had fallen into your eye with the sweat; possibly a little floater swimming gently across the back of your own retina.

Among this profusion of full-freighted greenery, houses were embowered: Australian enough in their lean low silhouettes and their wide verandahs, but also Tasmanian in their 'roses-round-the-door-make-me-love-mother-more' atmosphere. Their owners were terribly proud of them and were delighted if any visitor said they reminded him of England (or Scotland). They subscribed to the *Illustrated London News* and *Punch* as well as to the Hobart *Mercury* and the *Illustrated Tasmanian Mail*. Except when the English Test Team made its triennial visits the valley dwellers were vocally and unashamedly English in all their sympathies.

Yet Australia kept creeping in. Beyond the comfortable orchards and hopfields, above the little rose-covered weatherboard cottages and farmsteads rose the jungly eucalypt-clad hills. The herbage faltered and died against their tawny flanks. Trim rows of Lombardy poplars might line the banks of the Derwent, but in the distance purple hills crouched at the throat of each valley. In the winter their summits were streaked with snow. The girls were Australian too, riding horses bareback to distant paddocks. Sheep with their oblong incurious eyes crowded against the barbed-wire fences beyond the intensive cultivation. Bushfires, which many Tasmanians, despite all evidence to the contrary, continued to regard as a Mainland menace, made short savage forays into the secluded valley in the shimmering summer heat, leaving hillsides scarred and blackened by their blow-torch fury. And though the Derwent, green and pellucid, might flow as gently as Sweet Afton, it was joined right at Ruth Penny's homestead, Bushy Park, by the Styx, brown and turbid with the sap of wattle, cootamundra and ironbark.

My entry into this arcady was secured through the same 'Uncle' Arthur who had played so craven a part (according to Mother) in the 'plot' to get Dad removed from TAMECO. Apparently his vexation at Mother's hauteur or his general fed-up-ness with Dad's lolloping inefficiency didn't extend to the second generation. Specifically it was Arthur Dennistoun Wood's wife Lowiny ('Aunt Lone') who arranged the entry. Her two nieces Ruth Penny and Jill Page were attending St. Catherine's school for girls in snobby Toorak and of course we saw a lot of them at Cromford, Aunt Lone's funny little steep-gabled house on the disputed marcher-lands between Toorak and Malvern. For three or four years we all frolicked together in those other marcher-lands that divide childhood from adolescence; and when the girls began to gain their bumps and lose their freckles the friendship survived these assaults. So that when Aunt Lone suggested that her sister Nell Penny, Ruth's mother, would be delighted to include me in a bunch of youngsters who'd be going over to The Speck from Melbourne one summery Christmas holiday, I was delighted.

Jill and Ruth at Bushy Park, Macquarie Plains, Derwent Valley, Tas, were quite, quite, different from the two long-legged St. Catherine's girls in their grey cotton stockings, sky blue uniforms and straw boaters. They had suddenly become identified with The Land, and had a new authority. They rode horses, summoned reasonably deferential underlings, kept pet lambs; above all, they were part of a thick network of exciting new friends—most of them related to each other it seemed—who were unknown to me: Shoobridges and Watchorns and Warners and Parsons, all knit in a wonderful secret society of blood and self-absorption among their rose-rambled houses by the gurgling flumes.

I suppose an unattached male of whatever vintage is always useful to have around, but I was constantly amazed at the hospitality offered to me by the friendly families of the district, being honestly unable to grasp that they might perhaps have liked me for my own blue eyes. Bushy Park, where it all started, was a rambling, white weatherboarded house with a big wide verandah, set in a wonderful roses and spices garden bordered by the confluence of the Styx and the Derwent. The commingling of the waters here was intensely dramatic. The Styx, tawny as port wine, erupted into the cool greeny-grey Derwent like a severed artery, and for about half a mile the two waters flowed side by side sharply divided as by a liquid bundling board. Near the confluence the Pennys had erected a little gazebo whence you could watch this dramatic sight, or alternatively dally with a girl and gaze at Orion reflected in the Derwent, until the huge river mosquitos discovered you and banished romance with a sharp ping-g.

Ten minutes walk along a dusty gravel road, bordered with small paling-enclosed trees with the names of the fallen in hand-punched bronze clip-ons, lay the home of the Henry Joneses. They were much sought after because they had the only tennis-court near at hand. He was a lean leathery fellow with a big masonic tie-pin; she a motherly housewife with a massive superstructure and underpinnings that creaked alarmingly as she quanted herself from chair to chair breathing heavily. She was greatly in demand as a chaperone, and from the standpoint of us boys a very good one (i.e. no questions if you came back with the girl after ten minutes). Their daughters, like so many Aussie country girls, had terrific forehand drives and could also split the whitewash on the base-line with a cunning lob. The entire family, even the youngest daughter, had the most dreadful false teeth; as amazing in their brittle-china wobbliness as the poor diet which, in a valley of apples and citrus, must have made them necessary. I once told a story about Masons to Mr. Jones at a tennis tea party. He laughed so much that his uppers collapsed completely on to his lowers with a resounding clack, revealing for the instant before his hand whipped up to his mouth, an expanse of purply gum like a goanna's palate.

Next up the valley came A. S. Watchorn, a pawky paunchy gent who had pioneered the cultivation of tobacco. He lived a bachelor life in a small white weatherboard cottage, rose-bowered for himself alone. The ladies grew pensive when his name cropped up. Watchorn was a cunning fellow and a comic character with a wonderful way of cutting young fellows down to size. His cat-like middle-aged skill on the tennis court was exemplified in an awkward womanish-seeming service. Dropping with deceptive languor the ball would shoot disconcertingly sideways from the asphalt leaving one's own racquet lunging at empty air. He was also an expert in doubles at slipping a fast one down the sidelines past the eager youngster at the net. Dreaming of a smashing volley, you saw—half saw—didn't see—Watchorn's ball zipping quickly by on your blind side. As you crossed the court, cheeks burning, you would see Watchorn gazing fixedly at the sky and whistling tonelessly in aggravating insouciance.

We once went with Watchorn and Mr. Penny on a Homeric camping and fishing trip to the Great Lake high on the central Tasmanian plateau. It followed a pattern the men had established on innumerable earlier trips, and its humour was adequately symbolized by the notice 'No snoring aloud' tacked on the wall of the lakeside cabin. Their fishing technique was equally insensitive. With two or three companions, a deck of cards and a couple of dozen bottles of beer we would set out in the motor launch in the early mist-scarved morning, lash the tiller and troll, with the rods and lines speared out over the stern like radio antennae. The poker players, their beer inside them, would be jarred out of their concentration on the game only by the screech of an outgoing reel.

'There she goes.'

'Better reel her in while you're still ahead of the game.

'I'll see you. Or do you want to buy another?'

'Cards face down, you sharpers, till I get the strong of this beaut.'

The motor sputtered; the launch lay gliding in its own feathery wake, and cool deep waters slid silently by as someone dragged in the eight pound trout, a writhing silver and brown jack-in-the-box of scaly fire with glazing eyes. You didn't play the fish, you just dragged them in.

Upon my return from the Great Lake I fell madly in love, was spurned and briefly contemplated suicide or a trip to the South Pole. It was thus fortunate that at this moment an invitation should have come from further up the valley to waft me away from the superheated adolescent love-hate cats' cradle among the young people at Bushy Park. I think Mrs. Penny was glad to see me go, for I was becoming a damned nuisance with my moonstruck maunderings, always 'draped round a verandah post' as she'd say, or else boring Jill's brother Algie with a moaning supplication for help in my latest entanglement.

This time it was a Shoobridge, D.M. or 'Pat', a roly-poly florid kindly fellow who shared with his elder brother Rupert the hop farms and grazing lands over the next ridge. Shortly after leaving Macquarie Plains the little Tasmanian Government Railway crossed the Derwent and headed south and west up the valley of the Russell, eventually fetching up at the osmiridium mines near Tyenna at the foot of the imposing rampart of Mount Field West. Beyond this lay the unsettled and almost uncharted and undiscovered south-west corner of Tasmania: land of drenching rains, tangled scrub and lowering spindrift-laden skies.

Rupert—later Sir Rupert and president of the Legislative Council of Tasmania—had the big red gabled house up on the hill with the tennis-court and the apple orchards and the tawny paddocks. Pat's house, a more modern structure of red brick (in Mr. Lancaster's Wimbledon Transitional style) lay further down towards the river. Both brothers owned extensive summer pasture up on the central plateau, and what with wool, hops, tobacco, cattle and fruit managed to keep the wolf comfortably from the door even in the midst of the Depression. Mrs. Shoobridge—Mrs. Pat to the hired hands—was a kindly laconic woman with an instinctive understanding of a boy's problems. There were four youngsters, Norah, Mollie, Fergus and Jim. Whenever I stayed at Glenora I had the big room under the eaves. It was a real delight—an exhilarating sense of release as the exams at the University ground to a final halt—to contemplate in the mind's eye the creaming waves under the *Nairana's* bow, the little train clanking down through the purple olive-clad mountains, the arrival at Glenora, kids shouting, dogs barking, horses snorting and whinnying, Pat Shoobridge and his wife smiling, family dinner, a game of Russian pool and then the room under the eaves and five weeks of joyful abandon stretching out ahead.

They were wonderfully kind to the tetchy young student whose mother was 12,000 miles away and whose step-father lived in another world. What we did was perhaps not so wonderful except to me: riding, tennis, fighting bushfires, swimming, flirting, an 'oh-the-days-of-the-Kerry-dances' atmosphere, shrouded in a magic light both then and now. Then, because the Derwent Valley with its free and easy, take it for granted, democratic family-mingling out under the open Australian sky, was so utterly different from the cramped suburban realities of 4 Grace Street and the Procrustean framework of Kensingtonian ideas that Mother had endeavoured to impose on it. Now, because in retrospect the sunny open kindliness seems to have been more than ordinarily generous.

We went to the famous Campbelltown dance up in the centre of the island. Two girls and two boys left in evening dress in broad daylight to drive forty miles over the dirt and gravel roads. The car belonged to Johnny Elliott who was distinguished for wearing what we called a coat-shirt, i.e. it opened up the front instead of having to be wrestled on over the head as our English type shirts had to be. For this reason he was considered American and hence very daring, and he was certainly a demon driver. Competition among the girls for his driving favours was almost as keen as for those of Tom Stafford Smith, a wealthy and exquisite young man with an English accent and a head of thick wavy chestnut hair. If you couldn't be seen seated sedately beside Tom Stafford Smith in his immense and croupy old yellow Daimler you could at least scorch past your admiring friends, shrieking and head-scarved beside Johnny Elliott the demon driver.

On this trip to Campbelltown we saw the moss-dappled bridge at Ross and the great mansion of the Camerons, Mona Vale, with its reputed 12 chimneys for the months, 52 rooms for the weeks and 365 windows. It floated by in yellow sandstone Regency magnificence, a little theatrical against the tigerish fields and jagged blue mountains of Van Diemen's Land. We kissed in cars, danced all night, had eggs-and-bacon and hair of the dog at first light in a scarred old wooden country hotel sagging at the corners, and zoomed back into Glenora in a cloud of dust still in our long dresses and dinner jackets as the sun rose orange over the eastern ranges.

We picnicked at the Salmon Ponds near New Norfolk and illegally fed tit-bits to the fingerlings. We rode deep into the bush and chewed gum scraped from the cootamundra. We played endless and futile games of bridge, considered a safe and certainly a highly conventional form of amusement for kids. Auction was going out and contract gradually coming in and we wrestled with its complexities and devoured news stories of the great jousts in faraway mysterious battle-mented New York between Ely Culbertson and Sidney Lenz.

Sometimes we would all troop down to Hobart, the state capital, for a dance, a dinner or an Old Boys' reunion. Dear old Hobart Slow-bart, as the kids called it, had become more glamorous as I grew up. Now American tourists off a world cruise on the *Franconia* roamed up Elizabeth Street gawking in the store windows. 'Wonder what they see in little old Hobart?' said John Shoobridge, Norah's cousin. Had we but known it, the little town, perched dramatically on the steep woolly shoulders of leonine Mount Wellington, with the star-fish harbour at its feet, must have seemed romantic indeed compared with the carbon-copy cities of the Middle West and the Great Plains. We watched the tourists back on to their ships, went to our old school, Hutchin's, and changed with great daring in the Masters' common room into dinner jackets. Then off we went to another dance, this time in posh Sandy Bay, Hobart's S.W.1, where the girls had a sheen and we deserted the country cousins for their brittle charms. John and I took the girls home, kissed them passionately but fleetingly on the doorstep in a flurry of organdie and Houbigant's *Quelques fleurs*, and went on to an all-night café for sailors at Sulli-van's Cove. This was the original waterfront Hobart of 1820, all sandstone terrace houses, grey stucco offices and frowning bluestone warehouses, small and secret and neat like Weymouth or Lyme Regis. Our tattered evening attire excited stares and loud remarks about tonks and nanas from the turtle-sweatered longshoremen; but we were immortal and didn't care who knew it.

It was 2.30 a.m. on a summer's night and just the time for eggs and bacon and chips. It was still dark when we piled into John's little two seater and roared through sleeping silent Hobart and up on to the shoulders of Mount Wellington. The brown hill with KEENS CURRY outlined in white stones slid by in the gloom. Later that summer the University students were to change it overnight, with Egyptian labours, into HELLS CURSE. From The Springs Hotel at 3,000 feet we saw the sun come sailing in over the hills and the starfish harbour, and shouted and roared in sheer exhilaration. Then we drove back to the school, woke up the porter and changed into day clothes. After a huge breakfast at Hadley's Hotel—porridge and kedgeree and great steaming cups of tea—we went over to the Royal Tennis Club, a rare and recondite place to which we had entry by courtesy of Pat Shoobridge. We sat in solitary grandeur in the gallery watching Finch the professional play Stone the great amateur in a warm-up match. Within the covered court they bounced the ball skilfully off the walls, the balcony and the roof as they had in the days of Henry VIII; and suddenly we found ourselves nodding. We'd been awake for thirty hours. Couldn't go back to the Derwent Valley just yet; the girls wouldn't be ready. Well it was Saturday. How about an all day movie, if we *must* sleep?

We crept into a fleapit on Liverpool Street and dozed happily while the silver screen hopped and twitched and flickered. The usher woke us up when we'd slept the whole show round and demanded we buy an extra ticket. No fear, we said, and staggered out into the midday sun. We now needed a bath and a shave. I know, I said to John, let's bot on my step-grandmother up at 405 Elizabeth Street. She'll give us a bath. We parked the car across the street, opened the wicket gate, and crossed the six feet of front 'garden'; a strip of faded lawn with two decrepit hydrangeas (but blue, though, for they had buried iron filings at the feet of the once pinky cauliflowers). We mounted the step and twisted the bell in the middle of the vitrified mucous of the little front door.

Unfortunately it was Stella who answered, and she looked far from pleased. Stella was the wife of Major Robert Mowbray Winston Thirkell, otherwise Uncle Winston, my step-father's elder brother. She came from New Zealand, and was kind in a crisp bossy sort of way. It was she who now stood before us, rather than my soft-spoken step-grandmother with her sad voice and ill-fitting store teeth.

'Well!' said Stella unpropitiously. 'We *are* honoured! And what may I ask brings you here?'

'This is John Shoobridge,' I said. 'Where's Meo?' meaning my step-grandmother.

'In her bedroom,' said Stella, chucking her eyes up to heaven. 'You'd better come in.'

'We've been up all night, Aunt Stella. We'd just like a hot bath and a cup of coffee.'

Stella made way for us. 'Mamma will be most disappointed if you don't stay,' she said.

I mumbled something non-committal and led the way for John down the narrow passage, past the door to the tiny sitting room, past the door to Meo's big bedroom—mercifully shut—and out on to the minute glassed-in back porch: on the second floor since the ground sloped steeply from front to back. In this back porch were a tall-boy with a streaky mirror, two raffia chairs, a bed with a naked mattress stained from the loss of many cups of morning tea, and a home-made hand-painted hanging wooden bookcase in which were a shaving mug, a copy of *Captain Blood* by Rafael Sabatini, a moustache-cup and a small pottery saucer inscribed 'Dinna Forget' and filled with collar studs.

'Well,' I said to John hopelessly, 'this is where they live.'

He nodded, inarticulate with sympathy.

'I think you'd better stay.' Stella was standing in the doorway, with one arm on the jamb. 'You and John have a bath, then we'll talk about it.' She shut the glass-curtained door into the house and clumped down-stairs to the kitchen where we could hear her banging about.

John sat on the stained mattress and started to take off his shoes. I busied myself in the bathroom with the chip heater. I opened its fire-blackened little belly, shoved in scrunched up sheets of the Hobart *Mercury*, stuck wooden shavings and chips on top and added a dollop of kerosene from a dark brown bottle labelled Phenyle. I threw in a match. Whoomph! The tap started to ooze warmish water and I watched it moodily, reflecting on the tiresomeness of step-aunts-in-law.

Eventually we finished bathing, changed into slacks and open-necked shirts and were wolfing coffee and squashed fly biscuits down in the dining room when Stella shoved the *Mercury* under my nose.

'I don't suppose you've seen this,' she said. 'Perhaps when you've read it you'll agree it might be best for you to stay here for a bit.' Her finger pointed to the 'Letters to the Editor'. I looked at the signature 'Jan Hudspeth' and went cold all over. I passed it to John; consternation shook his visage.

'I never thought they'd print it,' he said.

'It's all over town,' said Stella thinly triumphant. 'And everyone knows who wrote it.' I put my face in my hands and did some thinking. It was complicated and it needed to be.

Jan Hudspeth was the cousin of my room mate at Ormond College, and a friend of both John's and mine. The letter was an ironical and irreverent—though not libellous—commentary on the agricultural theories and pet schemes of one Ebenezer Shoobridge. Ebenezer was the eccentric and garrulous uncle of Pat, with whom I was staying, and the great-uncle of John. We'd often heard Pat inveigh against the hare-brained schemes and the interminable garrulity of his uncle. Ebenezer, it appeared, believed that water could be made to run up hill. He had a scheme for pumping water by the weight of cars passing over a tread in the highway. He was believed to be a flat earthist. He was in fact a harmless old nut. We'd thought: what fun it would be to write a letter to the editor taking old Ebenezer apart. We composed the letter, blithely stuck Jan's name to the bottom of it and mailed it off. Libel, false pretences, uttering and forgery. It never occurred to us that the *Mercury* would print it without checking. Here it was staring us in the face. We suddenly felt naked in public.

Stella gave a laconic smile and twitched the newspaper out from under my hand.

'All over the town,' she repeated. 'I think you'd better lie low.'

'But,' we stammered, 'but how do they know we did it?'

'You silly goose,' she said. 'Jan telephoned the paper as soon as he read the letter. His father got in touch with the Shoobridge clan and the clues all led to you.'

'Yes, but what about proof?' I said lamely.

'It was just a bit of fun,' said John.

'A student hoax if you like.'

Stella pursed her lips. 'I don't think that's the view that will be taken by Mr. Ebenezer Shoobridge,' she said.

'Just the same, John,' I said, 'I can't go back up the Valley, not till this dies down.'

'If it dies down,' said Stella, rattling the teacups on her way out. We looked at each other across the table. John said,

'Uncle Pat's the one that's really in the soup. He egged us on to do it. Once old Ebenezer discovers it wasn't Jan, he'll blame Uncle Pat.'

'That's why we can't go back. At least you can, but I can't. I'm staying with your Uncle Pat.'

John sighed windily. 'He's a good old cock. He won't hold it against you. We'd better make our peace with Jan, though.'

At this point there was a great thumping on the stairs and down crashed Uncle Winston into the basement, his bald tonsured head shining and his bristly ginger moustache crinkled in a big smile.

'Day, Young,' he said. 'How about a cuppa for me? Hallo there young fella-me-lad. What's all this I hear?'

When we told him he roared with laughter.

'The Tassie police have got you up a well-known creek. Without a paddle,' he added, gulping down tea.

We looked at him, shocked at his heartlessness. Stella stood in the open door of the kitchen behind him with a damp tea-towel draped over one shoulder, and smiling cryptically, or so it appeared. Winston eased his coat off over his shoulders and sat sideways tilting the hind legs of the horsehair-stuffed chair with its fiddle back. His shirt and one side of his braces caved in a bit over the enormous crater that had been blown in his left shoulder on the Somme. After a while he started to laugh.

'I was only having you on,' he said. 'No one's going to bother much over a prank by a couple of kids.'

'Hey!' we said. 'Kids! Hey just a minute . . .'

'Well are they?' He slurped some more tea. 'You're both minors. Just keep quiet. Old Ebenezer will fuss and fret a bit, but that's his affair.'

'We'll have to apologize to Jan.'

'That's your affair.' We thought about this.

Stella cleared her throat and in the ensuing silence it sounded horribly loud.

'Don't you think Graham should stay here a bit? Not go up the Valley until it blows over?'

Winston shrugged his blasted-out shoulder. 'If you like, Young,' he said. He didn't seem much interested though.

I took a deep breath. 'I think maybe I'll go back up with John.'

Stella looked disappointed. Less from not having me as a guest than from having failed in her efforts to prevent me from doing what I wanted. Or so I thought. I could hear her in my mind's ear saying 'I *don't* think its gentlemanly to tell a joke like that when Wanda is in the room' (or Barbara or the Giblin girls or what have you).

John rose, 'Then if you'll excuse us, Mrs. Thirkell . . . ?'

Stella made way and as I brushed by her shoulder I smelled the damp tea-y odour of the tea-towel. Winston said, 'Drive carefully and remember me to Pat Shoobridge.'

We had to restrain our steps as we cantered upstairs and through the mucous door and into the street. We had to walk decorously across the car lines to the little two seater and start it up sedately. But once out of sight of 405 John gunned the motor and we both roared out at the tops of our voices, 'Oh boy! Oh boy! Am I glad to be out of *that* house.'

The Golden Valley

We lost no time putting as many miles of twisting tarmac as we could between us and Hobart. We scorched through Glenorchy, took the Claremont level crossing at a good fifty, shot through Rosetta scattering chickens and dust, cleared the hotel at Bridgewater and didn't slow down till the twin-humped, woolly-shouldered Dromedary was behind us, the fresh as opposed to the salt Derwent streaming by on our right, and the spires and false fronts and hitching posts of New Norfolk coming into view. Then and only then, when we began to see *our* Derwent opening up did we slow down and proceed at a more reasonable, even gingerly, pace towards Macquarie Plains and Glenora.

Much to our relief Winston proved to be right. At Glenora we were greeted with shrieks of merriment and 'Oh-you-are-awfuls' from the girls: from Ruth with her silky yellow hair, from Jill with her charming fringe, from Norah with her warm secret smile, from Jean, from Mary, from the boys at the swimming hole, from the grown-ups at tennis, even from Pat Shoobridge himself. Everyone, it seemed, was happy at old Ebenezer's discomfiture. All were prepared to agree that ours was a boyish prank which should be overlooked. We were back once again in the gorgeous golden Derwent Valley.

There was just one snag. Pat put it to us in his little study where he did the farm and station accounts and where the big map of Tasmania on the wall, with his broad back obscuring its moth-eaten sea-damaged south-east corner, sometimes looked like a cocked hat over his thick jolly head.

'I'll have to hand it to you, boys.' Tears of joy streamed down his fat ruddy face. 'You've made me feel years younger. Just the same it wouldn't do for us not to seek an amnesty.'

'Who with?'

'With Ebenezer.'

'How?' We looked blank.

'You'll write him an exquisite letter of apology,' he said.

'You mean admit it—in writing?'

'Yes.'

'But won't he prosecute us?'

'No fear. I've told him you got the idea from me. He knows. Anyway I'm not running for parliament.' He turned to John. 'But your Dad is.' John nodded glumly.

'I'll write the letter,' I said, 'and we'll both sign it.' This took most of an afternoon when we should have been playing tennis, but in the end it was done and mailed off. All we ever got was a typed acknowledgement, but by now the English Test Team was on its way and Uncle Ebenezer receded swiftly into the background.

Because I'd been born in England it was assumed by the Shoobridge family and especially by Pat, who was a tremendous sports fan, that I would back the English team. Radio coverage of the Test Matches was close to saturation point, and for hours the entire family hung over the set listening to the progress of the play. Partly because it appeared to draw attention to an amiable eccentricity, I was willing to play the role in which the Shoobridges had cast me and to appear as a fervent defender of the English team. But in reality I was hoping that the Aussies would win. It happened that the year was momentous.

I'd studied the newspaper reports and the accounts of the sports writers while the team slowly approached us across the Indian Ocean. I was struck with the aristocratic and unpleasantly arrogant bearing of the Captain of the English XI whose name was D. R. Jardine. They were 'out to get the Ashes'. It didn't seem to me that this was quite the way to play the game. Taking it a bit seriously, weren't they? Poor sports perhaps. It seemed, too, that they'd developed a team of bowlers who were going to bowl steadily on the leg side and get our batsmen into trouble. Wouldn't bowl on the off side, eh? Afraid our batsmen would hit them for six? Bradman, McCartney, Ponsford, Richardson. Who were these craven Pommies? Their names, it seemed, were Voce, Bowes and Larwood.

So much—and so much more horrific—has happened in the world of sport (to say nothing of the world at large) since 1932, that the furious storm of anger and abuse stirred up by 'body-line bowling' seems to belong to the distant days of gunboats and Jenkins' Ear. But it was real and terrifying enough to those who were in the middle of it; and because the Shoobridges had cast me in the role of ersatz Englishman there I was—right in the middle of it.

The initial performances by the English were distasteful and disconcerting, but not alarming or dangerous. They bowled on the leg side, yes; they tended to pitch the ball short, yes; so that it bounced a bit—flew, some might say—but was manageable. Clearly we'd been getting drunk on the great run-getting period of our history. Cricket had become a batsman's game. Individual scores of 300 or even 400 were not uncommon. The English aimed to correct the balance, to make it a bowler's game. Well, nothing wrong with that.

But at Melbourne it was noticed that our batsmen were starting to duck. The balls seemed to be not only fast, vicious and on the leg side; they seemed to be being pitched shorter and ever shorter, to fly up higher and ever higher. The batsman appeared to be not so much playing the ball, or even a game, as defending himself against a missile. And Jardine had a regular battery of fielders round the leg side. Did the batsman duck or snick a ball or simply raise his bat, then he'd be caught out. This isn't leg bowling; this is bowling —not at the leg, but at the body—why it's, it's *body-line bowling*!

At the Melbourne ground it was observed, not once nor twice but several times, that when a batsman missed one of Larwood's balls it would sail over the heads of the wicket keeper and the longstop and hit the boundary fence on the full. A low growl of disapproval came from the crowd and from the sports writers. This wasn't cricket, this was murder. Jardine kept his arrogant aquiline calm. He would give no interview to newsmen. The balls kept getting higher, harder and faster. Aussie batsmen fell like ninepins. Aussie tempers rose. Hey, someone said, as if suddenly realizing the danger, we might lose the Ashes! Cries of 'unfair' were countered by cries of 'Keep calm, Australia; be sports.' All's fair in love and war; and if cricket wasn't war what was it? Conversation round the Shoobridge loudspeaker was excited and loud though not yet harsh or strident. But I couldn't help feeling uncomfortable, defending these fellows.

At Adelaide one memorable day the blow fell, and in a trice Aussies and Pommies were at each other's throats. It was the Third Test. The English had already won two (by their unfair body-line bowling of course) and the atmosphere was tense with a big crowd at the Adelaide Oval. The Australians were batting and Jardine was alternating Larwood and Voce, with his usual battery on the leg side. Balls were flying viciously high and the crowd, very hostile, had started barracking. Jardine in crisp flannels appeared entirely unperturbed. His whole attitude and the cut of his jib suggested 'You just can't take it, you poor miserable Aussie bastards.' Our Captain, W. M. Woodfull, had already been hit painfully over the heart. Then in to bat went the beloved W. A. Oldfield, the greatest Aussie wicket keeper of all time; and also a sturdy tail end batsman. Bill Oldfield shaped up at the wicket and Larwood started his long express-train run. The ball left his hand like a sizzling rocket, the next moment there was a hideous thud and Bill Oldfield, hit on the head, dropped like a stone.

A great roar of anger burst from the crowd. The boundary fences went down like matchwood, and in a few seconds thousands of enraged Australian cricket fans were starting to stream across the ground. It looked as if Jardine and his team would be lynched then and there. But police, groundsmen and officials went tearing across to the pitch and strained with linked arms to hold the mob in check. Even they mightn't have succeeded if, Oldfield, still severely shaken, hadn't begged the crowd to return to the stands. For him they went, with menacing growls; for no one else would they have gone.

After a break the match was resumed but no one's heart was in it. Or in the rest of the series, for that matter. Victory had become meaningless. Let England take the bloody Ashes if that's the way they want to play. This wasn't cricket, this was legalized murder. Around the Shoobridge loudspeaker the wrath and resentment turned on me. Me and my bloody Englishman! Bastards they were! No hopers! Bludgers! In vain I protested. But you made me. . . ! I'd been born there, hadn't I? Bunch of bloody narks. I felt extremely miserable. I didn't think I ought to accept the Shoobridges' hospitality any more. Pat wouldn't even speak to me, let alone play Russian pool. Jim and Fergus were stormy-eyed; even Mollie and Norah were cool and correct. I went up to my big glorious room under the eaves, looking out on to the hopfields and the soldierly Lombardy poplars along the river, and the heavy-laden apple trees and the tawny hill-pasture and the purply blue mountains in the distance. I started to pack my suitcase. Exiled by body-line bowling.

While engaged in this melancholy rite, the door opened and in came Mrs. Shoobridge. She put her arm round my shoulder and told me not to be a fool, and that they all liked me and all wanted me to stay. I found myself blubbing like an idiot. After a while I went downstairs, and everyone was very kind and solicitous. Pat poured me a big tankard of beer. But the pretence that I was English was dropped and when the next Test came up we all concentrated on hating the Englishmen together. Much more satisfactory.

Cricket didn't recover for several years from the bitterness engendered by the body-line controversy. It united Australians as never before. But what was played—and discussed—wasn't cricket; but a kind of desperate internecine civil war with slit throats, knees in the groin and jabs to the kidneys. Well, if that was the kind of cricket they wanted, I knew where I stood. In the golden glorious Valley we were all Dinkum Aussies together; there was no room for a Pommie.

Chapter Ten

VARSITY DRAG

THE timid freshmen who had basked in the sun of their seniors' approval, or been abased by their frowns, came leaping back to second year drunk with power. Some, like myself, had learned to fit in the hard way; others, born with a natural flexibility, came off more lightly. As a second year student with my new 'wife', Geoff Hudspeth the engineer from Tasmania, I had the luxury of a study with a fire, even though it was barely ten feet square, and looked out on to the courtyard rather than to the breezy world outside. My bedroom also had its luxuries: a corner basin with one cold tap and a shelf with wire hooks underneath it from which to hang clothes. I pressed my pants by sleeping on them. The bathroom (one to a floor) was still 150 feet away along a brown linoleum corridor—but I now had status. I was a Second Year Man.

The way had not been easy. Success in the college and university amateur theatricals—that notorious cess-pit of the ego—had gone to my head. Storm signals were riding in the eyes of some of the seniors, but I was blithely unaware of their import. The first alarm came in the shape of a false telephone call at night. When I got down three flights of stairs and 300 feet of corridor the receiver was off the hook but it was dead. I pressed it hard to my ear, said 'Hullo' several times, then hung up and marched disconsolately back to the study. My arrival was greeted with hoots of laughter by Hudspeth. Unknown to me, the receiver had been liberally smeared with boot polish and I was blackened from temple to chin.

I should have taken this as a warning, but a combination of innocence and self-absorption prevented this. The next warning was more unpleasant. Once again it was the false phone call and once again I fell for it. But this time strong arms clad in football sweaters pulled me from the booth and despite my struggles four hooded figures carried me out across the yard over to the swimming pool into which I was unceremoniously tossed. By the time I struggled gasping to the shore my assailants had vanished into the night. Hot fury surging behind my damp and dripping abasement, I strode tempestuously through the College leaving a trail of water along the brown lino corridors. I had a general idea of the group from which my attackers were likely to be drawn and, when I paused outside their study door streaming with water and heart pumping rapidly, I heard their laughter. That was all I needed as a clue. I kicked the door open and burst dripping into their midst.

They affected a mild surprise, but I saw football sweaters and silk evening socks rammed hastily behind some books. With a great lunge I overturned the supper table. One of my assailants was a rower whose hair-raising set-piece was to lay tea in his study for a group of women visitors, with a silk table-cloth between the crockery and a highly polished wooden table. When all was ready he would nonchalantly twitch the cloth out, leaving the crockery trembling but still intact on the table. Girls used to shriek with delight. But having his own table overturned didn't appeal to him a bit. He howled with rage and soon I was on the floor being beaten up.

I wouldn't have lasted long, but the row brought the President of the Students' Committee, a venerable law student of twenty-four. We picked ourselves up off the floor while he gave us a tongue-lashing. By this time my enemies were looking a bit crestfallen, but I, burning with self-righteous indignation, demanded from the President a vindication of my Simon-purity. All I got was a dry look and a laconic 'Whatever they think of you, that's not the way to fix it'. I retired in shivering mortification—to the surprising and warming discovery that I had friends. When I'd changed and entered the study it was full of my 'Year' and they were 'out to get' the fellows who'd dunked me. It was, they claimed, an insult to our Year.

They decided to make an example of the rower with the silken table-cloth. They waited until he went out one evening, then broke into his bedroom and secreted themselves there. Others lay in wait in corridors. The fellow lurched in about eleven p.m. but as he put his key in the lock some sixth sense alerted him. He was aware of dim figures in the dark and he ran down the corridor into another bedroom and locked himself in. When our opposition realized what they were up against, proposals for an amnesty were made and for the rest of the term we eyed each other with wary circumspection. As for me, I took stock of myself and decided that I really must be rather bumptious and would have to do something about it.

About this time a wealthy Queen's student, one of the 'Methody boys' across the way, decided to buy a car. This put him far beyond the reach of ordinary mortals, but it put within *my* reach a Douglas Two-stroke for only £14. The machine was much too small for me and I had to ride it with my legs permanently bandy, but it gave a most heady sense of liberation. I rode all over town. I took girls on the pillion down to Frankston for a swim. I rode the bike to Ballarat and to Geelong for the boat races. It threw me, opposite the Yarra Bend Lunatic Asylum, in full evening dress, and I landed on top of my own silver cigarette case bending it beyond repair. I re-mounted and rode on triumphantly to the dance with muddied tails flying in the night breeze. But the fact that the motor bike could throw me without structural damage either to it or to me meant, clearly, that it was not a very potent machine. I needed a more powerful steed and one fell day I sold the Douglas Two-stroke and bought instead a bright red second-hand Indian Prince.

Then we discovered the bold bad nurses. They lived in the Residence of the Melbourne Hospital but were prepared to go out with students, to stay out after hours, provided you gave them a leg up over the brick wall and the *chevaux de frise*, and even to sneak out while Matrons slept. Such an adventurous and enterprising spirit seemed to us to promise excitement of a similar kind in another field. Add motor bikes and half a dozen Richmond beers and a sandy beach, and surely you had the makings of a really gaudy night? It didn't quite work out that way. The trouble was the nurses' acquaintance with blood, bones and sutures also made them more than ordinarily adept at the twistings and turnings both of conversation and of body designed to avoid the final posture, and in the end we clattered back on our bikes through the night frustrated in our main purpose.

The Indian Prince also proved frustrating, and a bad bargain and a bucking bronco to boot. The gear-lever kept leaping from its notch with a fearsome racing roar from the motor. It leaked oil, whereas with the dear old little Douglas Two-stroke you put the oil and petrol in together. It reared upward out of control if a twist of the clutch cable were ever so slightly misjudged. One afternoon, before an admiring crowd of undergrads, I acceded to an importunate request from Cyn Mason to take her up the Sydney road on the pillion.

Cyn was well-tailored to soften the excruciating sharpness of the pillion. She was a mannish sort of girl with a low rasping contralto, a part-time job as social reporter on *Truth*, the local scandal sheet, and a daring unconventionality in dress. She was the first girl to wear an evening dress of floor-length culottes. She drank beer out of a stein with the boys in the men's bar. She was utterly ruthless in the pursuit of scoops for her gossip column and had been known to back over-sensitive girls into a corner and snatch love letters from their protesting grasp. Her brash good nature, sifting through farouche ash-blonde hair and a Hogarthian profile, overwhelmed the men and it was always an honour to do something for Cyn. Accordingly when she commandeered a ride on my Indian Prince up to the Brunswick Town Hall I was most happy to comply and we tore up the Sydney Road together: she bouncing blowsily on the pillion, one arm round my waist and the other waving to startled or sympathetic citizenry.

'Good on ya mate!' roared the five o'clock swillers outside Johnny Naughton's pub.

But in essaying a U-turn outside the Brunswick Town Hall my front wheel became entangled in the network of criss-crossing tramlines at this Shepherd's Bush of North Melbourne. We were both thrown and the Indian Prince finished up bent and buckled against a lamp standard. Willing hands picked us up; neither of us more than bruised. But the Prince had to await the Rathdown Street garage mechanic and when he told me what the repair bill would be I sold the bike to him. We used to say, when a fellow showed signs of getting angry, 'Now, don't get off yer bike, I'll pick up the pump'. As the Cyn Mason-Indian Prince episode rushed round the University grape-vine, it eventually reached the ear of Frank Sullivan.

Frank Sullivan was a sedate Beau Brummel; a perennial dancing bachelor. All the girls adored to step on to the floor with him. With tails swirling, white tie in immaculate place, and face set in an expression of polite and vaguely ironic expertise, he really was a joy to watch. Though an extra-collegiate student of Newman, the Catholic college, Frank did not narrowly confine his attentions to the girls of St. Mary's, nor his discussions to evenings with the Christian Brothers, many of whose Irish teachers with their bigotry, their malapropisms and their long upper lips were a constant source of amusement to non-Catholics. Instead he moved with suave gravity from private talks with priests who had 'S.J.' after their names to social dinners in well-to-do Toorak mansions, to the University Union and the debating society; always with a twinkle; always correct and courteous in his attitude; but always with a strong though flexible wall of inner reserve. This was particularly evident in the annual season of balls, dances and proms.

It was the era of the revival of the so-called Viennese waltz, and of the spurious schmaltzy *Alt Wien* movie-musicals satirized by Christopher Isherwood in *Prater Violet*. Frank whirled his partners round the Melbourne ballrooms with exquisite nimbleness, delicacy and strength. Often the floor would insensibly clear, to give him space for his incomparable gyrations. But his name was never linked with that of any girl, and he remained an aloof, smiling, courteous enigma. He had, however, recently aspired to a wider interest in student activities, and he now announced from the editorial chair of *Farrago*, tongue in careful cheek : 'Miss Mason has announced that, whatever her partner may do, she has no intention of getting off her bike.'

I was enabled to buy and sell these motor bikes and take holidays to Tasmania, as well as look after my board, lodging and tuition by virtue of the comparative affluence bestowed on me by the Shell Oil Co. of Australia. Towards the end of my second year it occurred to the Managing Director, O. W. Darch, that he ought to take a look at me and see how the firm's money was being spent. Accordingly I received a summons to a weekend at the Darch residence, and was told that a car would call for me at Ormond College at four p.m. on a Friday afternoon.

The appearance of a Daimler limousine with a capped chauffeur —and a rug !—provoked a veritable cataract of raspberries, cat-calls and yoo-hoos. Half the men of Ormond were there to see me off and the inevitable dustbin lid, tied to the Daimler's rear bumper, had to be detached by the unsmiling chauffeur outside the Master's Lodge while I sat in glassed-in be-rugged comfort and my friends barracked me from outside. The chauffeur preserved a pointed silence all the way out to Templestowe, which was where the Darches lived, but the back of his neck was vocal.

Darch, as befitted a captain of industry, lived in an enormous pink brick mansion on five acres of rolling parklike hills overlooking the Yarra valley. The drawing room rose a full two storeys with a great vertical sweep of what must have been pioneer picture window, looking out to the furry camel-backed Dandenongs and, beyond, the purple horst of Donna Buang. Half way up the wall ran a gallery leading to the bedrooms clustered in a group at the north end of the house. This unorthodox, not to say highly un-English, arrangement, had been dictated by Darch's wife, an American from Swarthmore, Pennsylvania, with a lot of middle-aged charm, brown bangs, and a seductive American voice. It was to my young eyes one of the less likely outcomes of Anglo-American union. He was tall, big-domed and formidably silent. She was small, neat and outgiving. Indeed, if it hadn't been for her, the weekend would have been pretty grim.

For I was clearly 'on show', the fourth member of the unlikely quartet being a senior executive of Shell. He also was English and expatriate, in a different sense : very precise and glittery, with tight collars, striped shirts, and a clipped voice. He was inordinately proud of his French and kept the table in breathless suspense by an exposition of how important it was, in moulding the Anglo-Saxon soft palate and epiglottis to the maddening nasalities of French, to distinguish between the pronunciation of *puis* and *puits* (for example). He did it several times, demonstrating his excellence. I thought him a drag, and so, I think, did Darch, for he took me off to the billiards room and left his wife to discuss pronunciation with the executive. Here I could have recouped the general impression of open-mouthed undergraduate gaucherie undoubtedly conveyed. Unfortunately I'd forgotten the basic rule in billiards: always let your host win. Instead I gave a coruscating exhibition of skill, clearly the result of much misdirected energy at the University.

The Daimler took us all back to Melbourne early Monday morning and I thought I detected an atmosphere of frigidity. I may have been mistaken, and it may only have been due to my own awkwardness in the luxurious country-seat surroundings, with deferential house-boys, wine for dinner, and my exiguous clothes—including the patched underpants—laid out on the snowy bed by a French maid in high heels and a frilly cap. My discomfiture increased as the big Daimler rolled towards Melbourne, tyres squelching richly on the tarmac, when I remembered that I'd forgotten to leave a tip for the same maid. What would Mrs. Darch think? She'd shaken her charming bangs at me upon departure, but what would that mean in the light of my dereliction? I would of course write her an apologetic bread-and-butter letter, but I made up my mind then and there that a future in the Shell Oil Co. was too rich for me.

I think Darch (egged on no doubt by his colleague, who clearly didn't think much of my distinction between *puis* and *puits*) must have come to the same conclusion. At any rate when I told him a year later that I didn't propose to take up the offer of a cadetship in the organization—much as I appreciated its help in getting me through University—he gave a melancholy nod of his massive dome and said he quite understood. A few years later I met him in England on one of my visits there from Canada. He was living in Bloomsbury and sat wrapped in a travelling rug on a warm summer afternoon, sipping china tea with lemon, out of a Spode cup. His wife, her bangs only lightly peppered with grey, was as sprightly as ever.

* * *

Climbing slowly through the college hierarchy did in the end bring rewards of a sort. In our third year Hudspeth and I moved to a large corner study with a big fireplace, an outside view over Wyselaskie hall and also the incongruous residence provided for the theological professor, McLean. ('Ye may think the red brick doesn't blend with the sandstone,' said David Kennedy Picken, 'but it's more of a brick than a red ye ken'.) I was mounting the ladder of authority. Our fourth year saw us in one of the largest studies of all with great roaring fires, radio-phonograph and a position not markedly inferior to that of study I 40 where the literati hung out.

The inhabitants of this study generated an atmosphere of feverish wit which excited the envy and in some cases the suspicion of the less favoured, or the more sportive. The leader of the group ought to have been Ross Campbell whose study it was. Ross had been at Scotch College with us and had gone on to take first class honours in English. He was finally selected as Rhodes Scholar for the State of Victoria. He and the study upheld an excellent tradition, for his precursors had been Dick Latham, son of the Chief Justice of Australia, who was later killed in World War II, and K. C. Wheare, now Rector of Exeter College, Oxford and Vice-Chancellor of the University. Ross went on to Magdalen and later became a distinguished columnist in the *Sydney Morning Herald* and the *Sydney Daily Telegraph*. But at this time he was filling in the days before his departure for Oxford by tutoring in English and, like most of us, susceptibly embarking on a series of hopeless love affairs with highly unsuitable women. While he gyrated emotionally between the poles of hopeless involvement (girls) and witty detachment (Eng.Lit.) the atmosphere of the study was stabilized by the addition of other elements.

A disputatious ex-theolog provided the necessary note of crisp scepticism; for Ross, though witty, was apt to become too emotionally involved to be detached. He delivered a paper on Gloomy Deans in Eng. Lit. : Inge (Twentieth Century Blues); Farrar, of *Eric or Little by Little* (19th C. blues); Swift (18th C.) and Donne (17th C. or Jacobean). But he spoiled the effect, we thought, by allowing his involvement with the Victorian Era and its 'volleys of oaths' to enlarge the Farrar section at the expense of the others. What had started as an amusing essay became an exegesis of Victorian morality and sentiment.

The ex-theolog would have twitched his mantle blue much earlier, one felt, and gone capering off in a series of possibly irrelevant and probably tendentious but certainly balanced and crisply effective syllogisms. We had the suspicion, though, that he was a bit frivolous in the sense that no one as nimble in dispute could possibly be concerned with more than the surface of things. Besides, wasn't there something odd about a man who suddenly decided, in his late twenties, after a long training for the Ministry, that The Call he had received was not genuine? That God had dialled the wrong number? One could be tortured by doubts of course. Newman had been, to name only one; but our man with his crisp urbanity and his love of argument for its own sake—could such a will-o-the-wisp really be troubled by 'doubts'? We didn't mind his cynicism, but we wanted it to be based on something stronger than whim or a flighty fancy. The answer came in Geoff Sawer.

Into I 40 one day strode an unexpected apparition : thickset, darkly hirsute and with a gift for lightning complex exposition that held us enthralled. We remembered Geoff of course from school days. He'd been noted then for the fact that he started shaving before anyone else, and that he somehow managed to combine, to our envious admiration, brilliance at exams with witty story-telling. He was an odd ball, but no more. Now, five years later, here he was a full fledged Ll.B. and admitted to Ormond as a resident Tutor—who elected to share a study with undergraduates. His arrival—and this arrangement—were regarded with great suspicion by the heartier members of the College. For a man to hob-nob with seniors without having gone through initiation ceremonies : to partake of the sacred Ormond afflatus without having gone through the mill : above all, to share one of the best studies and perhaps engage in treacherous or subversive (certainly intellectual) talk behind seniors' backs—well, we'd have to jolly well *do* something about it.

Sawer was well aware of the resentment which his presence aroused. Nothing so enrages a conservative student as a really tough-minded intellectual. The ordinary swot or exam-fiend he can dismiss as a bore; the man interested in the arts as a queer. But a man who disdained even to be aware of his own ostracism; who joined, un-asked, in discussion on almost any subject; who demolished and obliterated his opponents with easy logic, while maintaining a not unfriendly smile; a man who, to cap it all, played a very good game of billiards : such a man was bound to be unpopular.

The Master realized this and very sensibly placed Sawer beyond the reach of the undergraduates' rage (and beyond the possibility of his baiting them) by insisting rigorously on his tutorial standing. He made Sawer sit at Head Table, and it was understood that he was not to frequent the Common Room. However he was allowed to continue his shared occupancy of I 40 with Ross Campbell, and the study quickly became the focal point of what little intellectual life the College possessed. Great was the joy of those admitted to this secret circle and great also the insatiable (and unsatisfied) curiosity of those outside and looking in. When the bull sessions (fuelled strictly on coffee and biscuits) enlarged to include *outsiders*—i.e. men who were not even living in at Ormond—curiosity and annoyance became about equally mixed. I was on the fringes and enjoyed the status which it conferred, but being a bit of a trimmer, I was also cagey of offending my more social or more athletic friends by complete identification. For this reason the Group denied me access to their really exhilarating bull sessions on, for example, sex in literature. I did, however, manage to infiltrate sufficiently deeply to get myself invited to one of the Bradshaws' parties.

To those undergraduates who aspired to drink life to the lees, aye, nor feel queasy, an invitation to The Bradshaws' Parties—there were many of them—was as much prized as an invitation to one of their more social colleagues to visit the mansion of Mrs. Benjamin Forsyth. Socially speaking I oscillated between these two poles.

The Bradshaws were young-marrieds in their mid-thirties who lived in a rambling house behind a tall cedar hedge in Kew. They had an undisclosed source of income—it was believed to be from a grocery chain—which in the early years of the Depression set them doubly apart. They also had a strong yearning to enter the world of bohemia and The Arts. To this end they were quite unashamed snappers-up both of the renowned and the raffish, on the fringes and in the midst of Melbourne's very modest and conventional bohemia. They were always willing to have a sprinkling of undergraduates and their girl-friends along as part of the decor—the University being considered vaguely *avant garde*. Melbourne bohemia was of the Garrick-Savage Club Variety: that is, highly institutionalized and self-conscious, riddled with social or journalistic hangers-on, and marked by such safe eccentricities as wide floppy black hats, flowing cravats and opera cloaks. Its leader had been George Lambert who affected long hair, a full ginger beard and a stock, and who modelled himself both in dress and in painting on the Augustus John of Edwardian days. One couldn't help feeling that Melburnians envied Sydney the Lindsay Brothers—but then Melbourne was always secretly envying Sydney. There was something about being in latitude 33.55 rather than in latitude 37.48 and away from the Southerly Buster, that made Anglo-Saxon blood—even 98.44 per cent pure—race madly. Sydney, we were reminded, was in the same latitude as Los Angeles; Melbourne of San Francisco. You could draw your own conclusions.

All Melbourne could produce in the way of non-representational art, and beyond the bravura of the society portrait, was the pale intimism of Max Meldrum, an attenuated member of the school of Bonnard and Vuillard. The lead given towards a national idiom by Streeton, MacGeorge and others of the Heidelberg School, was not picked up until a generation later, and in very different vein, by Drysdale, Dobell and Nolan. It all seemed exciting enough, though, to the Bradshaws; and to us youngsters the parties which their enthusiasm generated, and to which we could bring the girl-friend of the moment, and *no questions asked*, were deliriously unconventional.

Like most Australian parties of that era not dominated by social pretension, the key solvent was the homely keg of beer. An Aussie booze-up rarely went beyond that, and those who sampled the Old Court (Australian) whisky or Crystal Court (Australian) gin in a little cubby hole off the main room, or 'lounge', which had been cleared for dancing, were looked on as a bit odd. The 'niners' were normally set up on trestles, one in the lounge and the other in the back garden. In its own perhaps less brittle—and certainly less glossy—way the scene was very much like one of Gatsby's parties as described by Scott Fitzgerald.

Young couples lay smooching unreproved on the sofas under the bright lights, while men stood roaring and bellowing round the niner, deep in cricket and racing, and whether the racehorse Phar Lap had been deliberately poisoned by the bloody Yanks at Agua Caliente, or whether he just hadn't been able to stand the journey across the Pacific. Other couples stole off into bedrooms, being careful to lock the door, not for fear of being discovered but for fear of being pushed out to make room for the next couple. Around the niner in the garden a fight would usually develop and sooner or later *someone* had to walk along the top of the Bradshaws' twelve foot tall cedar hedge; and then he had to do it again but holding a schooner of beer in his hand. All the while the panatrope was blaring and cars kept pulling in and out with motors gunning in the night and headlamps cutting a swathe through milling, drinking roysterers, to light up a drunk asleep under a rhododendron or a couple, who hadn't been able to get a bedroom, locked on a rug under the hedge.

People made love uncomfortably in parked cars or drank beer on the sidewalk so that homebound citizens had to step fastidiously aside. And then some soulful fellow would start a fitful barbershop quartet out in the back garden, and the neighbours' windows would fly up and we'd be threatened with the police. At none of these parties, concerned though they were supposed to be with the arts, did I ever hear any coherent argument about painting or music or the theatre, though there was plenty of acrimonious debate on the merits of Aussie journalists, writers and poets—such as Edgar Holt —who had made a success outside Australia. For to the Kew bohemians, no less than to their more earthy brothers, the real challenge, the real excitement, the real possibility of success, lay 12,000 miles away in England. 'Home' in fact.

In all that milling confusion of bodies and booze there was only

SPEAKERS AT THE INTER-VARSITY DEBATES, HOBART, TASMANIA 1933. The Author, representing Melbourne University, is third from the left

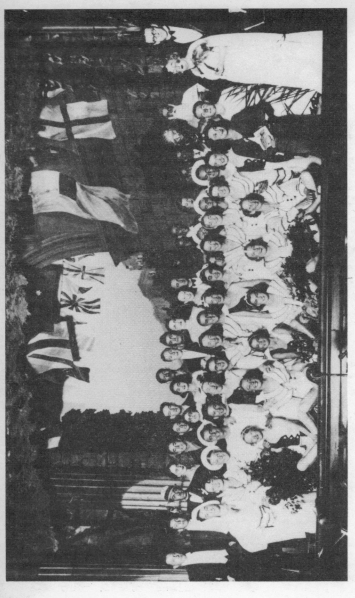

THE CAST OF *STUDE PRUNES*, COMEDY THEATRE, MELBOURNE 1933. The Author is standing tenth from the left; his future wife, Joan Burke, is kneeling eighth from the left

one place where you could be sure of quiet and an exquisite satisfaction in the eye of the storm. That was in the music room when Charles Zwar sat down—after customary and reasonable urging—at the Steinway, Charles was quite the most stimulating jazz pianist I have ever known. His style—one of firm and delicate tension—was in the framework of Duke Ellington, Carroll Gibbons, and the half-remembered Fred Elizalde. But the attack, the compressed poise, the bold rhythms so solidly maintained beneath the gorgeous arabesques were entirely his own. He had a high forehead, a thin face, a long bony nose and a slightly tremulous mouth. His concentration when playing was so paralysingly tense that he was known to all his friends and admirers as 'Ag'—short for 'Agony'. He played firmly but not loudly with a golden tone and many inventions. When teamed in double piano work, it was always *his* lid that lay open towards the audience. At the Bradshaws' parties, surrounded by a group of admirers who were quite content literally to sit on the floor at his feet, he rambled with delightful sophisticated ease, creating a little haven of quiet amid the brawling mob.

Ag was also a deft composer and his own lyricist, in the Coward-Cole Porter manner which we all affected in those days. We adored his innocently naughty songs and, though we couldn't sing them with his quivering urgency, we loved joining in the chorus: boys on the floor with girls in their arms; boys leaning over the piano; girls with their bosoms hanging over Ag's nimble fingers and heaving in concert with the plangent strings. Ag later went to England to gain the reputation that then seemed essential to Australians if they were to have any success in their own land. He became associated with Alan Melville and the two of them teamed up during and after World War II in the *Sweet and Low-Lower-Lowest* series. But those of us who had, as the saying goes, 'known him when', thought he rarely equalled the inspired relevance of his earlier songs: *You're my one wild oat* or *Look at the Damage you've Done*. Never mind; we hung on his words, issuing like cool flames from the trembling lips, below the thin sensuous nose; his music pouring from the attenuated powerful fingers that could stretch a twelfth with no trouble at all. Come to think of it, he made the Bradshaws' parties more memorable than all the drunken hoopla. Would that he had also attended the soirées of Mrs. Benjamin Forsyth.

These soirées, held in a large severe Italianate villa on the Olympian slopes of South Yarra, were something of an ordeal for the young. It wasn't just Mrs. Forsyth, it was her daughter Mrs. Price and in turn *her* daughters. The grandmother was a formidable dowager with a pile of silvery hair and a pair of piercing brown eyes. She moved in a world of charity balls, elaborate musicales, furred rugs, glassed-in chauffeurs and speaking tubes. The mother was, as someone observed, less brilliant than brilliantine, and she scrambled up the local social ladder with unexampled ferocity and determination. She could size you up as husband-meat, decoration or chore boy in the wink of an eye, and it was she who pulled the levers behind the elaborate facade of highly polished and calculating hospitality. The girls were the sheeny debs of my youth and one often met them at 9 Darling Street, a commodious and ample colonial house in South Yarra available for hire when Mothers launched their young, and where the socially acceptable deb dances were held. They made frequent trips Home (as well as Abroad) and one year returned from America with the first lacquered finger nails ever seen in Melbourne. Young men gaped but also felt vaguely uneasy. Briefly, the Price girls and the Price menage, though desired, as the unattainable usually is, proved too rich for the blood. Nowhere was this clearer than at Mrs. Forsyth's soirées.

Great waves of heady perfume and rich winey food, great gales of brittle laughter and conversation floated out into the winter night as one approached. Tails and white tie had been insisted upon as *de rigueur*, for the Prices were nothing if not starchy. Yet as you entered the great hall with its arched portico, its depressing dark-brown panelling and the heavier type of chinoiseries—porcelain jars, fretted wooden screens, red silk curtains, bhoddisatvas of dubious authenticity—tails seemed to your innocent eye unnecessary. For where was the orchestra? Where was the dance floor? (And where was the supper?) The bulk of the guests were of the older generation, looking, as they always do to the young, so terribly thick. Thick through the middle: men's rib cages lined with fatty tissue and protruding under waffle-piqué white waistcoats to push the reveres of tails back to the point where shirt-sleeve shoulders began to show; women's bosoms heavily cantilevered and wired into immense blubbery superstructures. Thick furs (some of them a bit nibbled), tall white collars on which elderly men impaled their jowls (the latter often with a bit of tell-tale white bristle still lingering); voluminous dresses of too much ruched and flounced satin and crepe which in the days before zip-fasteners bulged and strained at their hooks and eyes in the most unlikely and revolting way. Painted faces with downy upper lips that caught the powder; powdered faces where the powder flaked and gathered round the wrinkles; scarlet jabbering mouths in the middle, with stringy dewlaps. Sometimes the mouth was askew of the real mouth in imagined flattery, but frighteningly grotesque.

Among the pricked and powdered, ponderously moving like great whales or half-blind elephants and rhinos, flitted the young: pimply,

spare, willowy and ill at ease. No seats for them. At Mrs. Forsyth's
they sat on cushions on the floor (girls) or on the floor itself (boys)
with much damage to tails crushed and dusty on the parquetry.
Huddled there below the bums and bellies of the mighty they would
listen to a chamber orchestra perform the more showy works of Liszt,
Saint-Saëns and Tchaikowsky; or hug their knees lugubriously while
sopranos burbled the air from *Thaïs* or *One fine day* from *Madame
Butterfly*. One's attention wandered during these recitals to young
contemporaries sprawled languidly around below the knees and skirts
of the powerful, and one might hope perhaps for an assignation at
the enormous and very starchy supper which followed. Though
here again the young were at a disadvantage for the old elbowed
them aside in their rush for the trough, and gobbled and masticated
their food with horrible greed.

The split between the generations was complete. Conversation,
since it consisted mostly of gossip (no one gave a damn about the
quality of the performance that had just finished) was conducted on
two separate levels. Usually the young huddled into a corner with
their backs to the pots and bosoms, and flirted and hoped they would
not be noticed. In this they were usually not disappointed. Most agoniz-
ing of all was finding the hostess to say good night and thank you.
A backbencher trying to catch the Speaker's eye had an easier time
of it than an undergraduate in white tie and tails. With his girl
waiting patiently for him, in the evening dress she had made herself
and wished she could have imported from Molyneux or Patou, or
even afforded to buy at the local Myer Emporium, he sought in
vain to catch either the vulture's orb of Mrs. Forsyth or the glaucous
eye of Mrs. Price.

'Mrs. . . .'

'Just a minute, dear. Good night, Sir Hector, I'm so glad you
came. Yes, wasn't it? Yes, I'll tell her. My dear Hermione, must
you go? *Good* night, darling. Walter! How sweet of you!'

'Mrs. Price—I—'

'With you in a moment, dear. Why Joan dear, this is most kind
of you! Yes, she was in rather good voice tonight. I agree. The air
from *Thaïs*. Harold, how nice of you to have come! *Did* you? Dr.
Schnitzel! What a pleasure. Good night.

'Mrs. Price . . . Ijustwantedtosaythankyouverymuchforthelovely-
party.'

'Oh *thank* you. So glad you . . . Penelope darling! You're not
going? But, my dear, it's only eleven thirty! *Must* you. . . ?'

We bolted out into the night, free at last and fearful of missing
the last tram. Next time we would come into our own. At a dance
at 9 Darling Street perhaps, or at a great charity Ball in the Mel-

bourne Town Hall where youth, because the evening was so strenuous, was triumphant: gay couples in fancy dress whirling the night away while the older generation sat panting on the sidelines slumped in their gilt spindly cane-bottomed chairs sipping champagne.

Despite all this outpouring of energy we were immortal; we could go on till five in the morning. We still managed to hurl ourselves into the bookwork and swotting required to pass our exams and get our degrees. We worked all morning, played games all afternoon, danced all night. Yet between them all we found plenty of time to stew over weighty tomes in the library, to consult fellows in the next study who were on the same course, to con again with vexed brow the scribbled notebooks containing the winnowed wisdom of Professor Cowling and Professor Scott. The third year was the year of the thesis or dissertation, and in this Scotty proved far from helpful.

'I was thinking, sir, of a study of labour conditions in the sheep shearing trade in the nineties.'

'Vewy intewesting.'

'Would you approve of it as a subject, sir?'

'It is not my business to appwove or disappwove. It is the wesponsibility of each student to suggest his own subject.'

'But, sir.'

'—and pwepare it.'

'But would you agree that this would be a suitable *subject*, sir?'

'I would neither agwee or disagwee. Bit I would wead it when it was pwesented to me.'

'Yes, sir.'

I had selected, without much enthusiasm or any help from Scotty, a study of the history of South Sea Islanders on the Queensland sugar plantations. Almost at once I found that most of the important work had already been done by a woman who had written a history of the White Australia Policy. I pored lugubriously over her book. It seemed to me that there were perhaps a few nooks and crannies that she hadn't explored? Kanakas? Sir Thomas McIlraith? Sir Samuel Griffith? The annexation of Papua? Yes, I would take a fling at it. I soon discovered that much of the key original source material was not in Melbourne at all, but in the Mitchell Library in Sydney.

Sydney!

I looked up from my desk in one of the spokes of the immense wheel that radiated outward from the dais of the invigilator at the great Melbourne Public Library. I gazed at the immense circular glass and cast-iron ceiling modelled on that of the British Museum and I suddenly saw through the dirty glass the sparkling blue of Sydney Harbour; the blinding yellow sands of Coogee and Bondi; the great arc of the Harbour Bridge. A world of sub-tropical passion and languorous nights—and all in the cause of learning, too.

Sydney, here I come!

Chapter Eleven

SYD—NEE!!

EVERY Melburnian was secretly envious of Sydney. No matter how much we congratulated ourselves on being Australia's financial capital, no matter how much we boasted of our superiority in education, our leadership in religion, our solid reliability, our time-tested integrity (of which the politicians were forever reminding us) we had to admit that Sydney had what Melbourne lacked: glamour. This was just precisely what we didn't have. We could excuse the Sydneysiders their Harbour; pardon them their Bridge; forgive them for being the oldest city in Australia (1788 vs. our own 1834); even swallow, without too much resentment, the fact that they were bigger than we were. But the drama, the excitement, the semi-tropical aura, the air of being a metropolis, this we found difficult to accept and impossible to forgive. We tried the sour grapes approach. 'So terribly *American* doncher know mah deah' as Melbourne dowagers were wont to observe (Sydney was about as American as Barcelona or Antwerp). We tried direct denigration: 'They're so boastful, such terrible skites the Sydneysiders'. We tried ignoring them, but Sydney—big, brawling, bold and brassy, as Chester Wilmot has described it—had the unforgiving edge. We envied them while they envied us not at all. For who, except in periods of financial crisis, envies middle class virtue and solid common sense?

What made Sydney so different? I believe John Pringle may have the answer. He has written most eloquently of the three winds of Sydney.[1] The south wind that comes booming up from Antarctica to remind Sydney of her temperate zone and bustling cockney origin; the west wind that blows hot and dry from behind her back reminding Sydney of the presence of the enigmatic, incredibly old semi-desert of a continent at whose edge she huddles; finally the east wind, blowing in from the tropical Pacific carrying with it languorous suggestions of lotus eating. We in Melbourne had the

[1] *Australian Accent* by John Douglas Pringle, Chatto and Windus, 1958.

first two winds, the Southerly Buster from Antarctica, and the Brickfielder from the oven of Central Australia. But we didn't have the third. We were too far south, too much 'round the corner' from the Pacific. The piquant triple mixture was denied us, and we could only envy.

Sydney: New York in the South Pacific!

Sydney: Botany Bay and the convicts.

Which was it? Well, I would soon find out. I composed a careful letter to Cousin Hugh Poynter and booked a second class return fare, sitting up all night on the train. Cousin Hugh was the son of my great-grandmother's sister and hence my first cousin twice removed. But he seemed a lot closer than that because of his jolly conspiratorial manner, tonsure of rumpled greyish-white hair and shrewd brown eyes. He had landed in Australia by a series of chances as remote as those which had governed my own landfall. His father, Sir Edward Poynter, had been in his day President of the Royal Academy for which service he had received, in the rather excessive way in which the Victorians honoured the pillars of the established order, a baronetcy. On his death this had passed to Hugh's elder brother Ambrose, and Hugh would normally have expected to look forward to being known only as Hugh Poynter, Esq., O.Medj. (a decoration conferred upon him by the Sublime Porte, prior to World War I, for services to the Ottoman Debt). But Ambrose died unexpectedly and Hugh inherited, while his bride, the former Molly Dickenson of Binghamton, N.Y., became unexpectedly Lady Poynter. After the War Hugh joined Baldwin's, the big steel firm whose chief pillar was his first cousin Stanley Baldwin, and was sent to manage a new plant in Toronto, Canada. Five years later he moved on to a similar position as head of Baldwin's & J.C.M. (Australia) Ltd. in Sydney where he arrived in 1927. We were by this time old Australia hands having been in the country since 1920, and when Hugh came over to Melbourne on a business trip a few years later we told him so.

'That's all right,' he said, 'I'll make a dinkum Aussie sooner than you. I'm from Sydney!'

How we howled and roared. But how we appreciated that a Bart. and an O.Medj. should enter so gaily into the Great Australian Game. It was to this gay dog that I now addressed myself. His wife had died a couple of years ago and I thought—selfishly I suppose—well, that means there'll be room for guests in his house. Sure enough a most cordial answer came back and in high spirits I embarked on the *Spirit of Progress*, the crack train of the Victorian Railways which did the 197 miles to the New South Wales border in four hours. What a fine beginning to an exciting trip. The train drawn by its great 4-8-4 Pacific locomotive with the recessed chimney and wind baffles pulled smoothly out of dull old Spencer Street and soon we were growling purposefully up the long hill to the Kilmore Gap. At Seymour we wolfed the usual cold pies drenched in tomato sauce. When we climbed aboard again it was dark and we droned on through the Ned Kelly country—Euroa, Wangaratta, Glenrowan—and then there came the surprising and lengthy roar of iron on iron. Criss-crossed girders flickered by, the moon shone on a mighty river : the Murray, 800 miles east of where I'd crossed it at Murray Bridge on that trip to Adelaide—that dull provincial city—so long ago. We pulled into Albury, N.S.W., 'All change!'

It is only in the last five years that the break of gauge between Australia's two principal cities has been eliminated. A third rail has now been laid on the Victorian side, enabling expresses to travel the 586 miles between the two cities without changing. But in those days the proud *Spirit of Progress* halted at Albury, because the Victorian 5ft. 3ins. came to an abrupt end, and the remaining 389 miles of the journey were over the N.S.W. so-called 'standard' gauge (how that annoyed the Victorians) of 4ft. 8½ins.

But the discomfort of having to alight late in the evening and tramp the long mournful asphalt of Albury's platform could be mitigated by sneering at the N.S.W. rolling stock. This was then wooden and antiquated and rattly; the compartments were smelly and in the second class lined with straw ticking; the engine was a sad disappointment—old, stiff and dirty. But all was soon forgotten in the excitement of bowling through the Riverina at night. The station boards swam by in a nest of pricking lights : Wagga, Junee, Cootamundra, Yass. Fitful sleep possessed us and at some indeterminate time the landscape became grey instead of black and we were out of the endless plains and into the high N.S.W. coastal hills. The sun came up at Goulburn, deep in the forested ranges, and long yellow bars of light struck through the trees. A little later it was Moss Vale and we all piled out on to the early morning winter platform, rimed with frost, to bolt once again meat pies, tomato sauce and strong tea amid the yelling mob served by the sour waitresses, yawning at us in their grubby white uniforms.

Back in the coach with a full belly, what a comfort to see the rich undulating pastoral country slide smoothly by ! New South Wales, Cradle of Australian hopes. 'The Ma State' as *The Bulletin* called it in affectionate banter. Double tracked now. Bowral. Gosh ! That was where Bradman came from ! Imagine having seen that sign. Mangalore. Not Bangalore? No, you clot, that's in India. A huge curving descent near Picton and we're down on the coastal plains and very soon the outlying suburbs of Sydney come into view. Disappointing at first: red brick and terracotta rather like Melbourne, but of an immense, an unbelievable extent. Now squat mean-looking electric trains come hurtling into view. Trains on a Sunday morning? This is different. The houses thicken; the gantries pile up like a shuffled deck of playing cards; factories—miles on miles of them—then a maze of twisting shining rails, a knuckle or fistful of junior skyscrapers up ahead and looming over all the immense yet delicate arc of the great Harbour Bridge—largest in the world! (Alas, the Yanks had added three feet to the Kill-van-Kull Bridge in Greater New York so it cannot be the longest.) The view is blocked as we slide into an immense station. Beneath its clangorous glassed-in roof people pour out of the train like treacle into a drain. In the vast confusion a single familiar face with a shrewd liquid brown eye beneath a grey Homburg.

'Cousin Hugh!'

'Welcome to Sydney!'

* * *

'There's one thing I want you to know,' said Hugh as we drove in his big red Vauxhall up the approaches to the Harbour Bridge.

'Yes, of course.' I wasn't really listening. The slope of the great highway flanked by electric railroad lines, the huge spider's web of steel girders caging us from above, engaged my rapt attention. Cousin Hugh droned on through a shroud of rich cigar smoke.

'. . . of Linda. She's a very dear person. We see a lot of each other. And I'd like you to be kind to them.'

'Oh yes of course, Cousin Hugh. Um. Be kind to who?'

'To the girls of course.'

'Oh yes. Who are they again?'

'I've just told you,' he said with slight asperity.

We were right inside the enormous cage of the arch now. The Harbour glittered 175 feet below; traffic rushed by on either side.

'You can't have been listening. They're Linda's daughters.'

'Oh yes. I'm sorry. Are they young or old?'

Electric trains tried to ram themselves down our throat as they hurtled by. A big liner began to glide smoothly beneath the Bridge and all movement, including our own, insensibly achieved a new dimension.

'I'm never quite sure,' said Hugh. 'I suppose Jocelyn's about eighteen, and young Shirley must be sixteen now. As I said, I'd like you to be kind to them because . . .'

But it was lost in the roar of traffic which had now become an excited buzzing in my ears. Be kind to a girl of 'about eighteen'.

That was filling my holiday cup to overbrimming. Would I ever be able to keep my eyes on the books at the Mitchell Library? Hugging the knowledge ecstatically to my belly I observed our sedate progress through North Sydney and then up the Pacific Highway towards Wahroonga where Hugh had told me he lived. Still the same terracotta, the same petrol service stations, the long line of small shops and detached bungalows swelling into suburban shopping ganglia at Chatswood, at Killara, at Pymble; but all illumined now by the fierce light of adventure. The surrounding and occasionally intrusive bush was scrubby and the Blue 'Mountains' in the distance seemed to be an escarpment rather than our own romantic horsts and camelbacks. But they were blue! Supposing this girl was plain? Or had buck teeth? But no, she couldn't. It was impossible in the country of Governor Phillip, the founder of Australia; of John MacArthur who brought the first merino sheep to the island continent; of Blaxland, Lawson and Wentworth, the immortal trio who first breached the Blue Mountains; of Governor Bligh of *The Bounty*; of the New South Wales Corps and the traffic in rum; of Bathurst and the early goldfields; of the great rivers ringing with the names of early governors and statesmen: Lachlan, Macquarie, Gwydir, Castlereagh.

An afterthought struck me. 'Where's Linda's husband?' I asked. Hugh was now on his second cigar lit from the lighter in the dashboard above the red leather upholstery. He coughed.

'He's in South Africa,' he said shortly. Maybe it was the cigar smoke. It was on the tip of my tongue to ask, 'Is he coming back?' but some instinct held me in. Just as well not to be *too* curious.

We pulled off the main Pacific Highway into a steep and leafy street. Spring was in the air and something else: the languorous wind from the Pacific, sending its warm wet fingers beckoning through the flowering gums and the wistaria. The car turned into a big garden terraced with flowers and hidden by a tall locust hedge. Embowered among the trees was a large two-storey red brick home with a slate roof and mock tudor gables. An elderly Scots housekeeper with white fuzzy permed hair opened the door. But Hugh took me round to the side where an arched patio overlooked the flowers and the terrace and a reticent fountain. We walked up the slope towards the patio. Two women stood there: a plump middle-aged dowager with a Katherine Mansfield fringe, and a twinkly smile; a gawky girl with bands on her teeth. Hugh introduced me, to Linda and Shirley, put an arm round Linda and gave her a good kiss. My heart sank.

'Hullo, Shirley,' I said.

'Where's Jocy?' said Hugh.

'She'll be down in a minute,' said Linda, adding wickedly, 'she wanted to tidy herself up for Graham.'

I laughed uneasily and started to gas with young Shirl, when behind me a voice like bees buzzing in honey said 'You're Graham'.

I turned and there stood a tall but cuddly girl with genuine ash-blonde hair and warm smile. And an intoxicating voice.

'You're Jocelyn,' I said.

She gave me an appraising conspiratorial look. 'That's right. How did you guess?'

* * *

In a curious way it was like coming home because in Cousin Hugh's house were paintings and pieces of furniture and *objets d'art* which were part of the common inheritance of the vast Clan of which Hugh and I were both members. I'd seen such treasures no-where (except in our own little suburban house in Melbourne) since leaving my grandparents' home in London as a small boy twelve years before. And now, unavoidably, we come to The Clan, or rather to the MacDonald Sisters, for it was they who brought it into being.[1]

In the endpapers of Windham Baldwin's book there is a genealo-gical tree. It extends far enough down to include the author of the book among the 2 s. & 4 d. of Stanley Baldwin, and his second cousin, my mother, who is listed as 'Angela (Thirkell)'. It doesn't quite in-clude me and my brothers because we are of the next generation, though in fact 'Little' Baldwin is only eight years older than I am. But it does quite clearly show Hugh, his three wives, his first cousin-ship to Stanley Baldwin and Rudyard Kipling, and his first cousinship (twice removed) to me. It was of course these illustrious names which sickened me of distinguished relatives during my school days in Aus-tralia, for the very obvious reason that schoolmasters, scoutmasters, clergymen and others were always hinting—and not too subtly either —that because of these connections 'We expect great things of you, etc., etc.'

George Browne MacDonald, though his family came originally from Skye, enters the story as a circuit parson for the Methodist Con-ference. He married Hannah Jones from Wales, at Devonport in 1826 and he had one of those masterful Victorian families of eleven. We are concerned only with the four sisters who produced the illustrious progeny. These were Alice (1827-1910), Georgiana (1840-1920), Agnes (1843-1906), and Louisa (1845-1925). Alice married Lockwood Kip-ling whose son was Rudyard; Georgiana married Edward Burne-Jones,

[1] *The MacDonald Sisters* by A. W. Baldwin (Earl Baldwin of Bewdley), Peter Davies 1960, gives a good factual account.

the Pre-Raphaelite painter, whose daughter was my maternal grand-mother; Agnes married Edward Poynter P.R.A. whose younger son was Hugh; Louisa married Alfred Baldwin whose only child was Stanley. In his book *The MacDonald Sisters* 'Little' Baldwin gives few clues, at least to me, as to how four penniless daughters of a methodist parson in the Midlands should have attracted the attentions of a group of such diverse and unusual men: a museum curator, archaeologist and Indian civil servant; a masterful steel-master; and two distinguished painters, one orthodox and the other highly original. Looking at their portraits one surmises that it was a question of looks, intelligence and extreme toughness of character, plus a willingness (since they could only rise in the world) to take a chance on young and unknown men.

The next generation—that is, Rudyard, Margaret Burne-Jones, Stanley Baldwin and, to a much lesser extent, Hugh's elder brother Ambrose who was fifteen years older than he was—holidayed together as first cousins in and around Rottingdean in Sussex. My mother has described the adjacent family houses, grouped round the pond and the village green, in her book *Three Houses*:[1] the Burne-Joneses at North End House, the Baldwins at The Dene and the Kiplings at The Elms. The next generation after theirs may be exemplified by my mother, who was the daughter of Margaret Burne-Jones and J. W. Mackail, O.M., and by the author of *The MacDonald Sisters*.

By this time, however, as happens often in large families, the generations in their descent to modern times had got out of phase. Thus Mother, that is Angela McInnes and later Angela Thirkell, was born in 1890, but Hugh Poynter of the previous generation was born in 1882, so that they were contemporaries almost in the same way as 'Little' (b. 1904) and myself (b. 1912). But the great thing about a clan is that whether the generative steps descend by steep or shallow risers, the members of the clan can always get together and compare notes about the others. Family gossip on a large scale is a delicious enterprise and during my three weeks at Hugh's Sydney home, Tikinui, I learned a lot of amusing and some discreditable stories and also compared common attributes based on blood. There seemed to be quite a number of these. The residue of shared blood was small. Hugh had a quarter of the genes of the Rev. George Browne MacDonald, whereas I had only a sixteenth. But we discovered a common streak of raffishness including a love of sparkling burgundy and monopole magnums, yet at the same time a common vein of Puritanism which expressed itself in my prim and unnecessary distaste of the relationships between Hugh and Linda, and his distaste for the way we young people danced cheek to cheek.

[1] Oxford University Press 1931.

In point of fact what Hugh and Linda did was none of my damned business. Hugh had been a widower for three years and Linda was divorced. But young people, who are perfectly willing to entwine themselves on the slightest pretext, have a *pudeur* about middle-aged and elderly people showing affection or uxoriousness in public. Somehow in bodies so flabby and wrinkled it seems a profanation of their own ark of love. They have yet to learn that on the longest journey companionship is the greatest boon and, apart from faith, with which ever fewer are blessed as the century rolls by, the only thing that makes life bearable. In our prudishness we youngsters were horribly embarrassed by the nods and becks that passed between Hugh and Linda. It seemed a coarse and grotesque parody of our own yearnings.

'But I spose it's all right really,' she said one night, disentangling herself from my grasp. 'Because they're going to be married as soon as they can.' I nodded portentously.

They were married the following year and when I next visited Sydney it was to find the entire feminine brood moved into Tikinui, Linda with Hugh in the best bedroom, Jocelyn and Shirley in the two guest bedrooms and me on a camp bed in the 'sleep-out'. Later Hugh took his women round the world to show them to all the Baldwin and Mackail and Howard and Kipling relatives. They returned on the Dutch ship *Baloeran* with seven cabin trunks and in high spirits. Alas, it lasted only five years. Linda died and in 1939 Hugh married for the third time.

This however was a long way in the future and for the present Hugh was unmarried and living a pleasant, indeed to me an idyllic bachelor existence in a large and very comfortable house. We breakfasted together on orange juice and papaya on the patio beneath the wistaria with warm damp Sydney sunshine. About 8.30 he would leave to drive thirteen miles down to the great Bridge and over it into Sydney where, as President of Baldwins & J.C.M. Ltd., he had an imposing office in a fourteen-storey building which impressed me a great deal, for in Melbourne the 132 ft. building-line of those days held us to twelve storeys.

I couldn't quite grasp exactly what Hugh did, because whenever I visited the office I used to find him with his feet on the desk reading *Anthony Adverse* or *The Story of San Michele*. Quite unashamedly too, and a couple of smiling secretaries to beckon me in. Then we'd walk a few yards to the downtown garage, get into the red Vauxhall and speed across the Bridge and up to Linda's house in Pymble, pick up the three women and go back to Tikinui. I supposed that Hugh must 'know' people, or be 'very influential'. He was on the board of directors of a number of companies including Bond's Hosiery, and when he took us to the annual staff dance I noticed that he was treated with much deference by the company executives. Perhaps it was the name—Baldwin—or the Bart. Sir Hugh Poynter, Bart. That was a phrase to conjure with in still semi-colonial Sydney society.

Tikinui was crammed with remembrances of ampler Victorian days. In addition to the family heirlooms there were expensive and indeed opulent middle-eastern bric-à-brac picked up by Hugh in his tours of Turkey and Spain. A long low-ceilinged comfortable drawing room, reached by a step, was 'wall-to-wall' not in beige broadloom but in rich Turkey carpets, and Persian and Afghan rugs. Besides the normal piano and panatrope there were gate-legged hexagonal ebony tables inlaid with mother of pearl; scalloped circular brass trays from Lake Van and great shallow burnished copper pitchers from Isfahan; bits of mosaic from the Mosque at Shiraz; hookahs and hubble-bubbles beneath anaemic water colours by Poynter and Lord Leighton. Goya prints climbed up the stairway and the guest rooms had water colours by Philip Burne-Jones, the only and melancholy painter-son of his more distinguished father. All was oriental, otiose and just a shade showy.

It was the same at meals. We might have caramel custard instead of crême brulée, if that was all the cook could rise to, but we'd be sure to have sparkling burgundy or else Australian champagne. There were always cigars but never cigarettes. Hugh had pointy Turkish slippers and a flowered bath-robe of more than eastern splendour. The bookshelves were lined with first editions of Kipling's works, J. W. Mackail's *Life of William Morris*, my great-grandmother's *Memoirs of Edward Burne-Jones*, tales of Hajji Baba of Isfahan, Frazer's *Golden Bough* and wonderful old numbers of *Punch*. It was very difficult to work in such an atmosphere and even though I had set up a desk in my bedroom I'd be constantly enticed down by Hugh's racy talk or to dance with the girls to the panatrope.

After such evenings I would often find it difficult to get up in the morning. Hugh indulgently let me sleep in and I'd catch the train down to Sydney and my day's studying at the Mitchell Library. The first underground railway in Australia had just been extended and it was very exciting to ride high over the Harbour on the great arc and then plunge beneath the city's knuckle of skyscrapers to rush with a roar into Wynyard underground station, then cross the teeming canyons of Pitt and Castlereagh Streets and mount the steep hill towards Macquarie Street fronting the great open park of the Domain, and enter the very sober portals of the Mitchell Library.

I soon found that the documents I wished to consult were very handily contained in a small section of the library under the care of an indulgent middle-aged spinster who allowed me to take them into a small room where I had my own desk and chair, and might leave them there overnight. This kindness greatly assisted me in my study of the legislative labyrinth and the political maze through which the unfortunate Kanakas were dragged at the behest of the Queensland sugar planters until such time as popular pressure and union militancy forbade the importation of Polynesian labour.

I learned of the nefarious doing of 'Blackbirders'—freelance owner-captains of luggers and schooners who shanghaied unsuspecting Polynesians, crammed them below hatches in conditions not greatly different from those of the slave ships of the eighteenth century, and sold them as indentured labour for the Queensland sugar plantations. I learned of the activist lobbying of the Aborigines' Protection Society and the Church Missionary Society, and how they pulled the strings in far-off London that made the Queensland government jump through hoops. I learned how those wily old politicians, Sir Thomas McIlraith and Sir Samuel Griffith (caricatured by a local newspaper cartoonist as the two-headed 'Griffilraith'), persuaded the British government to support their annexation of Papua. All this and a lot more in the mornings, and sometimes even in the afternoon after a sandwich lunch, provided I could keep my eyes off the Domain and the towers of the Australian Mutual Provident Society and St. Mary's Cathedral, and my thoughts off the girls.

Often of course I couldn't and I'd wander dazed and bemused from the mountainous mass of words in the Library to explore the city. To me the metropolis seemed enormous. It had a population of about a million and a half in those days and must have seemed both provincial and antipodean to alien eyes. But to my own fascinated gaze it did truly seem like the New York of the South Pacific. Of course I hadn't seen New York then, or London or Paris or Rome. But to a twenty-year-old Sydney was the embodiment of all that a great city means to a young man: daring irresponsibility; the intoxication of loneliness; the sense of being one with a milling crowd; exciting anonymity and anonymous participation. Drama with a big D.

I took a tram to King's Cross and watched the equivocal women on their balconies greet the harbour lights, spearing in a long shimmer right across the water into the shop windows, just as they did in *Darlinghurst Nights*. This wonderful book with poems by Kenneth Slessor and illustrations by Virgil, was then enjoying a long run in *Smith's Weekly*. Reading it in staid old Melbourne it had seemed unbelievable. Yet here it was: the women in sweaters and tight skirts among the kosher beef shops, the salami and the liverwurst. Why, it might almost be Naples or Vienna!

I wandered up Castlereagh Street and thought how stimulating a narrow twisting canyon could be in comparison to our own grid system of streets 99 feet wide. The shopping crowds on the sidewalks seemed to me to be purposefully hurrying to great occasions. The clattering underground, as it burrowed under the heart of the city towards Central, was in my eyes glamorously divorced from the grey mass of creaking humanity which filled it, bound for a thousand identical suppers of cold cuts, limp lettuce, tea and tomato sauce.

Martin Place, flanked by the big banks and with its own Cenotaph I accepted at the Sydneysiders' valuation: Whitehall in the antipodes. I wandered along Macquarie Street where the city's cliff came to an abrupt halt before the raging surf of the Domain, complete with its own antipodean 'Speakers' Corner'. A short walk away, beyond the bus and taxi ranks, was the Archibald Memorial Fountain, that strange baroque monument to the combatively nationalist editor of the Sydney *Bulletin*. He had sponsored, fed, paid, bullied and cajoled the chroniclers of Australia's exhilarating march towards Federation: Henry Lawson, Victor Daley, Phil May, Low, Will Dyson, Norman Lindsay. What a grand group they had been! My adolescence yearned outward to them to be identified with a surge of self-identification which, because it had taken place a generation ago, had for me the sanctity of received writ. I didn't realize that because of this I couldn't live it all over again myself. These men had been participants when I was unborn or in my cradle. Could I ever be worthy of their noble rage?

I went with Hugh to Packie's Club, haunt of the flowing ties, spotted foulards, black floppy hats dear to John or Lautrec, silver-topped canes, flowered waistcoats and raging egos. In one room was Norman Lindsay's agonizingly Edwardian morality piece, drawn with wicked accuracy to play on the heartstrings of the susceptible and induce a formidable sense of *memento mori*. Three women in wide hats, tight bodices and flowing ankle length skirts, glared out with a haunted expression into the smoking room strewn with copies of the *Sphere*, the *Tatler* and the *Illustrated London News*. Beneath, the legend:

> 'We walk along the gas-lit streets
> In a dreadful row we three
> The woman I was, the woman I am
> And the woman I'll someday be.'

Kipling-Service-ese at its most effective.

Down at Circular Quay the ferries danced and twitched their way over to Double Bay, Rose Bay, Taronga, and Manly. The great bridge was supposed to have thrown them into the discard, left them rotting in ease by Lethe Wharf. But their criss-crossed wakes and busy belching funnels belied this as they skittered across the Harbour. Our 'Arbour'. I took a trip to Manly across its intertwined convoluted arms and twisting channels. The ferry stopped at one end of an avenue of Norfolk Island Pines. At the other end grey surf, surging across the Tasman from far-off New Zealand, pounded fiercely on a beach of sad grey sand. The mighty combers with their arching necks seemed to come from a great waste of ocean and as they crashed noisily into seething oblivion one forgot the city at one's back and saw only the terrible loneliness of the bottom of the world.

This mood somehow persisted when I returned to the city. The crowd became the faceless multitude; the incessant drone of the city became an angry meaningless roar. The busy hum of men became the aimless buzzing of insects. I was in a predictable mood of youthful misanthropy and should have traced its roots to a lovers' tiff. Instead I explored the city more ruthlessly, daring it to prove me wrong. I went on a great circular tour of the residential and industrial suburbs by electric train, fetching a long loop from North Sydney up to Hornsby and back through Pennant Hills to Parramatta and the smoking factories of Lidcombe and Strathfield. In thirty miles I was never out of sight of the endless panorama of red brick, terracotta, cement, steel and girders. Lonely lights blinked red, yellow and orange as burnished steel rails leaped in the glare. Spuming smoke raced livid across the sky from fires surging beneath it. The catenary caged in my speeding train. Crowds waited on a score of curving platforms, their faces obliterated by the *Sun* and the *Daily Telegraph*. Who *were* these millions of people and to whom could they conceivably belong? In fact they belonged warmly to a thousand cosy lounges with their cuppas and radios and H.P. sauce bottles in crocheted jackets, and it was only I who was lonely.

I tried another tack. I deserted the great ria or drowned valley which is Sydney Harbour and travelled north to the Hawkesbury. Here the intractable hardness of the Australian continent was vividly exposed in rocky geological contortions. The shores of the Hawkesbury were solid yellow-brown rock, thinly dotted with the interminable olive grey bush. The Hawkesbury itself was more enormous and more convoluted than Sydney Harbour, another drowned valley of immense proportions, squirming inland to a fortress of rock three thousand feet high. The Blue Mountains. Somewhere between the fringes of the encroaching sea and this forbidding eroded rampart of gneiss and conglomerate lay green pasture, fat cattle and placid rivers. Here the early settlers at last began to be self-supporting in foodstuffs after almost starving between the landings of the First Fleet in 1788 and the Second Fleet in 1790. They had tried with mattock and hoe to wrest a living from the land about Port Jackson and Botany Bay, but all they had found was rock and scrub and scenery. There was a little pasture along the Nepean near Penrith at the foot of the great rampart, but when the pioneer settlers tried pushing up the valleys that led into the interior they ended up, time and again, facing a vertical wall of rock. That tantalizing blue line. What lay beyond it?

At length Blaxland, Lawson and Wentworth succeeded in solving the mystery. They tackled the rocky tors instead of the valleys and emerged on a broken plateau across which, by precarious necks and saddles, they penetrated eventually to the rolling landward slope of the great fertile Australia which lies beyond the narrow coastal fringe. The Blue Mountains stood revealed as a great eroded scarp; not mountains in the true sense at all. The continent stood revealed as an enormous shallow saucer sloping gently inland from its seaward edge. The rocky indented shore was recognised now as a thin sliver of unrequited and perhaps unrequitable gritty stone. Penned in between the scarp and the sea for twenty-six years Australia could now expand across the ranges into limitless rolling park-like pasture with room for perhaps a hundred million sheep, grazing by great rivers which flowed inland towards the central desert. At once N.S.W. jumped from a semi-penal colony clinging to the edge of a rockbound alien coast, to the granary and the wool-shed of the world. The ironical touch was that, over a hundred years later, Sydney still exacted tribute in fullest measure from its rich productive hinterland and over half the people in the State lived along its tortuously beautiful harbour, among its rocky hills and sandy beaches.

Bondi on Sundye—as the Sydneysiders were supposed to say. What bliss at the end of the carline to find acres of gleaming golden sand, thick with sun-worshipping bodies or shaking to the tramp of magnificently muscled and fearsomely helmeted life-saving teams as they ran their reels out to sea. Their massive rowboats went dipping and plunging into the enormous surf, where the great breakers, twenty feet high, could tumble a boat and its oarsmen in the splitting of a second. But back they came for more. Sharks might and did cruise just out of the bathers' reach but the waves remained blackened with bodies and bobbing heads. Only when the shark patrol issued its shrill warning did the waters empty briefly, while the spotter plane cruised overhead. Soon the bobbing heads and golden sun-browned limbs were once more threshing the great waves, clad still in those days, in the regulation and fantastic 'neck to knee' insisted upon by the wowsers. Bondi, Coogee, Manly, Maroubra, Dee-Why. We visited them all, and then Hugh decided that we ought to see the Blue Mountains as well.

The climb up from the coastal plain was along the knife edge first located by Blaxland and his friends. The highway, the railroad and the telegraph line all strove, jostling to find a foothold on the narrow neck. At one point the remains of the Y by which the trains had crawled up the enormous wall before the First World War were still etched, a great overgrown scar, along the scarp's sheer face. Gorges dropped away on both sides as we rose and at last we were on a table-land, edges serrated and deeply gouged like a miniature Grand Canyon. Before us the Three Sisters raised eroded rock pillars from the bottom of the gorge. At a point named Govett's Leap, the whole world slid noiselessly away and we gaped across a flimsy railing into a 3,000 feet void where the depths produced their own blue to match the blue of the scarp. From far away came the faint roar of a stream dashing itself into spray as it fell over the edge of inland Australia on to the teeming coastal plain.

We lunched at Katoomba, the tourist centre for the district, where Hugh insisted again on sparkling burgundy. We young people thought it was terrific and after lunch, as Hugh drove sedately back to the city, his cigar smoke wreathing the red leather upholstery in a pleasant miasma, we fell asleep on the back seat from sheer exhaustion. He forbore to wake us to look at the views as he twisted gingerly down hairpin bends to the plains below. I expect he was missing Linda.

The fact was that all the young people had been up until the small hours being frightfully sophisticated and Twentieth-Century-Blueish at the leading nitery, Romano's. Whereas the overwhelming desire of young intellectuals today is to dress in hipsters, sweaters, duffles, sandals and beards, in the early thirties young intellectuals denied their talents with equal assertion but in an entirely opposite direction. Our great objective was to prove we were as good as the next bloke by dressing with the most elaborate and dandyish care. Four of us had gone to this very ordinary night club (no floor show, no liquor, bring your own under your coat in a hot water-bottle) dressed absolutely to the nines in white tie, tails and white gloves, the girls in floor-length dresses with deep décolletages and elbow-length gloves. It being the depths of the Depression, the tunes reflected this. We danced or rather trance-walked to *Just One More Chance, I Don't Know Why* and *Buddy can you spare a dime?* The orchestra kept lugubrious time with our Fate and we all preserved an air of extremely blasé indifference.

Nevertheless such is the energy that boils beneath even the staidest youngster's boiled shirt that we finished the night still raring to go as the place closed down. Two-thirty a.m. found us in a rented car exploring the old Sydney of convict and colonial days which still lurked beneath the giant arch, huddled together at the feet of its enormous southern pylon. We prowled the narrow silent streets among old bluestone lofts and chandlers' stores, terraced houses climbing steeply up the rocks with ironwork filigree dripping from curved zinc verandahs. We felt conspiratorial and old, belonging suddenly to 1788 and the First Fleet, which for Australia was antique night. When we staggered home at four a.m. after the customary interminable clinging goodnights, it was almost dawn; and at 8.30 we'd left for Katoomba.

That night it was early to bed, and the next day I left for Melbourne. Tearful women saw me off and my own ache accompanied me all the 586 miles down to chilly Melbourne and the virile hardworking south. The only man who seemed the same at the end as at the beginning was jolly Cousin Hugh, shrewd eyes twinkling, lit cigar waving as he receded from me under the grime-blackened roof of Central.

Chapter Twelve

STEPFATHERLY ADVICE

WHILE I was gallivanting around in this manner, my step-father, George Thirkell, was having a pretty thin time of it back in Melbourne. Once it was clear that, come what may, he was going to be eased off the TAMECO Board, Dad wasted little time in repining. Once the cord had been severed and he was no longer fighting for his job and his dignity, he ceased to heap curses on the heads of his antagonists. He stopped talking about 'Judas' and 'Pilate' and 'The Mafia' and became again his cheerful old self. Misfortune didn't curtail his daily visits to the Naval and Military Club; nor did he cut down on the invitations kindly extended to me to match schooners with him at the Club's bar whenever I was downtown from the University and he was at a loose end. This of course was much more often than I realized, because during my first year at the University I was so absorbed in my own voyage of discovery as to be more than usually insensitive to what was going on outside. I just hadn't hoisted in the fact that Dad, because he was out of a job, had time on his hands.

Not living at home, the cat's cradle daily development of domestic drama escaped me. Because he stood me drinks at his Club, and because, to tell the truth, I wasn't really interested in TAMECO (in fact, having spent so many uncounted hours hanging around at 'The Works' I wasn't sorry to see the last of them) I thought Dad was still an earning paterfamilias. I thought that the matter of his dismissal from TAMECO was something that would just 'pass away'. I was strengthened in this belief by Dad's rather pathetic efforts to remain on speaking terms with the men whom he said had betrayed him. Some of these men were members of the Club and when I saw Dad still nodding and chatting to them over a silver schooner of beer I was filled with indignation.

'How can you speak to those fellows!' I would ask in a fierce whisper as soon as I thought they were out of earshot.

Humping My Bluey

Dad would drain his schooner in pensive mood and then look at me mildly over the rim.

'Life's too short to nurse grievances,' he'd say. 'As you'll find out pretty soon.'

'But they betrayed you!'

'Poor devils, they couldn't help it. The others egged them on.'

But I had a feeling that if he'd been drinking with 'the others' he'd have found excuses for them too. He must be going to pieces.

'You mean,' I said, hoping to rouse him, 'Forgive them for they know not what they do? Eh?'

He gave me a foxy grin below the speckled irises.

'Something like that,' he said. 'Have another schooner.'

I nodded glumly. I should have refused and helped him to save his money, the money he hadn't got and wasn't now earning; but what undergraduate can refuse a free beer? I watched him sidle over to the bar. He'd put on weight lately and his suits, never Saville Row, now seemed to be bursting. I noticed for the first time that his hair was flecked with grey and his nose looked bigger and somehow coarser. His brown brogues with the Phillips rubbers were unshined; but the back of his coat—with the dowager's hump below the collar favoured by Australian tailors—was all too shiny. I suddenly saw him as the crowd of sympathetic or patronizing cronies in the Club must see him, as 'Poor old George; looks a bit seedy doesn't he?' The vision enraged me, partly because it reduced my own status, but also because it made me angry on his behalf that he didn't pick up his feet and square his shoulders; that he should go on talking to these vultures. He was then forty and I was nineteen. To appreciate the piquancy of the relationship we need to retrace our steps to my first year at Ormond College.

* * *

During one of my periodic weekend descents on 4 Grace Street to boast of my exploits at the University and to parade my new-found sophistication before my sometimes admiring brothers, I'd found an atmosphere which, even to a self-centred undergraduate, was thick with suppressed tensions. I thought at first of running a pipeline into Lance, Dad's own son and my half-brother. He was at that time nine years old and, being the 'baby', closer to Mother than either my brother Colin or myself. He had recently left Adwalton, Miss Adderley's prep school for boys (known to us as the Waddly-Paddly), and had enrolled with immense pride—fully justifiable in my eyes since I was an Old Boy—at Scotch College Preparatory School. His eyes were widening to the world and he might be able to tip me off as to what was afoot—the most obvious being that the rented Thürmer piano had gone from the drawing room, and I didn't somehow want to ask Mother why.

However I finally decided to seek Colin's advice. He was now sixteen and doing the School Leaving Certificate Honours examinations at Scotch. It seemed to me that whatever was in the wind, Colin would be more likely to be affected than Lance, and would also be more apt to guess at what was brewing.

'I think Mother's going to England,' he said.

'When?'

'Pretty soon. Before the end of the year.'

'How do you know? It that why the Thürmer's gone?'

'One question at a time,' said Colin testily.

It was near exam time so I sympathetically forgave him. His little desk was covered with spreadeagled books and I could see him swotting far into the night while I was about to go back to the University —smoking cigarettes too. I waited.

'The other day,' said Colin clearing his throat, 'she was on the phone to Mr. Ettelson to find out about marine insurance on the Sargent portrait.'

I looked solemn. Phil Ettelson was Mother's lawyer, and the Sargent portrait[1] was Mother's most valued possession. It had been drawn in charcoal by John Singer Sargent when Mother was twenty-five, and she was justifiably proud of it. If she was thinking of taking The Trip it would be the one thing she would wish to have with her: especially—it hit me like a bucket of ice—*if she weren't coming back*. Colin noted my consternation.

'I think so too,' he said. 'I'm to follow her when I've finished my exams.'

'What about Dad?'

He shrugged his shoulders. 'She has to get his permission to go.'

I sought out Mother. She was sitting at her little desk in the bay window looking out across the board fence to the neighbour's brick wall fourteen feet away.

'Mother.'

'Try not to interrupt when I'm working.'

'Mother, I *have* to talk to you.'

She swung round and faced me over her half moon glasses.

'Well, what is it, love?' she said with a judicious mixture of affection and exasperation.

'Are you going to England?'

'Yes, I am. Dad's not earning any money and it will be easier for

[1] See *The Road to Gundagai*. Same author and publisher 1965.

177

him if I remove the family burden. Not you, darling, of course,' she added looking at me quizzically. 'You've been a *great* help.'

'You mean I'm self-supporting?'

She gave an enamelled smile but didn't answer directly.

'I shall take Lance with me, and Colin will follow.' She turned round to her desk again, but I wasn't to be put off.

'When are you coming back?' I said to the back of her head. She whirled on me this time, pushing the hair up out of her eyes.

'When your stepfather can earn some money to support us all!' she said with the teary edge to her voice that always intruded when she felt herself crossed. My stepfather, I thought? You mean your husband, don't you? But all I said was

'Are you taking the Sargent?'

'Yes,' she said shortly.

'Why?' I persisted ponderously.

'Don't ask silly questions,' she snapped.

'I'm sorry, Mother.'

She did an unexpected thing; she to whom any show of emotion or affection was so hard. She rose quickly from her desk, gave me a brief hug and a peck and said 'You're a great comfort. Now I *must* get the tea.'

I went back to the University alone in a late night tramcar. I climbed up the four flights of stairs to my bedroom and looked out at the paddock with the college cattle, the decrepit and papery palm tree watered with uric acid by so many generations of Ormond men, the dark smudge of trees along the Sydney road and the traffic surging past beyond. The overcast sky was ruddy from Melbourne's great glow. So I'm going to be on my own. Entirely. A fearful joy strove inside me with a joyful fear.

Mother and Lance left on the *Themistocles* in November. Dad, Colin and I went down to Port Melbourne to see them off. Everyone was very cheerful, most of all Dad, and as far as I could see the illusion that Mother was just off on her Trip Home, and would return as soon as Dad was able to make both ends meet, was believed in and shared by us all. Or perhaps we just put it at the back of our minds and got on with the job. We commiserated with a drink at the Naval and Military Club and I went back to the University to study for my end of year exams, with a quite extraordinarily light heart. I had to admit to myself that the prospect of being entirely 'off the leash' was not unwelcome. For almost a year I'd been living up at the University, but 4 Grace Street and Mother had always loomed in the background as potential censors of many gay activities. But now . . . I caught myself singing as I crossed Sydney Road to my rooms.

Dad and Colin went back to 4 Grace Street, where they were to be temporarily cared for by a Colonel and Mrs. Biggs from Sydney who were provided with free lodging in exchange. No terminal date for this arrangement had apparently been made. Less than a month later Colin went off alone on the *Mooltan* to England. Once again there was the ferociously jolly little ritual down at Port Melbourne pier. The coloured paper streamers parted between deck and dock and the liner slowly moved out into the stream, her screws churning up a great surge of yellow sand and mud which raced towards us as she backed out to sea. But instead of nostalgia and the sadness of parting I felt an exhilarating sense of independence and freedom. I didn't see Mother or my brothers again for four years.

*   *   *

So here we are, I thought, Dad and I beached high and dry on Australia's strand, while the ark of the covenant is 12,000 miles away. We celebrated with a slap-up luncheon at Scott's Hotel. It never occurred to me to ask Dad where he got the money; the older generation always had money and, though in receipt of £260 a year from scholarships, I didn't consider myself well off, and was indeed unable to grasp the concept of money to spend. Mother's frugal habits after ten years at 4 Grace Street had borne fruit. I was constitutionally incapable of being spendthrift. The next week, the exams being over, the College was closed for the Christmas holidays, and Dad said why didn't I stay at 4 Grace Street until it was time for me to go to Tasmania?

What I saw at Grace Street disconcerted me greatly. Colonel Biggs' wife had taken over the house completely; on top of that, two unannounced children were in possession of my old room and the former Lady Help's room. The boy, a plump and pimply lad of fourteen, was moved from my room with curt and resentful apologies and went into Colin's old room at the back of the house. But that was the absolute limit of the extent to which the Biggs were willing to go to accommodate me. In all other respects the conjunction of Biggs memorabilia and the 4 Grace Street furnishing was a nightmare.

They'd left Dad the old front bedroom which had been his and Mother's, and had moved the oak table and Dad's stamp collection from his study into the bedroom. They'd brought down from Sydney a horrible double bed of mahogany veneer which they'd set up in the study; and along the shelves, in which were still the remains of Dad's precious collection of piston rings, gudgeon pins, radiator caps and headlamps (all shoved rudely into one corner), there now reposed Mrs. Biggs' bottles and unguents and the Colonel's tobacco jars, razor strops and shoe-shine kit. Their coats and dresses hung in Dad's huge old tottery cupboard that had come all the way from rural Richmond in Tasmania; yet Dad's trouser press (whose sure whereabouts I still sought from instinct and memory) remained in the bottom of this great closet. What was going on?

In the dining-room, where we all had our communal breakfast, the sacred books of my youth supported a vast freight of alien commerce. Above the noble worn spines of *Sard Harker* and *Butterscotia* were plastic gnomes, a small bakelite radio—kept on all day as far as I could see—a Kewpie doll in pink celluloid belonging to the odious little daughter, and a couple of hexagonal brass ash trays with decorations in varnished gum-nuts. In the drawing-room a bottle of Australian Old Court whisky stood before the peacock screen. The silver lustreware vases were now separated by sepia leather framed photographs of a strange man and woman fixed in improbable stares: a grey moustache like a band-aid; frizzy permed hair set in treacle. The naked overhead light was glaring and uncomfortable and I went to bed in a fine frenzy of annoyance and uncertainty. Of course Mrs. Biggs was in charge of the house, running it, I supposed, in her own efficient way. And naturally she would place her own family first. And of course Dad was bound to make some kind of arrangement for his welfare, with Mother gone. But I felt very out of it and wondered if 4 Grace Street had ever been my home.

The following evening the Biggs announced their intention of going to a movie leaving Dad and me alone in the house. I determined to woo Dad and find out where he stood. I poured him a whisky (Old Court) pulled out my portable H.M.V. gramophone and played him gems from Paul Whiteman's *The King of Jazz*. That, I thought, would send him. I played him *Happy Feet* and then *A Bench in the Park*. He kept his nose in his whisky, nodding absent-mindedly and occasionally tapping his feet to the rhythm. This was a good sign, but not enough for me to broach the subject. I decided to switch to Rudy Vallee. I put on *Confessin'* and then *Baby Bluebird*. No reaction. I wound up again. Records at 78 r.p.m. lasted only three minutes in those days and one certainly sweated at the handle of the portable H.M.V. I put on *Kitty from Kansas City*. Suddenly from the somnolent depths of Dad's chair came a lazy voice. 'Kitty Kitty Kitty,' it said.

> 'One of the committee
> Hit her on the titty
> With a hard boiled egg.'

I wasn't sure Rudy Vallee would approve of this. Dad sighed happily; I decided the time was propitious.

'Are the Biggs going to be here for long?'

'Eh?'

'Are the Biggs. . . ?'

'Ah yes; old Jerry. He's a good fellow. Be here a while I expect.'

'But how long?'

'Oh, long as we need them.'

'You mean until Mother comes back?'

He looked at me ruminatively over the edge of his glass. I had the feeling he was considering how far he could confide in me and I stiffened my face because I didn't want to be confided in. He got the point.

'Does it affect you?' he asked after a pause.

'Well, no, except, of course I realize we can't have a real home with Mother away . . .'

'And, anyway, you've got a home up at the University.'

'That's right.'

'So . . . ?' He poured another gurgling whisky into the silence. I fingered a record. It was *Beyond the Blue Horizon.* Somehow I didn't think I'd put it on. Dad gave a great terminal yawn. His waistcoat was undone in the chair and his tussore silk shirt gaped out. He had his slippers on and I was foolishly reminded of the scores of times when, as a boy, I'd unlaced his shoes, put on his slippers and fetched him his 'five-eighths of an inch in the bottom of a glass'. Could I get through to him now?

'Will they stay for a long time?'

He nodded sleepily. He gave another terminal yawn.

'Quite a while,' he said, adding, 'I think I'll wait up for them. No need for you to though, old chap, unless you want to.'

'Okay,' I said non-committally. I closed up the portable, putting the records away in the lid. They'd come in useful when I next went to Tasmania. I lugged the machine over to the door.

'Goodnight, Dad.' But he was asleep.

* * *

During the next four years I only returned once to 4 Grace Street and that was because of *force majeure.* I was at a dance at a big rented private house in the neighbourhood. Someone else took the girl home; I missed the last tram and hadn't the price of a taxi, so I walked in my evening clothes over to 4 Grace Street. It was about 1.30 a.m. when I rang the front door bell and for a while no one answered. The door was finally opened by a young military-looking man in pyjamas and dressing-gown. He had high cheek-bones and a hair-line moustache.

'Oh, hullo,' I said. 'Is Captain Thirkell in?'

'Who are you?' He looked startled. Behind him I could see our dear old oak linen-chest with the date A 1633 D on the lid.

'I'm Graham.'

'Oh. Sorry. Come in. George didn't tell me.'

'Who are you, for that matter?' I asked.

He smiled. 'Now don't get shirty. I'm Dave Tennant and I'm sharing the house with your Dad.'

'Where are Colonel and Mrs. Biggs?'

'There was a—disagreement, shall we say?' He gestured down the well-remembered corridor. 'Come in and have a nightcap. Quietly though. George is asleep.'

We went into the drawing room and he turned on the lights. Everything looked a bit tashed; yet someone, maybe Dave Tennant, had removed the atrocious overhead lighting with its tangle of naked wires festooned across the ceiling and down the mantelpiece, and substituted a couple of reading lamps. They carried flounced cretonne shades and didn't seem to go very well with the Morris wallpaper, the peacock screens and the gilt convex mirrors; but they were an improvement on the lighting. The furniture had been shifted about quite a bit, partly to accommodate the dumb-waiter or traymobile which, I noted, had now been set up as a permanent bar. I wasn't sure about this; it was nice to have a drink handy, but it seemed to me that the old system of having whisky in a demijohn in the larder and fetching drinks on a tray was preferable. Perhaps it was the Puritan *angst* at work in me again: unless a thing causes you pain or inconvenience it can't be good for you. But somehow drinks permanently in the old drawing-room didn't seem good either. Dave Tennant handed me a glass.

'Chin, chin,' he said. He smacked his lips. 'Ah that's better.' He eyed my festive attire. 'You look as if you've been out on the tiles.'

'Not exactly.' I wasn't warming to this character.

'I expect you wonder why I'm here.'

'Well . . .' not really, I thought: Dad needs a lodger. I was feeling very sleepy. Tennant said,

'I moved in here at your Dad's invitation about three months ago. I get a bed and he gets a 50-50 share-out in the cost of grub.'

'Who looks after you?'

'Oh there's a girl comes in once a week to clean up. The rest of the time, we're just baching.'

It looks it, I thought. My eyelids were starting to droop.

'You're sleepy,' said Tennant. 'Afraid I'm in your old room. D'you mind sleeping in the spare?'

'Okay,' I said. I was too tired to argue and also feeling considerably depressed. 4 Grace Street, which I'd once hated, now seemed to be reeling backwards out of my reach and, to my surprise, it made me uneasy.

Tennant rose. 'Think I'll hit the hay too. By the way, George gets the use of my car. I drive him. He's been a bit stuck since TAMECO took away the firm's Chrysler.'

'Where do you garage it?' was all I could manage. I was yawning now.

'Next door but one, at the Hambleys.'

'What happened to Mr. Capuana?'

'He died.'

'Oh. Well, goodnight.'

'Afraid there aren't any sheets, but you won't mind sleeping on blankets will you?'

I shook my head, stumbled down the passage and into the spare room. Without troubling to undress I slumped on the bed and was instantly asleep.

I was awakened by Dad. He was dressed only in a terry cloth bathrobe, without buttons or belt, clutched tightly round his belly with one hand. His slippered feet and hairy legs protruded. He was unshaven and there was an expression of impish joy on his face.

'What time is it?' I asked.

'About eight, young fella-me-lad. Just caught the old postie on his rounds.' He bounced gaily if awkwardly on the balls of his feet. Our post box, like most in Australia, was fixed to the front gate; not, as in some other lands, a slot in the front door. I had visions of Dad capering across the dew-laden lawn to the scandal of the neighbours, and I screwed up my censorious young nose.

'Were you out at the gate?'

'Of course. And caught a big fish too,' he crowed. 'All in among the bills and receipts and Dave Tennant's billets-doux.' He waved a piece of paper aloft.

'Show me,' I said ungraciously.

He waved it in front of my eyes. It was a cheque made out in his favour by an electro-plating firm, and it was for £4 10s. Somehow this made me inexpressibly sad, and I could feel the tears starting to prick behind my eyeballs.

'Better get up,' I said gruffly.

Dad grinned and pocketed the cheque.

'Right,' he said, 'eggs this morning!'

He gave a conspiratorial V sign and strode from the room still clutching the bathrobe to his belly.

Breakfast, cooked by Dave Tennant, was a lugubrious affair. The toast was burnt, the scrambled eggs leathery and the whole atmosphere of my old and hated home seemed slap-happy and disconcertingly wrong. Also I was still in tails at 8.30 in the morning.

'I'll drive you back to the University,' said Tennant solicitously. 'You can't be seen in that get up.'

'Is Dad coming?'

'No. He'll be in later,' Tennant paused. 'He usually likes to stay in bed and gloat, when a cheque arrives.'

I looked at him stonily. 'I'll be ready when you are,' I said.

I went into Dad's bedroom to say goodbye. He was lying naked, face down and half-covered with a sheet. His voice came muffled from the pillows.

'Be a good fellow, will you, and rub my back? There's coconut oil on the bed table.'

I took off my tail coat and rolled up the sleeves of my stiff shirt. I unscrewed the cap of the coconut oil and poured a generous dollop on Dad's pink back.

'Round the neck and shoulders please,' he murmured into the pillow, as I started to rub and knead. I was on the third ration of oil when I heard an imperious horn outside. That'll be Tennant, I thought. You bastard, you can just wait. (It never occurred to me that he wouldn't.) I kept up the rhythmic kneading and stroking and Dad just lay there grunting with satisfaction from time to time as I hit a sensitive or gratifying spot. Soon Tennant stood in the doorway, his eyebrows raised. I went on massaging.

'George,' he said. 'I've got to get into town.'

'Mhm,' said Dad.

'I promised to take Graham.'

'Mhm.'

I straightened up and wiped my hands on the bedsheets. 'Well so long Dad,' I said. 'Will we be having lunch at Scott's?'

'Mhm.'

'Good-oh.' I walked out into the daylight and got into Tennant's tiny yellow M.G. sports car which drove me, with many metallic rip-roaring farts, up to the University. The drive was melancholy and rather silent principally because I didn't feel like talking. I stiff-armed Tennant's opening gambit which was

'Always wish I'd had time to go to the Uni.'

After that the only observation he made was that George's back seemed to be getting worse. He dropped me outside Ormond about

nine-thirty, my attire, much to his astonishment, arousing only
the mildest curiosity among my fellows. As we shook hands he
said

'You and I must go cruising in this bus together. St. Kilda Esplan-
ade. You know? It's wonderful for picking up the sheilas.'

'Yes,' I said, 'we must do that some time.'

I sketched a half salute and trundled into the College while Tennant farted off down the drive and, so far as I was concerned, into
limbo.

* * *

I didn't go back to 4 Grace Street after that; Dad and I met instead
once a fortnight at Scott's Hotel over a lunch which he couldn't
really afford: stout, oysters, steak, imported Stilton cheese. Charac-
teristically he never asked me to pay. I used to look forward to this
ritual with gloomy anticipation. It was usually preceded by a visit
to Dad's office. After his fall from TAMECO he had found a small
room which he shared with a salesman of bathroom fixtures. It was
down the steep hill of William Street as it slipped towards the railway and the docks and I used to go there to pick him up on these
feast days. The office, of which he had only one corner, was full of
pedestal basins in vitreous china, urinals, both standing and wall
type, monel metal faucets, shower roses, flexible nickel pipes, and
a single bath—daringly new, because instead of being supported on
dragon's claws it was flush with the floor. Hung on the walls were
sample toilet seats in wood and plastic. Dad had framed in one of
the seats a photograph of the TAMECO official who he said had 'betrayed' him.

One day I arrived for the feast to find Dad in the company of a
very red-faced soldierly man swaying gently on his feet. Dad said

'This is Major Cornwall.'

The major looked at me with great pop-eyes like organ stops and
bared a set of crooked teeth. He then asked in a loud hectoring
English voice,

'Shall I be bloody rude to him, George?'

I must have looked very startled; I certainly felt it. Who was this
total stranger?

Dad said quietly, 'I wouldn't do that, Rupert.'

The Major sat down heavily on a toilet fixture.

'Sorry and all that,' he said. 'Whacked today, to tell you the truth.
Been drinking a bit.'

I looked enquiringly at Dad.

'Major Cornwall's wife has left him,' he said meaningly. 'She's in England. A friend of your Mother's, it seems. They've been talking.'

'How do you know?' I said. 'What about?'

'What about!' said the Major with great scorn. 'Are you dense, boy?'

'Now look here. . . !' I began, but he raised a beefy hand.

'No offence,' he said in an oracular boom. 'What about, is us, of course, *us*!' He pointed to Dad and then tapped his own chest. 'And how we know, is *this*!' He brandished a letter in the air. 'My wife. Writes to me just occasionally. Says she's not coming back to me—knew that anyway—and Angela's not coming back to George either. What d'you think of that?'

I glanced at Dad for guidance but he was looking pensively out of the window. Major Cornwall's exophthalmic orbs continued to bore in on me.

'I don't quite know what to think,' I said. 'It's nothing to do with me—directly.'

'How d'you mean?' he said belligerently. 'She's *your* mother isn't she?'

'She's *his* wife!' I cried pointing to Dad, 'and his business, not mine. If she wants to tell him anything let her do it.'

'Tut tut, the naughty temper,' said the odious Major.

'But he's right, Rupert, all the same,' said Dad. 'It's just . . .' he turned to me and our eyes met across the little thicket of nickel faucets, bath plugs, soap dishes and shower roses. 'Rupert thought you might ask her. Write I mean.'

'But why can't you?' I pleaded in a blaze of distress.

'Oh I will of course,' he said hurriedly, 'but I thought a word from you as well . . .'

'Okay I'll write then,' I said miserably. His face brightened. The Major harrumphed but otherwise had the sense to say nothing. The silence began to grow at an alarming rate; after a while it even reached out and grabbed the Major by the throat. He heaved himself unsteadily to his feet.

'Think I'll get along,' he said. He jammed a pork pie brown velours hat on to his head, lurched through the doorway, and half stumbled the three or four stone steps down into William Street.

'Poor Old Rupe,' said Dad. 'Let's go and have some lunch.'

Poor old you, I thought. We had lobster and chicken à la Maryland and a couple of schooners of beer. Throughout the feast we hardly exchanged a word.

I wrote Mother a plain letter simply asking her if she was going to come back and when. The answer was a three page tirade against Australia and against Dad so blistering that I tore it up. I tried never to mention the subject again. Whenever Dad asked me I'd say that I hadn't heard yet, and why didn't he write himself? It would be better coming from him. But he didn't write and she never came back.

This combined incidence of Major Cornwall and Mother's letter upset me a great deal. I felt that Mother had a point on her side but was being dramatic and unreasonable. I felt that Dad was being too feckless and supine about the whole business. If he wanted her back wasn't it up to him to do something? His lassitude annoyed me and I began to see less of him; but, as a sort of insurance, much more of his cousin and my step-cousin Terence Crisp.

My early encounters with Terence had almost ended in disaster. In the heart of the city lurked a host of innocent joys, among them The Man in the Window and Cole's Book Arcade. The Man in the Window stood inside the Leviathan Stores (A Square Deal). He was about eighteen inches high, but wore a man-sized borsalino hat. His papier-maché smile remained fixed and glistening, but a mechanism made his outstretched hand tap on the inside of the plate glass window to attract the attention of passers-by. In this he was eminently successful and citizens gazed at him for minutes at a stretch, blocking the sidewalk and being bumped and shouldered aside until it was time to go to Cole's Book Arcade. Here two other little men, with heads proportionate to their bodies, operated a winch on which display cards slowly came into view, held for a moment teetering on the brink and then plunged down inside the cabinet. The Cole's men were simply Lilliputian reproductions of Gog and Magog (themselves reproductions of the London originals) that glared down from the walls of the Arcade itself. This led to the related conclusion that the Man in the Window was like Terence, who was of less than ordinary height. I blurted out this amusing thought at Sunday supper one night when Terence was at the table. It never occurred to me that he might be offended. Mother gave me a pretty sharp look.

'But it *is* like Terence,' I blundered on.

'I think I'll have to be leaving, Angela,' said Terence after he'd downed his banana custard.

'How *could* you be so stupid!' said Mother. But a laborious explanation was necessary before the light finally dawned. I wrote a letter of apology to Terence. 'I'm sorry I said you were like the man in the window at the Leviathan. You are much bigger than that, and I didn't mean to be rude . . .'

At this point Mother looked over my shoulder. At her suggestion the letter was torn up and a fresh one drafted which simply apologized for 'the stupid remark I made last Sunday'. This letter was duly mailed, but it was some weeks before Terence forgave me. His forgiveness took the form of a visit to Cole's Book Arcade.

The Arcade, once you were inside it and past the little men with the eternally winding winch, was a world of extravagant display such as only a true showman could have devised. The immense variety of books crammed into a confusing profusion, scarcely equalled even by Foyle's of Charing Cross Road, spoke of a city and a country avid for reading matter from the great world outside, especially the world of England and Home. Among the bewildering array of books stacked on trays and desks, on trolleys, on rungs reaching from floor to glassed-in ceiling, were perhaps two or three dozen Australian titles. Of these by far the most enthralling was the book which old E. W. Cole, complete with patriarchal beard, had published himself to advertise the wares of his Arcade. It was called *Cole's Funny Picture Book* and it had a rainbow printed on the cover, in the spectrum of which arched the following ditty:

> Long ago the rainbow was a sign, 'tis said
> Now 'tis the sign of Cole's Book Arcade
> Old and second-hand, Common and Rare.
> You can get almost any book you want there

Inside, the book was a rich lode of comic information copiously illustrated by wood and steel engravings.

> When is a door not a door?
> When it's ajar.
> Right, you're a witch!

The Foolish Damsel. During the day, when it is warm, she wears clothes from her hat to her buttoned boots. (Illustration by steel engraving). But at night when it is cold the silly girl wears a dress which exposes her shoulders! *She is a Slave to Fashion!*

How to amuse your friends at a party. Ask them if they can turn a glass of water upside down without spilling it, using only a sheet of writing paper. When they say 'No,' place the sheet of paper over the filled glass and quickly invert it. Your friends will be amazed! (There was a mess before we mastered *that* one.)

A wonderful ballad against cigarette smoking illustrated by a picture of a weedy youth in a very un-Australian bowler hat— clearly a direct import from the grimy slums of London in the 1880s:

> This is the puny youth who smokes
> The deadly cigarette which chokes
> All round him with its poisoned fumes

And fast and sure his life consumes.
With fingers reeking from its stain
With stunted form and weakened brain
And giddy walk this arrant knave
Goes gaily to his early grave . . .
Poor little fool, he does not know
That if to manhood he would grow
He must renounce the fatal snare
Of nicotine and thus beware
Of smoking cigarettes composed
Of nasty scraps all decomposed.

This eighty years before the warnings about lung cancer.

Following the Cornwall episode I rather latched on to Terence. I felt in some dim wrong-headed fashion a share of the responsibility for Mother's continued absence. At any rate I was uncomfortable. But at the same time, though I didn't want to see much of Dad, I felt the need to keep a link with his family and, as Terence was an ardent theatregoer, this was fun.

Terence was about ten years younger than Dad and ten years older than me; an amusing bachelor lawyer whose disconcertingly waspish good nature had survived my youthful blunders over his stature. He was a tiny puckish fellow and sensitive about it; but he was a wonderful theatre companion, and his help in breaking down Mother's taboos on non-puritanical enjoyment had always been greatly appreciated.

'If you don't keep quiet I won't take you to Gilbert and Sullivan!' she used to say.

It may seem strange that this threat should have been effective; that the illicit attraction of moviedom's forbidden fruit banned by Mother should have been counterbalanced by the thrills of *Pinafore* and *The Mikado*. But so it was. I think the reason was that the lean jowls of Bill Hart and the kohl-rimmed eyes and vampish hair-do of Theda Bara didn't seem to bear any relation at all to life as I knew it. The eight-by-ten glossy prints pinned in the show cases outside the 'picture palace' seemed stiff, unreal and a little threatening. Though I used to want to go to the flicks 'because the other fellows did', the outside of the picture palaces somehow repelled rather than invited, whereas the real theatre was so warm and alive. I used to stand outside the Victory picture palace gazing solemnly at the garish posters, but I didn't really want to go in. The light was chill and repellent; the woman in the box office had the unblinking stare of a lizard; the interior, glimpsed through parted velvet curtains, revealed a shimmering, silvery shadow-show, backed by a rich surge of pianola 'stride' music, and I felt uncomfortable and self conscious. G. and S. was safe and warm. No use to say that Zasu Pitts was more exciting than Buttercup, she wasn't as funny; or that Pola Negri was more exciting than Yum Yum, she wasn't as enjoyable. The real theatre, with Terence as companion and guide, was at once spectacular and intimate.

Behind the warm splash of His Majesty's marquee, lay the trembling excitement of the great red plush curtain, glowing at its fringed and folded base with the penumbra of the footlights. All around was the daring sussuration of the audience, the programme girls in their black bombazine and frilly aprons, and the more than oriental strains of an orchestra tuning up. Cooled to a sudden hush by the overture, we waited breathlessly for: the curtain! Up it twisted, pulled by magic hands: and out into the auditorium surged a rich smell of dusty boards, grease paint, sweat, and fusty stuffs. The show was on! Beyond lay a wonderful world where people were brightly coloured and larger than life. From their company, even at a distance of fifty feet, I used to emerge with chest thrust out and a feeling of participatory grandeur that made the promenade with Terence down the after-theatre sidewalk like treading on air.

His Majesty's was only one of eight 'legitimate' theatres which operated full blast during a Melbourne season. The fare was all imported; I don't recall a case of a play or musical by an Australian being staged. It was also, a great deal of it, frothy and vapid to a depressing degree, much of it being a poor echo of London's West End drawing room comedies—the dregs of Pinero and Frederick Lonsdale—with imported principals and local supporting cast. Alternatively there was American Musical Comedy with the crisp accents and the strange, indeed almost Martian, New York humour falling flat on its face in Australian utterance, but somehow successful because it was supposed to be smart to like it. Anything from London and almost anything from New York secured our sycophantic adulation. We were a provincial society hanging on by our eyelashes to the extreme periphery of the bright world beyond. I used to wonder vaguely why we were always more excited about a play from overseas than about one from Australia; but the strings of bright lights overwhelmed all doubts.

His Majesty's shared the big shows with The Princess. Both were large and spacious theatres built in the heyday of Melbourne expansion in the eighties. King's was devoted more to straight shows, and with the old Theatre Royal was the home of that highly un-aboriginal activity, the Panto. The Panto, along with hot plum-pudding at Christmas time when it might be 100 in the shade, had been imported, holus-bolus, by these invincibly Anglo-Saxon denizens of the Antipodean bush, to remind them of Home. The best Panto was *Sinbad the Sailor* in the midst of which a comic djinn rushed up to the footlights and announced 'Me come from Fitzroy' (a 'tough' suburb) 'where they beat the tom tom!' Roars of laughter at this sally but from me a ferocious frown at the temerity of the djinn on stepping outside the framework of irreality and rending the gossamer veil of illusion. But the really spectacular shows were staged either at His Majesty's or The Princess, and it was here that Terence and I saw the great swagger musical comedies of the late twenties and early thirties with their Ziegfeldian opulence and brassy music. If the Antipodean version was muted or at second remove, we weren't aware of it. Mother considered musical comedies a borderline case—somewhere between films and stage plays—and therefore did not prohibit attendance. But she thought they were vulgar, so didn't go herself. I thought they were terrific.

It was the golden age of the musical comedy before it incurred the displeasure of those concerned with social realism. In its brittle innocence the musical comedy reflected a view of life light as thistledown, yet with a relentless glitter. It was full of young men in blazers and tennis flannels, young girls in bandeaux, jolly uncles and funny aunts in a world of tea and cakes. I loved it. In the earlier thirties the tunes of musical comedies tended to become dark, reflective and mournful; but in the twenties they scintillated with an effortless irrepressible gaiety, and later, as they moved out of the drawing rooms into the African desert, Ruritania or the Canadian North, they generated a broad flowing romance which demanded total acceptance, or nothing. Terence and I mostly went to Saturday matinees in the cheap seats and emerged groggy with wonder into the slanting light of Melbourne's afternoon, vowing that the world we had seen out-shone all others.

During that wonderful period we had seen *No, No, Nanette* (who can forget 'Tea for Two'?); *Lady Be Good*; *Sunny* ('Whooooo stole my heart away?'); *Wildflower*, and we fell in love with Marie Burke the leading lady, who never knew it, poor soul. Then came the great colour spectaculars where librettists wandered far afield to catch romance in an age which hadn't yet realized that it was just around the corner. We warbled 'The Indian Love Call' from *Rose Marie*, that improbable tale of a Métis girl and a Mountie dreamed up in Manhattan. This throaty lament ('I am calling you-who-who-who-who-whoo!') is forever memorable because Dad's mother, who had come over from Tasmania to stay with us, became confused between *Rose Marie* and *Mary Rose*, both of which were running in Melbourne at the same time, and emerged very cross from an afternoon of Barrie whimsy when she ought to have been regaled by the music of Rudolf Friml. We chivvied her for some days with 'The Indian Love Call'.

The Desert Song hit like a thunderclap a Melbourne already softened up trom avid reading of P. C. Wren's *Beau Geste* and E. M. Hull's *The Sheikh*. Scores of mating pairs on St. Kilda Beach could be heard chanting 'Blue Heaven and You and I' (and sand kissing the moonlit sky). We even roared it out around campfires into the deep Australian night. We really lived in the desert in those days. Ho! The Riffs were coming—either Abd'el-Krim or the chorus from The Princess theatre. The Blue Water sapphire, missing from Brandon Abbas, lay at the bottom of the garden in 4 Grace Street, Malvern, and hundreds of Jerusalem artichokes were uprooted to prove it. The Sheikhs pounded through the sand on their Arab stallions, with swooning maidens slung across the pommel. Whether they were Sheeks or Shakes Terence wasn't entirely sure, but there was no doubt that they were all really gallant British Army officers in blackface who, once they had reached their tents in the desert, would disclose themselves to the swooning maiden and to the trusty Australian scout who had believed in them, had followed them blindly against fearful odds. Then the Sheikh would down a bottle of *vin ordinaire* with Hank and Buddy, and a couple of officers of the Spahis with pillbox hats, waxed moustaches and impeccable manners, all served by a balloon-trousered Zouave.

On the heels of this magical fantasy, and while we were still shouting 'Ho! The Riffs are abroad', *The Student Prince* hit town. We exchanged the earlier for the more saccharine later Sigmund Romberg. With the indulgent Terence I watched James Leddy sing 'Deep in my Heart, Dear' to Beppie de Vries, and heard a rousing chorus of at least seven thousand extras on the stage of The Princess chant 'Drink, Drink, Drink'. But *The Student Prince* paled into insignificance with the arrival of *Show Boat*. This was the musical to end all musicals, and we didn't see anything as wonderful until *Oklahoma* seventeen years later.

In 1929 a new theatre had been opened in Melbourne, The Comedy. It was of smooth brick and 'modernistic' facings and looked about as much or as little like a theatre as the Royal Shakespeare at Stratford-on-Avon. It indubitably proclaimed its decade along with the jazzy facade of our first junior skyscraper, the Manchester Unity Building. But however exciting, it couldn't make up for the departure of the Theatre Royal, home for years of an Australian legend, Nellie Stewart; roughly, our own Marie Tempest. Certainly she was as beloved and equally certainly she didn't have to act (and didn't) but just be herself. When we saw her she was in her early sixties, blonde, raddled, invariably charming with a cerise cupid's bow mouth, and a pair of china-blue eyes sunk deep in impenetrable purple caves. She played, or rather revived, the performance each year of Nell Gwyn in a play called *Sweet Nell of Old Drury*. It was a great favourite with the students to whom it was known as 'Sweet Smell of Old Brewery', and they used to attend, sometimes nightly, drum with their feet on the floor—as in the marathon performance of *The Drunkard* in San Francisco—bellow out the lines before Nellie Stewart could reach them. She took it all with great good nature and tripped forward with a disarming Dresden doll modesty to curtsey at the curtain.

An even more popular figure was Gladys Moncrieff, known to Melbourne press and theatregoers as 'Our Glad'. Glad had first hit big Australian headlines with a robust performance as Teresa in *The Maid of the Mountains* and she was a fixture in musical shows throughout the twenties, her biggest success being *Rio Rita*. In this show, she sported black hair lacquered in spit curls close to the cheek, a high colour and, as always, a tremendous personality. She had a voice like the blade of a scalpel and could split the ears of the groundlings at five hundred paces, in an accent unashamedly and wonderfully Australian. Badly injured in a car smash in 1938 she retired from the stage to reappear during World War II in a revival of *The Maid of the Mountains* and to entertain Australian troops in New Guinea. Even as late as 1951 this indomitable woman went to Korea to sing to her own Australians once again.

Sometimes the curtain would rise on another spectacular, a boy-meets-girl romance of an ethereal sophisticated fragility where the hero and heroine would suddenly melt into each other's arms and glide away on feet so nimble, sparkling and intricate that we could scarcely believe they touched the floor. The pair, beloved of all students, male and female, were Madge Elliott and Cyril Ritchard. They were as popular in Australia as Fred and Adèle Astaire in less remote lands. They made you feel, as you shuffled around at your early dances, that you too could waltz away on feet of electric thistle-down—maybe not today—but one day soon . . .

No theatrical centre is complete without vaudeville, and Melbourne had two variety houses: The Tivoli and The Bijou. Both were on Bourke Street and both for many years completely out of bounds to us. Mother relented later in respect of the Tivoli, which was after all basic family fare, (though for families, well understood, who came from South Melbourne, Northcote, Collingwood and other unsavoury districts). The featured performer was Wee Georgie Wood, a blonde homunculus from whose old-young face came ditties and jokes suitable for feminine ears. But the Bijou, that was a different thing altogether, for the Bijou was the home of Roy Rene, otherwise known as Mo. Here attendance had been at first thoroughly clandestine, in company with the uncomplaining Terence.

The act had originally started out as Stiffy and Mo (who, according to student ditties, went for a row, in a po, to Bendigo) but Stiffy had dropped out and now it was Mo by himself. It was an outrageously, vividly vulgar performance. Mo affected an exaggerated Jewish make-up: a white face and a parted black chinbeard. His lisping mincemeat of the English language cascaded in a profusion of illuminated droplets over the footlights across the orchestra pits and into the laps of the audience. They loved it. Mo wore the traditional baggy pants of Vaudeville which he manipulated with a variety of obscene and unprintable gestures, to shrieks of merriment from stout matrons in the stalls. He twisted his body into incredible knots, sidled forward palms upstretched, blew raspberries at the audience. Anything to do with backsides, lavatories or couples in bed was grist to Mo's mill and balm to his devoted audience. It was Jewish comedy of the Yiddisher-boy type, the little man against the world; it was a mixture of the male team in American Burlesque (except that Mo was his own 'straight' man) and of the Crazy Gang in London; it was innocent in its very obviousness and in the depravity of its crude, crass *doubles ententes*. Terence and I used to emerge from Mo's shows with belly muscles aching and eyes wet with tears of sheer joy.

Dad, so far as I could learn, never went to the theatre. Maybe he couldn't afford it, though he could somehow still afford the bar bills at the Naval and Military Club. But his generosity was incurable, and he had an undeniable charm which he exercised on old Digger cobbers from Gallipoli and the Somme who were always passing odd commissions his way. He thus managed to keep his half of the little office going down on William Street. Through him I too became the recipient both of old soldiers' generosity, and of a very severe fright. I was off to Tasmania one Christmas vacation when Dad said: Why spend money on a boat fare when he could get me a free ride on an airplane belonging to one of his friends? I accepted promptly and presented myself at the airport complete with baggage, goggles and borrowed binoculars.

The plane turned out to be an amphibian Saro Windhover and we set off from the lower reaches of the Coode canal with the full intention of flying to Tasmania. I was the only passenger (because Dad was a friend of the pilot). We flew high over Port Phillip Bay, across Barwon Heads, the river far below like a stream of ink between white sand banks, and headed out to sea. Forty miles from shore the pilot, who was in front of me, suddenly whipped round to examine gauges behind my head. I saw on his face unmistakable traces of rising consternation. We lost height rapidly and with much coughing and spluttering turned and headed back to Melbourne, landing on the Coode canal just in time to catch the afternoon boat.

* * *

As the University years wore on I saw less and less of Dad. It finally occurred to me that I ought to repay his lunchtime hospitality and I had him up to Ormond College. He roamed the buildings, made friends with the boys and derived immense enjoyment from watching a water bagging battle from my study window. But the meetings grew fewer and in the end we tacitly avoided any mention of Mother at all. I knew she wasn't coming back but wouldn't say so to him. He knew she wasn't coming back but wouldn't admit it to himself. Sometimes I'd glimpse him among the lunch-time crowds on Collins Street, a portly figure now in a shiny suit with frayed cuffs, and a stained grey Homburg; and I'd duck into a pub to avoid meeting him and then feel ashamed of myself for doing so. Thus it dragged on, but the end came quite painlessly for us both.

At the age of twenty-one my own father once more re-asserted himself after sixteen years, though, as it were, involuntarily and by indirection. A month after my twenty-first birthday I received word from an insurance firm that a policy on my life, taken out on my behalf at the time of my birth, had now matured. I could use it, said the insurance firm, in a variety of ways. I could convert it into an endowment policy for £1,000, much recommended for young men; or a term policy for £1,200—say a pay-fifty life; or into straight life, which would be worth £1,500 but would only benefit my heirs and assigns (who were *they*?) and was not a good way to build up an estate. Of course, the company added, as an afterthought and in small print, I could convert the policy into cash, but this was something they really didn't recommend; besides it would net me only £250. *Only* £250! Visions of affluence and of trips round the world floated before me. I at once wrote to the firm and asked them to send the cash to my bank in Melbourne.

It was only then that the name of my benefactor suddenly rang a very far off bell. He was, I was informed, a Mr. Graham Peel, now residing in Bournemouth. He was my godfather and I had been named after him. He was also my father's best friend and musical collaborator before my father met and married my mother. It was a pale Edwardian pre-echo of a sort of Benjamin Britten-Peter Pears partnership, with A. E. Housman in the offing instead of George Crabbe. The poems were from *A Shropshire Lad*; Graham Peel set them to music and my father sang them in Edwardian drawing rooms and concert halls. They are of a faint and anaemic beauty and a sometimes haunting nostalgia, and manage to convey musically Housman's morose self-pity tinged with a wistful melancholy at the evanescence of youth and life. *Summer Time on Bredon* is my favourite but *Is my team ploughing?* and *Loveliest of Trees* come close. Of course I didn't hear these songs sung until much later, for Mother would have nothing of James Campbell McInnes (or Graham Peel) in the house. Family legend had it that Graham Peel had begged my father not to marry my mother. The two men were meant to continue their fruitful partnership in Edwardian ballads. Marriage would be a disaster. Graham Peel was certainly right on both scores. The marriage ended in divorce after less than six years, and Peel didn't write another song after his association with my father ended so abruptly.

But now here he was beckoning to me across a trough of years. And here, too, was my own father, a shadowy figure on the sidelines, in my memory still the lonely giant in the strange R.F.C. hat that I had last seen in Kensington High Street sixteen years before; a lifetime for a growing boy. I felt suddenly an irrational surge of affection for the distant figure. I knew he was living in Canada and I decided to write a 'thank-you' letter to Graham Peel and at the same time find out from him my father's address.

His reply was chilling. Yes, my father was in Canada. No, he didn't know exactly where. Even if he had the address he wouldn't have given it to me. He and my father had parted many years ago. He had refused to see him on his last visit to England where my father had given a recital at Wigmore Hall. He wished me well—in guarded terms. I was astonished and subdued; he seemed to be writing me off, almost as if the ban which he had inexplicably placed on my father should apply to me. I was prey to mixed feelings; Graham Peel was clearly a generous old boy—or had been—yet here he was, stiff-arming me. The adult world: how queer it was.

All of a sudden I thought of Cousin Hugh Poynter. He'd served with Baldwin's in Canada and he would know. I wrote off and a cheerful reply came by return mail from Sydney. Yes, my father had certainly lived in Toronto when Hugh was there; he'd seen him on a number of musical occasions at Massey Hall and at the University. They'd nodded and exchanged a few words, but not spoken at any length because of possible mutual embarrassment, and anyway Molly—though I might be surprised to learn this since I knew that she was an American—had rather frowned on divorced people. My father was connected with some opera company, Hugh seemed to think. No, so far as he knew, he had not remarried.

I filed the information away at the back of my mind, but now that I was almost a graduate and ready, like most of my fellows who had grown up in Australia, to take The Trip Home, it seemed to me that I ought to go eastabout rather than westabout. Instead of the standard P. & O.-Orient route via Colombo and Suez, I would cross the Pacific to Canada, cross Canada to Toronto and find out after all these years just who the man was who had fathered me and what he was doing. Besides, next door to Canada were the United States: exciting prospects loomed.

At our next ritual luncheon, I broached the subject to Dad. Though I was now twenty-one and he had no legal rights or controls over me, I felt that I ought to let him know what I planned. His response was unexpectedly cheerful. He quite understood; thought I ought to go; would have done the same if he'd been in my position; have another plate of oysters, old chap. But as we left Scott's Hotel, he put his hand on my arm. This was a rare thing for him to do, for neither of us relished demonstrative actions or physical contact. I braced myself, but all he said was

'After you've seen your own Dad and you go on to see your Mother, just tell her I want her to come back.'

Chapter Thirteen

LINDISFARNE

MEANWHILE, throughout the rushing University years, there was always a friendly haven in the country where I was welcome at the simple drop of a postcard. After their tour round the world in 1929 Nell and Basil Hall had returned to Ballan, high on its windswept plateau pierced by hummocky extinct volcanoes. This wonderful couple, who had received my brother and myself for countless boyhood holidays, now continued to offer their hospitality to me. Their own relatives had moved into the old family home in which the Halls had once lived; but they had found another farmstead to rent about ten miles away under the shoulder of Mount Wallace, one of those low basalt-encrusted hills which some cataclysm had blasted the top off long before the dawn of history. The Ballan plaeau was filled with these flattened, exploded husks of old volcanoes, which had lost their Fujiyama outline even in truncated form, so long ago had they been burst open.

The country was more open than that to the east of Melbourne: there were no sinuous gullies choked with tree fern and bedded with the sharp unforgiving sword grass. The rolling hills were but lightly treed and led gradually up to low flat-topped mountains which, since they themselves rose from a plateau, were often of a considerable height. The tough springy Australian grass was knit here and there with clumps of tussocks and covered with a dappled carpet of fallen brown eucalyptus leaves. Through the olive enigmatic bush, coloured parakeets, rosellas and king parrots whizzed like red, yellow and green shooting stars, or cackled and scolded in the branches. The wattle bird gave his horrid rasping cry in the noonday heat. Black cockatoos with scarlet crests, white cockatoos with sulphur combs and grey galahs with pink helmets covered the dead trees with soot or snow, and arose at gunshot in screeching mournful flight. Only the golden cascading liquid note of the magpie remained the same.

The eucalyptus, though sparse, was of the commercial variety and in the hills behind Ballan, settlers in the bush-lots made a living out of eucalyptus oil. Beneath an ironbark roof supported on saplings was a zinc tank filled with boiling water over which lay great masses of leafy eucalyptus branches. The fire beneath the tub was fed by the same green eucalypt and while the distiller stirred the pot with a long stick there arose from the shack a sharp medicinal odour as of hundreds of people with heavy colds squatting on beds over steaming bowls with towels on their heads. You could of course put yourself right into the sickroom by merely biting a eucalyptus leaf, either the round heart-shaped blue gum or the long thin white gum. But these little factories in the hills perfumed the bush for hundreds of yards around with perpetual analgesic steam. Once condensed, the oil flowed out of a small copper pipe into old beer bottles which, suitably re-labelled, sold in Ballarat.

Lindisfarne was a grey stone and stucco homestead, based essentially on four rooms, but augmented by a verandah on two sides and a trailing wing to the rear which housed the dining room and kitchen. The 'guest room' was simply a box at the far corner of the stables and woodsheds about a hundred yards from the house. It contained a camp bed, a small chest of drawers, some large metal hooks, a tiny deal table with a candlestick, and one window that looked up the hill through a thin cluster of pines in which the breeze was always whispering. The room itself was lined with pine boards and smelled wonderfully fresh and pungent. This room was always mine when I arrived on my motorbike, fatigued by the ravages of university life; and it was here that young Barry, now at ten the eldest of the four Hall children, used most kindly to bring me a cup of morning tea and a couple of Nice biscuits soggy from the slopover of the tongue-curling walk across the yard.

I first went to Lindisfarne alone with Basil to help him to move in. The family was still in Melbourne waiting for the painters and plumbers to finish; and we spent a wonderful two weeks baching together and replenishing the cook pot with rabbits and grouse. Our enforced though unwelcome companion was a jobbing carpenter from Ballan named Pile, a professional comic character. He put on his hat backwards and pretended to be ex-Prime Minister 'Billy' Hughes addressing a meeting; he squatted on the floor with a brace-and-bit as a cane and he was Harry Lauder; he quoted at length from *Hamlet* and *As You Like* It, ingeniously if unwittingly garbled like the orations of The King in *Huckleberry Finn*. At length the job was done and the family moved in.

Pleasures at Lindisfarne were simple in the extreme. There was swimming in a willow-choked water hole from which the house supply was pumped up-hill by a spindly Alston galvanized iron windmill. There was shooting with Basil's twelve bore double-barrelled gun, which once included a six foot copper-head snake. A wounded rabbit had bolted into one of the innumerable warrens with which the property was pocked; on rushing to the hole I found myself facing the copper-head, reared up on two feet of distended scaly belly, and nervously despatched him. I took him home in some triumph but Nell believed, in common with many Australian country women, that no snake died till nightfall and she made me hang the copper-head over a wire fence. By morning the crows and kookaburras had got at him, and all hope of a snakeskin belt vanished. Finally, there was the heady experience of driving Basil's 1930 Plymouth into Ballan for groceries and mail, and the fearful joy of getting it stuck across a culvert on the main street and wondering if the local cop, who kindly came to help me out, was going to ask to see my non-existent driving licence.

Back at Ballan the parties went further afield. Sunday tennis now alternated between Bungeeltap and the Lanes' Station, Moorac, about eight miles away across the plateau. Whereas Bungeeltap snuggled comfortably down in a cleft surrounded with great pine trees and majestic white gums, Moorac stood bleak, forlorn and windswept on the edge of the plateau. To reach it one passed the spidery three-hundred-foot tall lattice towers of 'the beam wireless'. This, together with its twin at Rockbank down on the plain, was the Australian end of the ambitious globe-girdling 'All Red Route' whereby wireless communication was to be ensured between 'the Great Dominions' from Daventry in Britain to Yamachiche in Canada and Ballan in Australia. The manager of 'the beam' was a good family man who was nevertheless not quite with it, though by virtue of his position invited to all the parties.

More with it, partly because they were bachelors, were the two radio engineers, undoubtedly the worst tennis players I've ever seen. They were so bad that even I could beat them at the age of sixteen and they grown men. One was plump, self-effacing and bald; the other was hawk-nosed, wore pebble lens spectacles and was very romantic because he'd worked in Fiji and New Guinea. Colin and I had once been invited to spend a weekend at 'the beam' with the engineers and as a special treat mounted to the top of one of the enormously tall towers. I horrified them all, including myself in retrospect, by crawling out along the lateral beam which capped the tower like the cross-bar of a T and there singing 'It Had to be You' suspended three hundred feet over the iron hard grass.

Our host at Moorac, Bill Lane, was a tall shambling fellow who looked more like a professor or a physicist than a station owner. From his front door he could gaze down a widening cleft in the plateau edge until, far below, the Rockbank plains spread out and in the distance were the spires and towers of Melbourne. On a very clear day he could see fifty or sixty miles across the sea glinting in blue slits along the shores of Port Phillip Bay. But he was morose and disobliging. You didn't feel with him somehow that he had seen terrible things, kept his lips lightly compressed and buried horrors at the back of a tidy mind. What you felt about Bill Lane was that he was at odds with the world and would rather have been reading a book in the Melbourne Public Library.

I used to think that the reason he was so cantankerous was because his wife was such a delightful and uninhibited hostess. She was blonde and pert with a very fetching drawl, which would be described today as Kensingtonian but which, this being Australia in the twenties, was clearly built on a do-it-yourself basis. She was an indefatigable dresser-up and the most vivid fancy dress balls of that sizzling era took place at Moorac with herself as chatelaine.

Australians, in common with most Anglo-Saxons, will go to no end of trouble to dress up and once they are in costume (as innumerable shipboard dances bear witness) rapidly lose their inhibitions and act like ersatz Latins or Slavs. Moorac was filled with eighteenth-century gentlemen, swaggies, Spanish señoritas, comic coons in black face, men dressed as devils and women dressed as men; and it's odd to reflect that the young among us went roaring on through the night at such parties fuelled strictly on orange squash and soda.

Further over in the foreign territory that bordered the railway line from Ballarat to Geelong lived the Austins, at Darra: he a short, chunky, tough man over whom hung an aura of desolation: she, tall, black-eyed, dramatically and beautifully and prematurely grey. They played tremendous tennis and Nora Austin let me talk to her, which was a wonderful alternative to lonely pursuits. For the fellow who excels at flogging the mind, who has perhaps wit and a sharp tongue and is not much good at games, generally finds himself gravitating towards the women and away from the men. The men were of two types. There were those like Les Austin who could ride hard and well, dig post holes, lasso a brumby, dip sheep, cut down a tree, play a thundering good game of tennis and remain barely articulate. Compared to their laconic observations my nervous outbursts always seemed excessive. Too much froth, or as Les Austin used to put it after an unusually long oration, 'Wipe your chin, son.' The other men were the gay blades who were courting daughters of the squatters and whose conduct we observed from afar with an unblinking lizard eye.

Towards the end of my University years I made several trips in to Ballarat, the big country town around the outskirts of which you could still see the lunar landscape produced by the fossickers and diggers of the great 1851 gold rush. Their contours were softened now by time, but trees sprouting from weed-choked holes still testified to the frenzy of eighty years earlier. Ballarat itself had done its best to put the past behind it. With its wide main street flanked by late Victorian verandahed hotels and Edwardian-baroque banks, its neat little tramcars and its comfortable suburban villas on the shores of Lake Wendouree, it was the embodiment of staid provincial worthiness. And then one evening on Sturt Street I suddenly ran into Sheila Kelsall.

Sheila was a little older than I was, had freckles, a shock of wavy honey-blonde hair, blue eyes and the nicest smile I'd ever seen. We'd first met when I was still at school, for Kevyn and I had been billeted on the Kelsall family when we took the School Play—Ian Hay's *A Safety Match*—to Ballarat. She mothered us like a big sister, darned our socks, played Five Hundred with us, kept her young brother under control, and even made our beds. The beds I'd never forgotten because of that ultimate symbol of suburbia, the hollow bolstercase, upholstered in claret slub repp with satin bows at the end, into which all the pillows were unceremoniously shoved. When the bed was fully made up it looked like nothing so much as a demonstration unit in a furniture store and you were afraid to sit on the edge of it, let alone lie on it. All this now came surging back—bolster and all—on Ballarat's main street as I wrung her hand.

'You've got a moustache now,' she said roguishly.

I blushed. 'How's Tom?' For I remembered her boy-friend Tom Hollway, dark and intense and bursting with politics. Sheila's face lit up like a theatre marquee.

'We're getting married.'

'Congr— Gee! that's wonderful.'

'Tom's going to pick me up at Usher's,' naming the local coffee palace and tea parlour combined. 'Why don't you wait and see him?'

Tom was waiting and looked as if he had a skinful of dynamite. I congratulated him heartily on his achievement. He patted me on the shoulder and showed us to a marble-topped table with wiggly cast-iron legs. We ordered tea and cinnamon toast. The conversation was stilted and I got the feeling that Tom had something of great importance to say to Sheila, and didn't want me around.

'What are you doing?' he finally said to me in a testy perfunctory way. He was blue-chinned and could obviously grow a moustache much faster than me—if he wanted to.

'I'm at the University.'

'Hell, I know that,' he said irritably. Sheila's eyes looked cautious.

'I mean when you leave. You have your finals coming up haven't you?'

'Yes. Well, really, I haven't much idea. I might try the law. I've often thought—'

'Why don't you?' he cut in. 'It's got a future, eh Sheila?' She nodded and her honey locks fell over her face. This seemed to put him in a better temper.

'Before you go,' he said with what I thought was unnecessary emphasis, 'you may as well both be the first to know that I've decided to contest a Ballarat seat.'

Sheila clapped her hands and my mouth fell open.

'But you're only twenty-six,' I said ungraciously. I was all of twenty myself.

He grinned. 'That's right and with my new wife here to run my campaign for me I'll be home and dry.' He turned to Sheila and there they were lost in admiration for each other. All at once I felt very out of it. I pushed my cast-iron fiddle-back chair across the tile floor. It made a horrid screech, but they didn't even notice. I rose and said, 'Well so long. Nice to've seen you and good luck in the election.' They nodded dreamily. I don't think they even saw me go.

Tom Hollway won that seat and became the youngest man ever to be elected to the Victorian State legislature. Twelve years later he became the State's youngest Premier and Sheila the First Lady, but by that time I'd been in far away Canada for almost as long.

* * *

Back at Lindisfarne life rolled on and as my departure from Australia loomed nearer I took to solitary walks, sometimes with a gun, to impress indelibly on my mind the memory of this harsh old continent. I positively willed myself to etch on my memory the dry tawny hills, the sterile stony gorges, the blue line of distant mountains and the steep slopes clad in the woolly fur of the eucalypt. Chance favoured me, for one day in the May (i.e. winter) vacation, Basil asked me if I'd like to come down to Geelong with him for the day. This was quite an adventure, for a hundred mile drive across the grain of the country in the dirt roads of the early 1930s was not a journey one undertook lightly. I wondered what was afoot, but Basil, though cheerful, was uncommunicative.

We galloped in a great plume of yellow dust across the rolling parklike uplands and then through dense eucalyptus where the leathery fronds hanging listlessly down were dusted with the powder of earlier cars, and where the antediluvian bush came alive because of its tart and pungent scents. Suddenly we were at the edge of the great cliff; the tired grey bush fell away into clefts, dissolved at our feet into a bubble of bushes held in the crannies of steep gorges; and there 1,200 feet below us lay the great lava plain with the rocky You Yangs sticking up like fists and fingers, and the blue of Port Phillip Bay beyond. The true Australia Felix.

We came twisting down the scarp in a series of far from voluptuous curves, breasted the small dry hills of the Anakies and reached the edge of the Moorabool valley at Gheringhap. The railway crossed on a lofty and noble viaduct; but we went tortuously down the stony gorge to a ford, bumped through brown muddy water and climbed slowly to the other side. When we topped the rise there lay the redbrick scatter of Geelong with the Ford factory towers glinting in the sun, and smoke pouring from the foundries.

We had lunch at Mooney's hotel in the centre of the city and then went out to where Basil said he had some property to inspect. It was a suburb of weatherboard houses and corrugated-iron roofs behind saltbush hedges and facing wide treeless streets. I sat in the car while Basil disappeared inside one of the little houses. Around four o'clock his business was done and we started out on the long dusty climb back to the plateau and Lindisfarne. On the way I delivered myself of some disparaging remarks on suburbs. Basil was silent for a while and then said,

'I'm sorry you think that, because we're going to live there.'

I was dumbfounded; at my own crassness and at the dreadful prospect of Basil and his family moving from Lindisfarne to a suburb of a provincial town. Of course, I reflected, he probably wanted to be near his old school, Geelong Grammar, for the boys' sake, if he had to move. But why did he have to move at all? Finally, as we struggled over the last rise of the great scarp and rode once more easily along the plateau, I blurted it out: 'Why?'

'I've struck a rough patch,' he said, frankly. 'We can't go on renting Lindisfarne.'

'But,' I faltered, uncomprehending, 'why should that have happened?'

His brown jaws creased in the well-known smile and the fine strong teeth clamped more firmly on the pipe.

'They tell me it's the depression,' he said. 'The slump. Call it what you like. We just have to pull in our belts that's all.'

As the car bounced on towards Lindisfarne, with the sun at our backs, I reflected with some shame, probably unnecessary, that I was perched on my little island of gold in the raging sea. It was modest enough; £250 from an insurance policy. But here was I planning a trip to Canada while Basil was going to have to move into a bungalow in a suburb of Geelong and write articles on fishing for the *Argus* and broadcasts for the A.B.C. to keep the aspidistra flying. The rest of the way home I was very silent so that, as we pulled into the garage and turned off the motor and the kids came shrieking with joy out across the yard, it was Basil who had to lean across and clap *my* knee and say,

'Come on now, cheer up! Worse things happen at sea.'

Chapter Fourteen

MORTAR BORED

THE terrible and awe-inspiring final exams were held in the blazing February dog days in Wilson Hall. A month later the results came out. I was astonished, though much gratified, to learn that I'd gained First Class Honours, the Exhibition and the Dwight Prize in English. The results surpassed all my hopes. A further month and I received my degree from the hands of Sir James Barrett, the Vice-Chancellor of the University. After the ceremony I went down to a fashionably inexpensive photographer in 'The Block' and in my borrowed plumes—for no one would ever think of *owning* their own cap and gown—sat for my degree picture: a rather supercilious young man.

The question now arose, what was to be my career? I had a long talk with David Kennedy Picken. He very kindly, though rather alarmingly, insisted that I accompany him for this purpose on a walk through Royal Park. With hands clasped behind his back, curly tonsure and bald head hidden under a rakish black Homburg, body bent forward in his customary purposeful lope, he padded incongruously with me up the cinder track that led from Royal Park to the Zoo. A little horse-drawn tramcar, crammed with screaming and waving children, overtook us and trotted by, on its way no doubt to the Elephant ride and Molly the Monkey. Digger refused to be distracted but loped steadily on.

'Ye'll be wanting to apply for the Rhodes no doubt', he said as he quickened his pace.

'I'd thought rather of the Millett, sir.'

He stopped dead and looked at me with intense concentration from beneath his shaggy brows.

'Indeed? Indeed?' We resumed the lope. 'No doubt ye'd have a better chance at the Millett, for no prowess in sport is involved and I really don't believe you're much of a darb at sports, eh?'

'No, sir. I'm not.'

'But just the same, it would be a great honour for the college if ye captured the Rhodes. I think perhaps ye'd better try for both.'

'Both, sir?' I felt alarmed. Would there be no end to oral boards and exams?

'Aye,' said Digger, quickening his pace. 'Both.' We were walking now by the big aviary. The sun was westering and the birds were screeching and caterwauling in a most inconsiderate way. Digger had to raise his voice to be heard above them; the macaws were especially diligent interrupters, some of them clinging to the wire with their claws and beaks to shriek at us as we went by.

'Ye see,' said Digger, 'the Millett is chosen in August and the Rhodes in September. If ye didn't get the fairrst ye could try for the latter. The question is what are ye going to do while ye're waiting?' He bent a keen eye on me as we trundled on abreast, past the snake house and in the general direction of Molly the Orang Outan.

'I'd thought of getting a job on the *Argus*, sir.'

'The *Argus*? Who put that idea into your head?'

'A newspaper friend, sir.'

He stroked his battleship chin. 'H'm! I don't think that would be the best idea. Jairnalism. I don't care for it.'

We walked on in silence for a few moments. A small crowd had gathered outside Molly's cage offering her peanuts through the bars. She took them with a large prehensile hand, shelled them with her feet, sniffed them and threw them back at the crowd.

Digger chuckled. 'Almost human,' he said absently. Molly whipped out an old sugar-bag from the rear of the barred premises and draped it over her head like a clumsy mantilla. Digger suddenly barked

'Would ye like to be a junior tutor?'

I was nonplussed. I saw myself, with only a tenuous lead, trying to keep one jump ahead of fellows whose colleagues I had been in my final year. I sought counsel from Molly; but she drew the sugar bag right over her head and 'retired'.

'Well?' said Digger sharply. 'We could continue your board and lodging at Ormond and offer you £120 a year, as your Shell Bursary wouldn't be operative.'

I said what was on my mind.

'Do you thing I can waste a whole year waiting, sir? After all I'm twenty-one.'

Digger gave a strangled chuckle.

'Ye'll be dying of old age in no time,' he said.

We turned round, leaving Molly behind, and began to retrace our steps through Royal Park, now bathed in an angry red from the rays of the slanting sun, striking almost horizontally through the gum trees.

'I think ye should take it on,' he said. 'Ye can be wurrking at your Dwight at the same time. Tutoring in history will keep your hand in and I like to see a man occupied.'

'May I let you know tomorrow, sir?'

When I got back to college I sought Geoff Hudspeth. He was in his shirtsleeves in our study, undershot chin unshaven, green eyeshade slantwise on his brow, cigarette streaming smoke up into his eyes, and a slide rule in his hands. He was in his final year at engineering while I was free as air with my B.A. behind me.

'Half a mo,' he said as I opened my mouth. 'Tough problem.' He pored over the slide rule for a moment, drew a smashing curve on his architect's drawing board and hurled the eyeshade up to the ceiling.

'Shoot.'

I told him what Digger had proposed. He was amazed that I should be hesitant. £120 a year *and* board and lodging! And I wouldn't have to dip into my own savings.

'On top of that,' he said, throwing his slippered feet on the desk, 'You'll be sitting at head table in Hall, and you know what *that* means.'

'No,' I said dully, 'what?'

'Cream, boy, real live cream! You'll be living like a king.'

I really wasn't all that keen on entering for the two great scholarship competitions. The last three Rhodes Scholars from the State of Victoria had all been Ormond men; the most recent being Ross Campbell the literate and witty inhabitant of I 40. Not only had they all been Ormond men; they had all been intellectuals with only the most superficial interest in, let alone skill at, games. Rumblings of discontent had already been heard in the Letters to the Editor column of the *Argus*; and a muted snarl of disapproval had reached us from the depths of the 47-inch chests of the Trinity College rowing blues. I considered that the dice were loaded against me. Also Rhodes men were required to evince qualities of leadership and high moral purpose which, it seemed to my own appraising eye, I conspicuously lacked. I didn't think, to sum up, that I was quite the sort of fellow Cecil Rhodes had in mind.

As for the Millett, though an entrant didn't require proficiency in games or a sense of moral duty, it had its own drawbacks. The applicant had to have first class honours. Well, I had those. But he also had to set forth in great detail his plans for the three years that the scholarship ran and also his proposals for a career. I wasn't at all sure that I'd be able to do this honestly. I really had no idea what I wanted as a career. Journalism attracted me enormously, but would such a frank admission gain me the approbation of the selection board? I hardly thought so, and yet at the same time I'd find it hard to dress up my proposals in a manner that would impress the board. If they didn't see through me on the written submission, they certainly would at the oral.

The Millett also held a macabre horror for us because of what had happened to an earlier winner. This man combined fantastic learning ability and an agile brain with the sudden enunciation of the most startling blasphemies. His furrowed brow and boiling of unruly red hair seemed to hint at sulphurous desires, but his scholastic record was so consistently brilliant and, curiously, his game of tennis so mathematically exact (without being spectacular) that we all overlooked his darker side. Two years earlier this man had won the Millett, and departed amid our envious stares for England. A year later he was brought home all the way back to Australia in the company of a male nurse. He had had a complete and catastrophic breakdown. He was taken from the ship to a Home and was never seen by us again. This naturally threw a pall of gloom over the Millett and over potential entrants.

However, the tutor's job was money for jam—I hoped. And why shouldn't I try my hand at the two scholarships, especially if the Master and the College wanted it? I'd graduated before my twenty-first birthday. I had Uncle Graham's insurance cheque for the trip. My career—and my father in Canada—could wait surely for one academic year?

Having made my decision, I notified Digger and, in order to keep abreast of students of my own age with whom I'd been hobnobbing in the same lecture room, I started to feed my moustache with a nourishing oil.

Life as a college tutor proved to be demanding only in the exercise of intellectual agility. I had to keep one lesson ahead of the students who were taking European History and Eng. Lit. and while this meant a lot of late nights swotting up the set books it didn't really mean that I had to exercise my brain: rather, my cunning.

The game was perfectly understood by the students who solicitously refrained from asking questions they knew I couldn't answer. However the college got good value, because whatever the quality of my tutorials they were costing less than a quarter of the fees of the regulars. Of course it could be argued that I had only a quarter of their capacity: but I think Digger's Scots parsimony was well satisfied with the bargain and I noticed that the regular tutors gave me the heavy chores to do, such as correcting exam papers or the essays of those competing for the entrance scholarship into Ormond.

Being a tutor did mean, as Geoff had forecast, that I would sit at Head Table, and that we had real cream with the porridge, caramel custard instead of 'sinker' and egg-and-bacon instead of 'Choppasteak'. But in other respects I remained a student. I continued to share my study with Hudspeth. I ducked out of the senior common room into the junior common room as soon as I decently could after Hall, and I continued to be amazed at my own temerity in instructing my contemporaries on the basis of so little extra knowledge. The blind leading the blind, in fact.

I was not a little annoyed at having to purchase a new gown. Digger had made it clear that the noble tattered remnant which distinguished me as a Senior Man had no place on the back of a junior tutor. I bought a secondhand gown from my friend the resident tutor in medicine. He played the flute and disapproved of my jazz records, but he was not averse to making five quid out of me. He threw in a free medical examination and told me, as he pocketed my fiver, that I had a heart murmur, but didn't need to worry. His news alarmed me greatly and indeed dominated my mind until Mother sent me out from England the latest Duke Ellington Album.

The knowledge that I possessed this wonderful album spread like wildfire throughout the university and I found myself unexpectedly popular. Football blues who, from their bulgy height, had scorned my intellectual pretensions, now invited me to smart Toorak parties and to weekends at Portsea—that cesspit of sinful iniquity and sandy beach fifty safe miles down The Bay. Girls whom I'd never met—or glimpsed but fitfully in the distance—approached me without shame in broad daylight on the most populated part of the campus, in and preferably between lectures when crowds were elbowing each other to and from the classrooms. Would I come to a party they were having and bring my records? Would I? Well of course I would, and I wasted a great deal of time traipsing to and from such gatherings in the belief that at last I was being sought for my own dear self. When I should have been preparing myself for the Millett and the Rhodes by leading an exemplary life and swotting hard I was out many nights and most weekends with my Ellington Album, now augmented by the Dorsey Brothers, Joe Venuti, Cab Calloway, Jimmy Lunceford and the Boswell Sisters.

It is pleasant to be able to record however, that many of their tunes have stood the test of time and, thirty or so years later, are still recognized for the masterpieces which we of course all thought they were: 'Hot and Bothered', 'The Mooch', 'Black and Tan Fantasy', 'Mood Indigo'. Ellington—the early Ellington of the Jungle Band— didn't *send* people the way the pop singers do today. He was played then only to aficionados, not in enormous one-night stands at the

Streatham Empire and the Golders Green Hippodrome. You rarely danced to him. You sat and listened, preferably sitting on the floor, in groups of ten to twenty. Everybody kept deathly quiet and after the record—only three minutes each in those pre-LP days—there would be a lengthy and intense discussion of Coleman Hawkins' saxophone solo, the hot riffs of Sonny Greer on drums, Bubber Miley's staccato trumpet or the extraordinarily inventive arabesques of The Duke himself. He quite often hit wrong notes (sacrilege to say so, of course) so his technique or lack of it you took for granted. It was his musical invention that staggered us all.

I soon realized that possession of the album loaded me with the expectation of profound knowledge—which I didn't have. I began to subscribe to *The Gramophone*, that delightful spare-time activity of Compton Mackenzie and Christopher Stone, and to *The Melody Maker*, the gospel of the jazzbos and out-of-work musicians who hung around Archer Street behind far-off Leicester Square. I became an Authority, a pundit and finally a bore. At the end of six months my records were worn to throaty fuzziness and ideas for my future were now indelibly muddled by the quite ludicrous belief that I could become a professional jazz musician. I think if I could have been more honest with myself I'd have realized that my student affluence (courtesy now Ormond College, Uncle Graham *and* the Shell Oil Co. Ltd.) was giving me—in the midst of the Depression too—a false sense of security and perhaps a false sense of values. It might have been better for me if the Depression had really hit me (it did a year or so later). Oh well. Never mind. After all I wasn't marking time was I, I was awaiting the Millett and the Rhodes. And the College approved, didn't they? Why, Digger himself . . .

I had celebrated my twenty-first birthday with a dinner given to seven of my college cronies at Sammy Artwell's rather disreputable pub in the Sydney Road. Mother had sent me a cheque for £50. More backsliding! My pals gave me a leather tobacco pouch. When the beery innocent revelling was at its height Mine Host put his head in.

'Yer'll have to sign the book.'

'What book?'

'To show yer from outa town.'

'Do you expect us to tell a lie, Mr. Artwell?'

'I dunno about that, but if the johns raid the place and you're charged as found-ins, it ain't just you that's gunner get into trouble. It's me.' He tapped his thick chest with a meaty forefinger. 'Ain't supposed to be drinkin' in a pub after six y'know.'

'Okay Sammy,' we shouted. 'What do we do?'

'Sign here—just put some country place after your name. Any

place. But no foolin' now. Some of the young fellows put London and Paris and stoopid places like that.'

He handed me the book and I passed it round the table. We wrote Wangaratta and Colac and Dimboola and Bairnsdale and Deniliquin, giggling stupidly, and watched with a grey impassive face by Sammy. Only when someone spilled beer on the book and made the entries run and spread did he lose his temper.

'Gawd stone the crows!' he cried. 'It's the last time I have you young barstids in here again.'

I arose in my wrath. 'Mister Artwell,' I said with tipsy dignity, 'Such language affronts us. You will kindly apologize.'

'I'll see you in the dunny first.'

'Now Sammy,' said one of my guests, Charlie Newman, 'Cool off. you want your bill paid, don't you?'

'My flamin' oath I do and I'll . . .'

Rat-tat-tat!

Sammy's suffused face drained instantly of blood and his eyes assumed a watchful expression. His great fat body was tense and aware.

Rat-tat-tat!

We looked at each other in consternation. Sammy breathed heavily.

'Thought so. The cops. Now fer Gawd's sake don't forget where yer from.'

Rat-tat-tat!

Sammy waddled out to open the front door. We heard him drawing back the chain and an unfriendly voice 'Evening, Sammy.'

'Evening, Sarge.'

'Just checkin' up. Mind if we look around?'

'Take yer time, Sarge. Just a small party of lads from up the country.'

Back in the private room we all strove hard through the beery fumes to remember where we were supposed to be from. And what if we couldn't remember? Or got it wrong? Or if they guessed— of course they couldn't, could they? that we were really just innocent Melbourne University students, innocently breaking the law.

'Evenin'.' The sergeant—a beefy man with a tall patent leather helmet—gave us a nod full of bogus bonhomie. We nodded back. I felt that as host I should rise; the others swivelled round in their chairs to get a better look at The Law, but remained seated. We all registered what we hoped were expressions of polite enquiry. The sergeant kept his helmet on, placed his hands on the back of an empty dining room chair and leaned forward, taking in, as he did so, the cluster of empty and half empty beer bottles on the table. Useless to attempt to hide them. Anyway we didn't need to. We had our alibi, didn't we?

'Havin' a party, eh?' said the sergeant.

We nodded.

'All you young fellows bona fide travellers?'

We chorused assent. Sammy Artwell's huge moon-face loomed through the side door; in the gloom of the corridor we could dimly see Mrs. Sammy in a wine-coloured dressing gown and mules, with her hair in curling papers.

'Where's yer home?' said the sergeant looking at me.

'Wangaratta.'

'M'hm. And you?'

'Colac.'

'M'hm. Howzabout you?'

'Deniliquin,' said Weary Dunlop.

'Deniliquin?' said the sergeant. 'Are you from outa the state then?'

'Not exactly.'

'How do you mean not exactly. Deniliquin's in New South, ain't it?'

'I really meant to say Echuca. I got mixed up.'

The sergeant scowled slightly. 'And you? You from New South too?'

'No, Sarge. I'm from Wangaratta,' said Charlie Newman.

The sergeant turned ponderously to me.

'I thought you said *you* was from Wangaratta.'

'We're both from Wangaratta,' I said glibly.

'Is that right!' said the sergeant. 'Well I think you're both a coupla fibbers. How do you like that?'

'I don't like it at all, officer,' I said with hauteur.

'Don't officer me,' he snapped. 'I think you're a mob of young fellows down from the Uni. That's what I think. I don't think you've been in Wangaratta in yer life, eh Sammy?'

'I'm sure I couldn't say, Sarge,' said Sammy impassively. 'It's all in the book.'

'The book!' said the sergeant with biting contempt. 'And what does the book mean? Look at the names in it. John Smith, Bill Smith, Bill Jones, Jack Robinson . . .'

'But those aren't the names we put down,' said Charlie Newman. 'We put down our right names.'

'Your right names and your wrong addresses,' said the sergeant.

Charlie rose to his feet. He was a law student and a footballer, and stood six foot four in his socks. Eyed speculatively by the sergeant he poured a foaming schooner of beer.

Humping My Bluey

'Sergeant,' he said, 'I made a mistake. I'm not from Wangaratta at all. I'm from Warracknabeal—in the Wimmera, y'know? Sorry and all that. But anyone could get mixed up with names like these.' The sergeant grunted. 'Our host is having his twenty-first birthday and we invite you to join us in wishing him good health.' He handed the foaming schooner to the sergeant.

After a moment's hesitation the policeman removed his tall patent leather helmet and put it on a spare table. Then he grasped the schooner, drained most of it at gulp, belched and said 'Good 'ealth.'

We solemnly raised our glasses.

'Just the same,' he said 'You boys are from the Uni, ain't ya?'

'No, no' we shouted in chorus. 'We're from Warracknabeal.'

He gazed at us in mock incredulity.

'Not all o' yer?'

'Yes, all of us.'

The sergeant picked up his helmet and moved towards the door.

'All right,' he said with a ponderous grin. 'But keep quiet, and, Sammy, see they leave by the back door.'

After this episode, the excitement of eating down town instead of chomping at the wholesome but predictable fare at the University gripped me. I began to explore the Soho of Melbourne situated up the hill, towards the Parliament Buildings, on Exhibition Street. It was modest enough, goodness knows, but it excited us enormously. The two places that the University youngsters found the most exhilarating were the Café Latin and Mario's. The Café Latin was run by two Italians, Signori Triaca and Borghese. Borghese was in charge of the kitchen and one rarely saw him except when the swing-door was kicked open to reveal steamy visages shouting over the preparation of the lasagne, the spaghetti and the canneloni. Triaca was the front man with the glad hand and the brilliant toothy smile and the eye on the cash register. He dressed incongruously in ginger brown tweeds and wore a tiny fascist badge in his lapel.

As the European crisis deepened and the iniquities of Hitler and Mussolini began to be talked about even in far-off Australia, Signor Triaca's fasces became less and less attractive. Besides he didn't have a licence and you had to climb up steps to reach him. We deserted him for Mario who had a licence and was at street level. Mario was blond, suety and pie-faced with an aureole of grey-white hair, black olive eyes and a manner 'as smooth as a baby's bottom', as Charlie Newman put it. He was particularly kind to students, allowing us to use his bistro for assignations and never complaining if we sat for an hour or two over a single glass of dry vermouth and some stick bread. His reward was our undying affection, immense word of mouth publicity among the parents, and the patronage of the University and café society for dinners, receptions and weddings. It was a single room fronting a curtained window on to Exhibition Street, square tables for four with checked cloths, and mirrors on the wall decked with hand-painted views, by his wife, of Lake Como and Lake Maggiore. The food was Italian tempered to the Australian taste which meant not too much olive oil or cheese—just enough to give the sober matron from Kew or Malvern or St. Kilda the illusion that she was at a *trattoria* in Florence or Milan. We thought it extremely romantic. But Digger spoke to me with good-natured asperity

'We don't see you much in Hall these days, for your evening meal.'

'Well no, sir, I have been a little neglectful.'

'Aye. Don't be too neglectful. We want an example set for the younger men.'

'Yes, sir.'

For a few nights I'd attend Hall and Chapel religiously, and then spend the evening studying for my dissertation. For the catch in the Dwight Prize (£25) was that, even if you had gained first class Honours for your B.A., you were required to do another dissertation for your M.A.; and this had to be handed in *before* the selection was made for the Millett and the Rhodes. I therefore neglected Melbourne's bohemia and strove with might and main over the novels of Thomas Love Peacock. My choice of these picaresque productions of the early romantic period had been dictated entirely by chance. When Mother went to England she had left behind her a complete set. The names appealed to me: *Gryll Grange, Nightmare Abbey, Headlong Hall*. I was fed to the teeth with Dickens and Scott. Mother had read them aloud to us every night for close on ten years, but this true labour of love (or of *à la recherche* of her own *temps perdu*), far from inculcating in me an affection for these classics, had made me vow never to read them again. Peacock seemed a change; respectable and O.K. for Eng. Lit., yet also a little *recherché*. I spoke to Professor Cowling, who concurred. Soon the study was lined with novels of T. L. Peacock and I had a large loose-leaf notebook in which I jotted down far from original observations.

But cheerfulness kept breaking in and when to the joys of Mario's were added those of the first Melbourne University Revue (for the Lord Mayor's Fund, of course) I began once again to see less of T. L. Peacock and of dinner in Hall and more of Mario's and the Comedy theatre a few doors down Exhibition Street. The students thought they were exceptionally fortunate in having for the revue, as their universal artistic uncle, no less a whizzbang than Cyril Pearl and his girl friend Irma Janetzki. How glamorous, how sophisticated, how daring and bland they both seemed to us. They moved among the callow youngsters—mature, internationally expert sophisticates in their late twenties—as gods. We would have done anything for them.

The revue was to be called *Stude Prunes*, Cyril's idea. Brilliantly witty, we thought. He brought his girl friend into Ormond College, and sat down in the sacred I 40 and with Alan Nichols and Ross Campbell and me. He rewrote the entire script, filling it with wizard wheezes from top to toe. I suppose it must have been wonderful for him, a journalist and traveller with a mordant wit and a newspaperman's flair, to have at his beck and call the inventiveness, high spirits and rudeness of a score of clever undergraduates. To say nothing of their adoration and affection. He subsequently went on to become the editor of the Sydney *Sunday Telegraph* and author of *The Wild Men of Sydney* and *The Girl with the Swansdown Seat*, so that he fully deserved to be the only begetter of our revue, which he just about was.

Pearl was a swart thickset fellow with a sallow complexion, a pendulous lower lip, an untidy Chaplinesque moustache and a great shock of long black hair. Assuming wrongly that his appearance connoted inarticulate decadence, the bully boys—the rowers, the footballers and the Toorak socialites—attempted to engage him in heavy-handed witticisms. He sliced them off at the ankles before they knew what hit them. The Gurkha with his kukri on the Western Front and the Scimitar of Saladin were as nothing compared to the ease with which Cyril Pearl vanquished his attackers.

His effortless superiority was perhaps easily come by since most of us were five or six years his junior. He was also bad for us to be exposed to; for we sought to ape him, and, being neither as quick witted nor as ruthless, failed lamentably. Cyril had a tough punning humour developed to a fine-honed edge. His appearance, usually without a hat and often accompanied by Irma, was to us more intoxicating than a lecture by Professor Scott, a visit to the Bijou or an evening at 9 Darling Street.

Cyril Pearl introduced us to T. S. Eliot and Ezra Pound, to Surrealism and *Les Six* and a host of iconoclastic intellectual and artistic people and ideas which went to our heads like champagne. If the three ages of students in relation to their professors are aptly summarized in the apophthegm : They say. What say they? Let them say !; then it was Cyril who most gloriously and irresponsibly sealed us in that final posture of defiance and excitement. He questioned *everything*, as a matter of principle; he taught us to share his avid lust for causes, even if we couldn't match his piercing Socratic thrust. Thus he was bad for us as well as good for us.

Rehearsals for *Stude Prunes*—which included a skit on the League of Nations, a mock ballet set to Ferde Grofé's *Metropolis Suite*, innumerable blackout sketches crammed with *doubles ententes* and an inevitable chorus-line of co-eds—took place in the Comedy theatre. Cyril Pearl had taken over responsibility for the book, many of the lyrics, the programme (Irma did the design for the cover) and the advertising campaign. Music was in charge of Ag Zwar, with an assist from a blues singer named Marge Stedeford who wooed them all by singing, 'torchily', seated alone on a cushion over the footlights, with Ag's whispering piano somewhere in the rear. Cyril rested lordly in the second row of the stalls in the darkened Sunday afternoon theatre while his disciples draped themselves conveniently at hand, and lesser lights like myself (only two sketches and four speaking parts) were relegated to the back of the pit.

This particular Sunday I was with Charlie Newman in the excited darkness, when the chorus made their entry to the supplicating gestures of the choreographer. I was immediately struck by the appearance of the girl fourth from the left. She was tall with a big shock of titian hair, a reserved expression but a wonderful figure—what a combination—and a lovely mouth with a dimple in the lower lip. As the girls—dressed for some reason as Don Cossacks—pranced across the stage to the music of Ag Zwar, I nudged Charlie Newman.

'Who's that? Fourth from the left.'

'Who . . . Let's see. Oh yes. That's a sheila called Joan Burke.'

'Joan Burke?'

'Mean to say you don't know her?'

'Never seen her in my life.'

'She's extra-collegiate—second year arts I think. Want to meet her?'

'My oath I do.'

'Good oh. Come behind with me at the interval and I'll give you a knock down.'

He was as good as his word and after the usual preliminary parrying and thrusting she agreed to come with me to Mario's, suitably accompanied, and drink an innocent vermouth. Five years and twelve thousand miles away from that Sunday May afternoon at Mario's we were married. But at the moment this was hidden in the future and I didn't think to thank Cyril or Charlie or anyone but myself for my good fortune. Rehearsals now proceeded with all the jealousy and the back-biting, but little of the professionalism, which distinguish the real theatre. I moved in a double intoxication: the show, my new girl friend. We ran for a week. We made a lot of money for the Lord Mayor's Fund. Suddenly the Millett loomed.

It turned out that there was no written examination; only an oral board. I was annoyed at this, having spent what I considered to be a great deal of time in preparing cunning drafts of essays on The Directorate, Bismarckian policy, and the Congress of Vienna, to say nothing of the novels of T. L. Peacock. I emerged from the oral with a slight sinking feeling, confirmed a week later when it was announced that an extra-collegiate mathematical genius had gained the coveted prize. There were sympathetic murmurs and one or two claps on the back as I walked through Hall that night in my gown on the way to Head Table. Digger didn't seem to be greatly perturbed.

'Ye had the examinee's ability,' he said with devastating frankness, 'but perrhaps harrdly the true scholarrly approach. We must keep our eye on the Rhodes now.'

Alas, with the Rhodes a month later it was the same story. I did well at the oral and later learned that it had been a very close thing; but not close enough. I was edged out by a man who was about as good as me scholastically but who was also a footballer and active in S.C.M. affairs. Scotty, who'd been on the selection board, told me much later that he had spoken up for me, but that the Board had judged—perhaps rightly—that on the whole it was about time that the State of Victoria got away from the long line of Ormond intellectuals.

This time I really was upset. I had believed that I would gain one of the scholarships and had oriented my whole year to that end. Here it was October and the year appeared to be wasted. What had I achieved since graduation in March? Nothing, it seemed to me. I'd spent the year fooling around at my tutoring job and wasted a great deal of time in meaningless extra-curricular activities: debating, amateur dramatics, jazz (Heavens, the amount of time I'd wasted over *that*!) social climbing—yes, I had to admit it. But what availed the enamelled smiles of the Toorak matrons when it was seen that I had no job and (though an amusing boy to have around, no doubt, as an extra young bachelor on a weekend) no prospects either? My anger burned against Digger. It was he who had wanted me to go in for the Millett and the Rhodes, and all for the kudos and prestige of the College. He who had dangled the bait of a tutorship to keep me in trim. Ah, but wait a bit; I didn't *have* to accept, did I? I could have gone straight into a cub reporter's job on the *Argus*. I could have gone into a cadetship in the Shell Oil Co. Instead I yielded to the siren call of a year in comparative indolence—admittedly following three years of extremely hard work—in which I could relax as a Senior Man loaded with laurels, or strut around the campus as a brilliant young man about town of independent means (for so the dregs of my scholarship and Uncle Graham's insurance policy now made me feel). It was my fault as much as Digger's.

Mortar Bored

And now I realized, which I hadn't in my dance through bohemia and café society in white tie and tails, that the selection board for both the Millett and the Rhodes had been watching me narrowly all the time, gauging my suitability, as displayed in my daily conduct, to be considered as a candidate. What had they seen? A young man who had appeared on the stage of the Comedy theatre impersonating Adolf Hitler in a foolish student revue; a man who had participated in a ludicrous and offensive jape whereby 'The Baron' had been foisted on the worthy bourgeoisie of Tasmania; a man who had light-heartedly, indeed almost frivolously, rejected an opportunity to serve in a Great (semi) Australian Enterprise—Darch would have told them that; a man who, while preparing to be a Leader of Young People, was known to dash down to Portsea and Sorrento in fast cars, and to drink gin on the beach while listening to the latest hits on an H.M.V. portable; a man clearly lacking in the ability to influence others, as witness his failure to prevent Sam White being dumped in the pool; a man whose political judgement was questionable (hadn't he brought Billy Hughes to the campus?); and of course the child—poor fellow, he couldn't help it—of a 'broken home'.

A dark picture indeed. My reception by Professor Cowling, Head of the English Department, added to the gloom. He had read my dissertation on the novels of Thomas Love Peacock. Really, it was rather poor stuff; quite superficial. What had I been doing all this time? On top of that it was written in long-hand and was appallingly hard to read. I forebore to observe that taking down notes from his lectures on Milton had ruined my hand for life, in case he should retort that a man on a £250 a year scholarship ought to be able to afford to get an MS typed. He would not, he said wearily, withhold the £25 Dwight prize money; but that was because it would be administratively awkward to do so rather than because he thought I had earned it. He handed me the cheque in prim disdain and I departed fuming—half of me resenting his innuendoes and half of me prepared to admit grudgingly that he might be right. No wonder I'd failed at both scholarships. No wonder I'd wasted my year. The fact that I had met the girl who was to be my wife and wise counsellor was naturally lost on me; as was the fact that I'd gained a great deal of general experience, cemented old friendships and made some new ones (as well as some brittle acquaintances). I railed at myself. Timon of Athens had nothing on me. And then, about a month after my rejection, while I was still threshing around wondering what to do, I received an unexpected letter from my grandfather in far-off England.

It was unexpected for two reasons: first because he didn't often write except to send me the odd cheque; secondly because of what he said. His opening gambit was to congratulate me on *not* being selected for the Rhodes. In bitter amazement I hurled the letter into the corner of the study. But a moment later I picked it up and read it carefully. The Rhodes Scholarship, said my grandfather, Professor J. W. Mackail, O.M., was a misnomer. Rhodes had been guided by specious values and involved in doubtful ventures most of his life. He was a narrow, power-drunk, uncivilized oaf and the use of the word 'scholarship' in connection with him was laughable. Rhodes scholars were not true scholars in any sense of the word. They were more properly bursars, designed to perpetuate a type of man for whom there might have been room in the days of Edward VII, Elgar's Pomp and Circumstance, and (*pace* Cousin Ruddy) the white man's burden and lesser breeds without the law. Such men were not needed now. There would of course always be room for men of character and men of genuine intellectual attainments. But the qualifications laid down by Rhodes did not necessarily produce men of that stamp.

'Good though they may be,' he said, 'they are not as good as they might be.' He himself, a Fellow of Balliol and a lifelong frequenter of Oxford occasions, had witnessed with distaste the irruption of Rhodes House into the peaceful and fastidious atmosphere of dreaming spires. Rhodes House, with its overtones of muscly outback Christianity, colonial politics and men with queer wide-brimmed hats. Why, the first Trustee of Rhodes House had been a Canadian—and from New Brunswick too! We all knew what *that* meant. One had only to think of Lord Beaverbrook. He hated it all. He was delighted that I had not been selected. It would be the making of me. He looked forward to seeing me in England one of these days.

I read and re-read the letter in a tumult. I couldn't know that my grandparents and my great-grandmother had all been tremendous pro-Boers at the time of the Boer War and had incurred the severe censure of the villagers of Rottingdean in Sussex for their failure to celebrate the relief of Mafeking. I couldn't know that he was just venting his spleen on the Empire Builders. I'd waited so long, groomed myself so hard for the Rhodes, that I just couldn't accept its sudden denigration, by him. As for my grandfather's views on colonies and Empire, why, they were downright anarchistic! Wonderful of the old boy to write, though. He was now 74. I'd better get to England and see him before it was too late. Immensely bucked I sat down and started to make plans for a long journey, to be powered by Uncle Graham's insurance cheque.

I'd go to Sydney first and see Cousin Hugh and the jolly girls. Then I'd take a ship to Canada via Fiji and Honolulu. What an *unusual* way to take The Trip, people would say. Most of us go by Colombo and Port Said. Oh, but I came *out* that way, I'd reply (omitting to mention that I was barely eight years old at the time). No, this was a much more romantic way, didn't they think? You know, the vast Pacific? Oh yes, very romantic. Then I'd cross Canada by the C.P.R., from Vancouver to Toronto, and discover my father, whom I'd not seen since I was five. My, you *are* an interesting boy ! Yes, it's true too, that Canada's in many ways more interesting than Australia. Less isolated. And then 'The French'. Oh yes, well I plan to visit Quebec and Montreal of course. And it's so close to America too ! Well yes, I'm going to visit New York, and maybe Boston and Washington as well.

Then after that, I'd cross the Atlantic to a grand reunion with Mother, Colin and young Lance (he'd be thirteen now) and of course all the relatives I hadn't seen since childhood—my grandparents, my uncle, my aunt; and a host of half-remembered friends and parents of friends.

And then? Well, I'll have to see. I'll probably travel around Europe for a bit; you know, visit the art galleries in Paris and all that. Or I might return to Canada to be with my father. But what do you plan to *do*? Haven't exactly decided yet, but I'll probably go into newspaper work (in the end it turned out to be the improbably named *Mail and Empire* in Toronto). But you've been in Australia a long time. Yes, nearly fourteen years. Hasn't it got into your bones? Of course it has; but, you know, only young once . . . must travel . . . have a little money . . . Are you coming back? Oh yes, I expect so; don't know really. Yes, probably.

I went to pay a farewell call on Joan. She shared a studio with another girl in a loft in the centre of the city. I'd been away, having my last stay with the Halls at Lindisfarne, and hadn't seen her for some weeks. She greeted me with unpropitious if understandable coolness and when I unfolded my plans for travel she infuriated me by saying that I was simply using travel to mask my own uncertainty about my future. I hadn't made up my mind—maybe couldn't was a better word—what I wanted to do, or was able to do. So I was going on a trip instead. Substituting movement for action. She quoted Horace at me. 'They change their climate, not their nature, who run beyond the sea.' It would gain me nothing. At the end of all my travel I'd be just as unsettled as before. Why couldn't I get a *job* and do something worthwhile?

I flung out of the studio in a fury, and for a long time didn't even write to her. It was only after I'd been in Canada nearly five years that correspondence—becoming passionate over time and space—convinced us both that we should meet again and marry. As it was, I went on to fling out of Melbourne, also in a fine fury. Shaking the dust of the dull old city from my shoes; and on towards broad horizons. Dad saw me off at Spencer Street in the *Spirit of Progress*.

'Don't forget,' he said. 'When you see your Mother tell her I'd like her back.'

I was sickened by this litany and could only gulp and look awkwardly at his sad brown face and long bloodhound nose as it receded beneath the smoke-grimed girders and the dusty glass.

Sydney was a blur. The Poynters were just back from their round the world trip and we were rather a tight fit in Tikinui. I was welcome but perhaps not all that welcome. I chafed to get away. The ship was to be the R.M.S. *Aorangi* (The Cloud Piercer in Maori— Mount Cook in English) of 18,500 tons, bound for Vancouver on the now long since defunct Canada-Australia line. Hugh gave me an introduction to the Managing Director of the Bank of New South Wales who was travelling first class (I was travelling third). We said a not too tearful farewell at the docks at Darling Harbour.

'Don't stay!' I cried. I didn't, I said, want to be on the seaward end of the canopy of streamers which, stretched from deck to dock between loving hands, would eventually strain and part and flutter down into the bilgey water as the ship took to the stream.

'Don't submit me—and you—to that!' I cried.

But the truth was that I didn't want to be seen waving from the third class, for it was full of men in sweaters and braces and open-necked shirts. I was ashamed of my tiny cabin with its two flat bunks—almost as hard and narrow as those in the *Nairana* going to Tasmania. The cabin was made gorgeous and gushing with perfume. Barbara Cohen, the girl who had beaten me for the Exhibition in History, had kindly sent an enormous bunch of roses all the way from Melbourne. The steward cocked a supercilious eyebrow. Why waste it all on a fellow who can only afford to travel third?

I locked the door and sat down on the bunk. The last of Sydney; the last of Melbourne; the last of Australia. Fortunately the porthole was on the far side away from the dock, so that I was spared the sight of the widening wedge of water and the fluttering streamers. I saw instead the rusted side of a collier from Newcastle discharging its cargo in Darling Harbour. When the Plimsoll mark began to slip sideways across the porthole I unlocked the door and scuttled through the bowels of the ship, amid an infinity of interlacing tubes and wires suffocated with white paint. I gained the foredeck just as the great arch of the Harbour Bridge was sliding overhead. Down in the tiny third class lounge a Canadian deportee was playing 'Over the Waves' on a cracked piano. I went down to listen, and by the time

I came up again it was dusk, and the deck was starting to heave beneath my feet.

So, carrying with me a burden of woe and frustration as well as a freight of hope and excitement, I sailed outward across the Pacific into the rising sun, while the old grey cryptic continent slipped slowly backward into oblivion.

THE HOGARTH PRESS

This is a paperback list for today's readers – but it holds to a tradition of adventurous and original publishing set by Leonard and Virginia Woolf when they founded The Hogarth Press in 1917 and started their first paperback series in 1924.

Some of the books are light-hearted, some serious, and include Fiction, Lives and Letters, Travel, Critics, Poetry, History and Hogarth Crime and Gaslight Crime.

A list of our books already published, together with some of our forthcoming titles, follows. If you would like more information about Hogarth Press books, write to us for a catalogue:

40 William IV Street, London WC2N 4DF

Please send a large stamped addressed envelope

HOGARTH LIVES AND LETTERS

HOGARTH FICTION

Graham McInnes
The Road to Gundagai

New Introduction by Robertson Davies

Lauded by John Betjeman, birthplace of Germaine Greer, home of Dame Edna Everage and source of Foster's lager, the city of Melbourne is regarded as one of the most gracious in the world. But not by the novelist Angela Thirkell – uprooted from England in 1919 with her two sons, Graham and Colin McInnes – who viewed all Australians as being both down and under. The boys, however, took to Australia with gusto, and this is the memoir, wonderfully, wittily told, of their adventures in that strange, compelling land. *The Road to Gundagai* shows us 'boyhood in essence' (Angus Wilson), but it is, too, a portrait of a beautiful city, an astonishing country, a devastating mother – 'a work of literary art' (*Times Literary Supplement*).

Colin MacInnes
All Day Saturday

New Introduction by Tony Gould

Everybody loves Mrs Helen Bailey – everybody, that is, except her husband Walter, who sits alone in the Australian sun, polishing his guns. For Helen, a faded *femme fatale*, destiny seems to hold only embittered passion, infertility and a lifetime of tea parties. But one Saturday a young stranger arrives – and the lives and loves on the Baileys' sheep station are altered forever.

A novel which may surprise those who know Colin MacInnes through *Absolute Beginners*, *All Day Saturday* is, at once, a telling portrait of a troubled marriage, a comic evocation of life in the Bush, and a classical drama – where the fates of many are decreed in a day.

Colin MacInnes
England, Half English

New Foreword by Paul Weller

'an album for posterity' – *Paul Weller*

The author of *Absolute Beginners*, Colin MacInnes is also famous for his pungent criticism. Here he turns his attention to the Fifties – one of the first commentators to grasp the massive influence upon Britain of new peoples, colours and rhythms. Whether writing about Elvis Presley or Sidney Nolan, race riots or prostitutes, literature or skiffle, MacInnes displays the hard-edged brilliance and broad-minded compassion that will be appreciated as much by his new fans as by those who look back nostalgically to that exhilarating decade.

Eliza Fay

Original Letters from India (1779-1815)

Edited by E.M. Forster

New Introduction by M.M. Kaye

Forster called her 'a work of art'; 'how I wish I'd known her,' says M.M. Kaye. Seamstress, teacher and luckless merchant, Eliza Fay set sail for Calcutta in 1779 with her hopeless husband – only to be thrown into gaol by Hyder Ali on arrival. It was but the beginning of a lifetime of adventure: in Europe, Asia, the United States – and, constantly, back to her beloved India. 'Tremendous', 'prepotent', she poured all her fortitude and chagrin into these glorious letters home.

Fergus Hume
Madame Midas

New Introduction by Stephen Knight

Madame Midas is a woman who knows her own mind, but not her own heart. Charming, of humble origins, she stakes her claim in a land of pioneers and soon returns to Melbourne laden with gold. But the streets of that city are paved with envy, betrayal, cruelty and crime. Slowly but surely, Madame Midas hardens to the touch.

Sought after for years, *Madame Midas* is now republished for the first time since original publication – bringing to an end a century of notorious neglect. It is a rivetting, salutory story and, like *Hansom Cab*, a sharply realistic picture of Victorian times – a nugget of pure gold.

Frederic Manning
Her Privates We

New Introduction by Lyn Macdonald

'It is the finest and noblest book of men in war I have ever read' – *Ernest Hemingway*

On July 1st, 1916, the Somme offensive began. This is the battle from behind the lines, of those sardonic, humorous troops honoured from *Henry V* to *The Virgin Soldiers*. No grand heroics here, but as they try out their French on village beauties and wangle a cosy billet, dodging shells and sergeant-majors, Privates Bourne Shem and little Martlow build up a friendship which supports them through terror and pain to the edge of the grave.

E.F. Benson
As We Were

New Introduction by T.J. Binyon

E.F. Benson's eye roves back to those nostalgic days of pincushions and paperweights, of 'Floral Lotto' and soulful renditions of *The Lost Chord*. Starting from the top – with a trenchant picture of Queen Victoria – he unfolds the extreme oddities of his own family and of the people he encountered in their vast social circle. Gladstone tells us how to pack a sponge bag, Tennyson talks of braces, Whistler challenges Moore to a duel – writers and artists share the stage with famous beauties and doughty dowagers in these unparalleled memoirs of late Victorian and early Edwardian England.

Richard Cobb

Still Life

Sketches from a Tunbridge Wells Childhood

Still Life is a classic memoir. In it, Richard Cobb takes us through the streets and houses of his childhood – down Poona Road, along by the Grove Bowling Club, and on past the taxidermist's and 'Love, Fruit and Vegetables' shop – recapturing, with the innocence of a lonely boy, the snobberies and eccentricities of secure middle-class England in the Twenties and Thirties.

'strange and wonderful' – Hilary Spurling, *Observer*

'a rare treasure' – John Carey, *The Sunday Times*

The Hogarth Press

Graham McInnes, brother of Colin — both sons of the
formidable novelist Angela Thirkell — here tells the story
of his youth in Australia in the Twenties and Thirties.
His boyhood is evoked with all the captivating spirit of
the born raconteur: his schooldays at Scotch College,
donning a Digger Hat to enact the unmilitary ritual of
National Service, life at university — more sedate, except
for an unwitting and near-disastrous arson — and the
discovery of the characters and beauties of the land of
youth and opportunity.

Here is a magical and hilarious portrait of being young in
God's Own Country. It is also a touching farewell to a
charmed way of life, for Colin is set to sail for England,
and Graham to embark on a search for his father and a
new life in Canada.

'A deft, at times brilliant, talent'—
Elspeth Huxley

Graham McInnes (1912–70) became a distinguished
diplomat, art critic and novelist. *Humping My Bluey* is
one of three volumes of his classic autobiography, the
others being *The Road to Gundagai* and *Finding a Father*.

New Introduction by Barry Humphries

Cover illustration by Amy Burch

ISBN 0-7012-0594-6

9 780701 205942